SQUEEGEE
ART
revolution

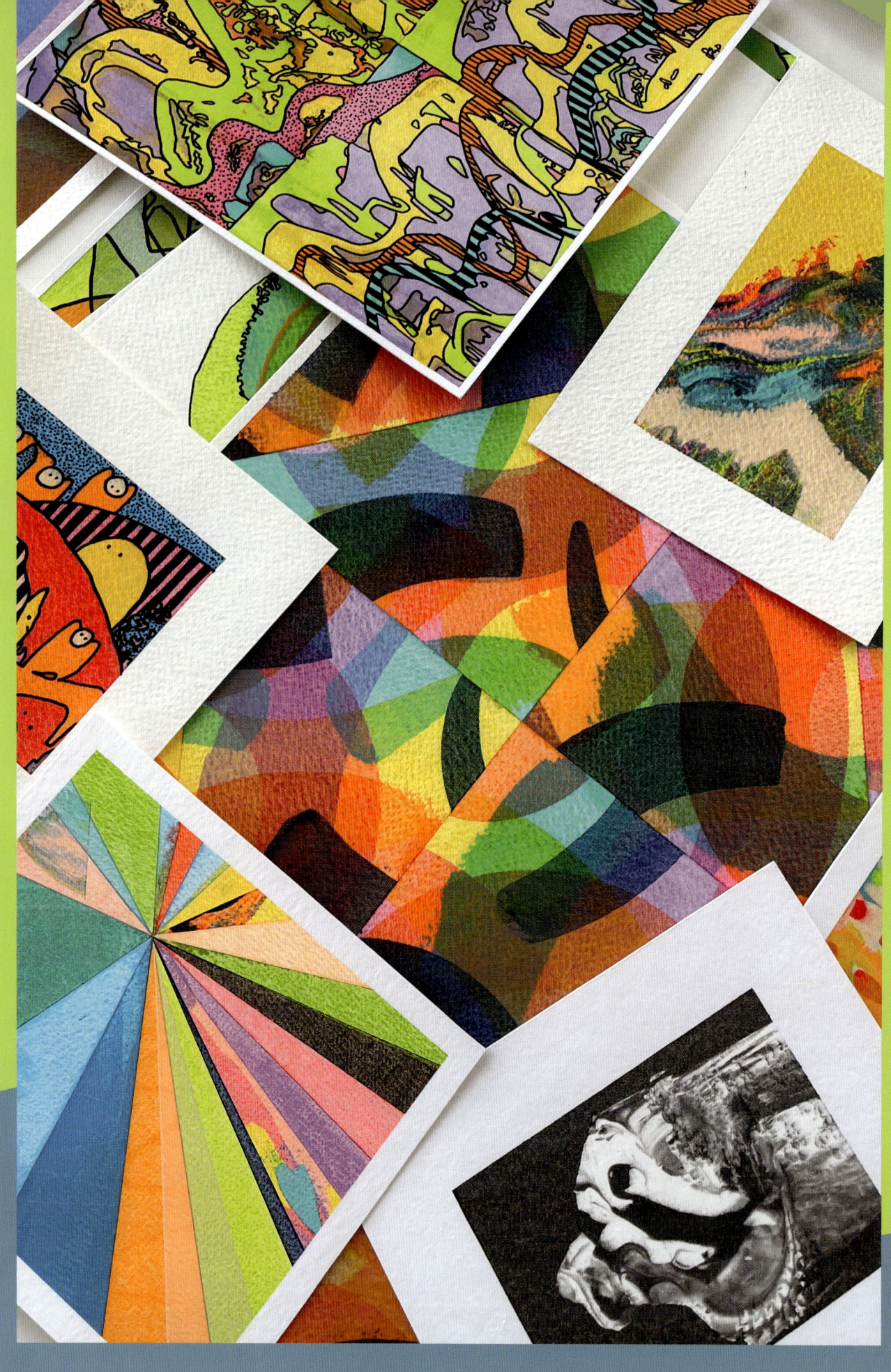

SQUEEGEE ART *revolution*

SCRAPE YOUR WAY TO AMAZING ABSTRACT ART

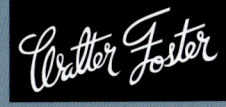

CONTENTS

Introduction   6

THE BASICS OF SQUEEGEE ART   9

How I Discovered Squeegee Art   10
Materials: Basic Equipment   12
Optional Materials   18
The Technique   22

PROJECTS   33

01 Jelly   34
02 Jelly × 4   38
03 Dynamic Shapes   42
04 A Dance of Color   46
05 Pop-Art-Party I   50
06 Pop-Art-Party II   54
07 Hidden Surprises   58
08 Sunrise Mountain   62
09 "Noonlight" Mountain   66
10 The Marble   70

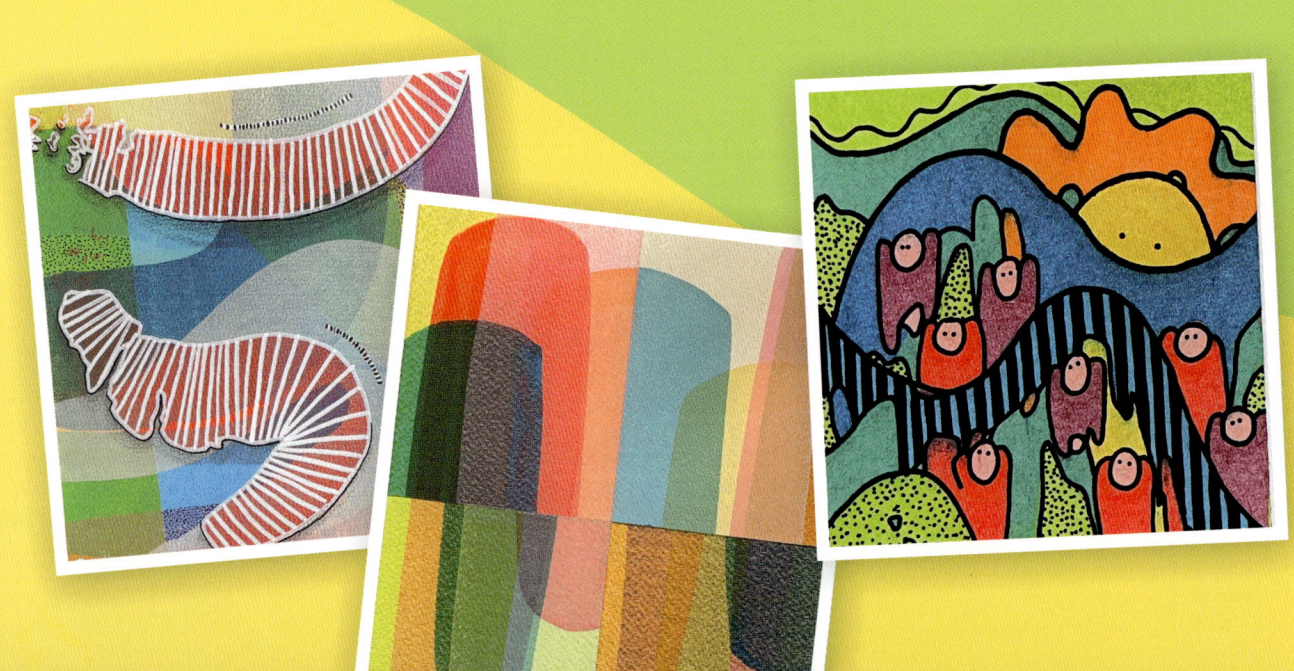

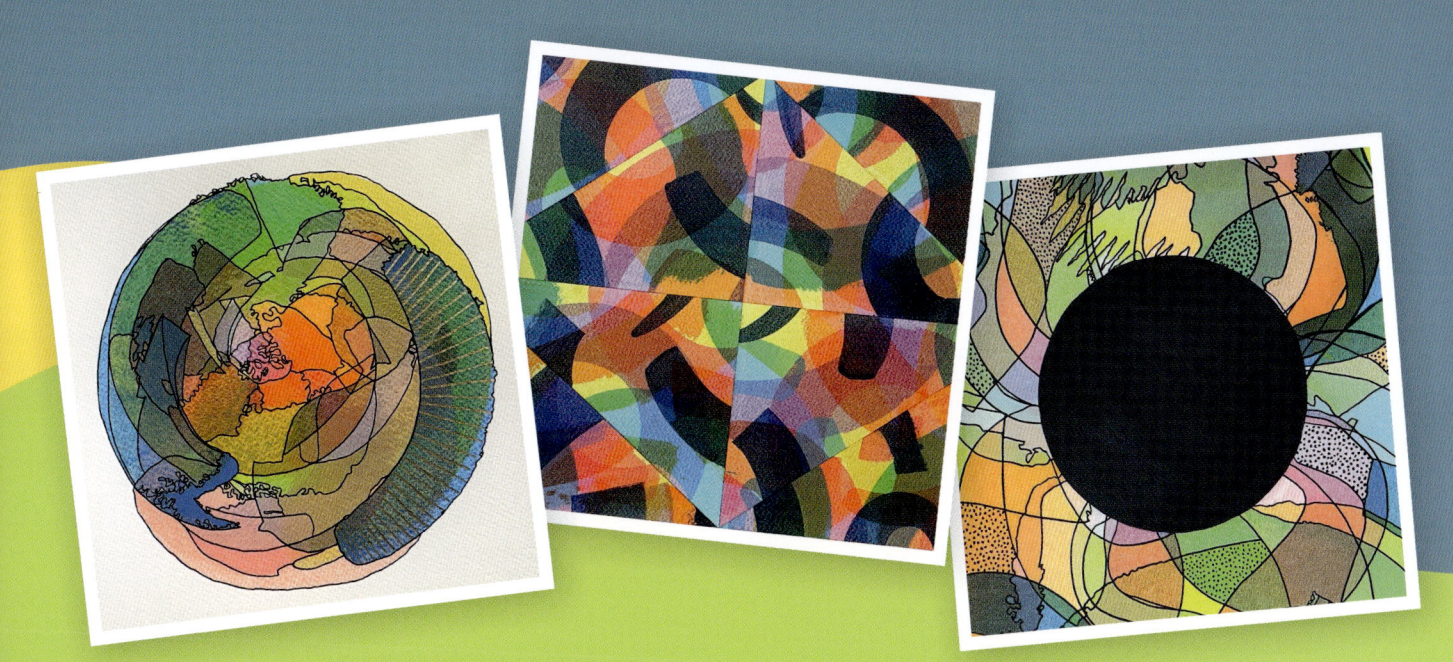

11	A New Planet	74
12	An Explosion of Color	78
13	Creative Love	82
14	The Color of Bliss	88
15	Ribbons in the Wind	92
16	Firework	96
17	Rays of Color	100
18	Chaos Diamond	104
19	A Collection of Mini Paintings	108

20	Black Hole	114
21	Melting Roller Coaster	118
22	Colorful Greetings	122

| Acknowledgments | 126 |
| About the Author | 127 |

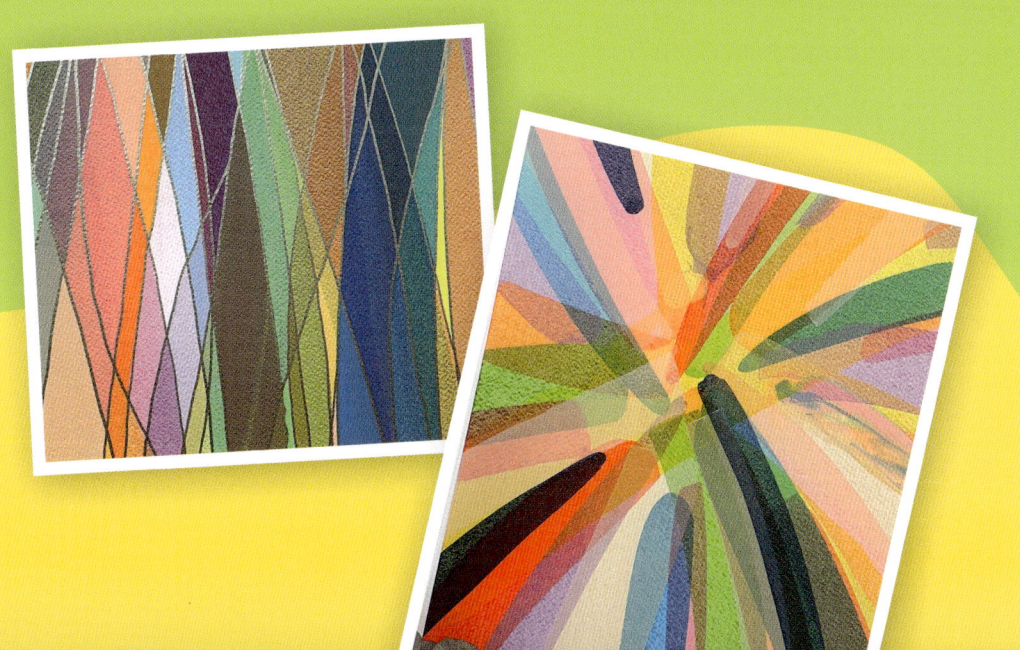

INTRODUCTION

I started to paint and draw at an early age. My dad was a gifted landscape painter, so you could say this passion for creativity was passed down to me. I can still remember how proud I was when I won a painting competition when I was nine years old, and my drawing was featured on my elementary school's monthly menu. My mom has kept that menu to this day.

Art and creativity were highly prized, and also encouraged, in my large family. I did plenty of crafts with my granny and my aunt. My aunt also taught me how to draw, my dad introduced me to the basics of depth and perspective, and my granny taught me how to stay curious and experiment. I've painted and drawn on every material you can imagine: paper, walls, clothes, and shoes. In short, anything I could get my hands on. I started sharing my work online shortly after my parents bought our first computer.

At high school and university, I had an on-and-off relationship with my art. Back then, I had no intention of becoming a full-time artist: I wanted to be a designer.

Then one day, I came across a few watercolors online. They blew me away. They were pictures of a starry night sky, with colors that reminded me of the Northern Lights. They were so magical and fascinating that I felt driven to create something myself. Taking my inspiration from these pictures, I started out with watercolor painting, though my initial attempts didn't turn out all that well. I kept on trying. I didn't have a lot of experience with watercolors, so you can imagine the chaos that ensued. After many attempts, my pictures gradually improved and somewhere along the way, I started to like them. I loved watercolor painting. I loved the process, the colors, the depth, and the results. That feeling of inspiration, experimenting, failing, and then experimenting over again until, finally, everything came together. Then falling in love with something else and starting over.

It's thanks to this determined, creative, experimental attitude that, after plenty of highs and lows and trying out lots of different techniques, I discovered squeegee art. I experimented so much that I got completely immersed in it. Whether it's painting, drawing, or crafts with my granny, the most important thing for me now is having fun. If I'm having fun, everything else follows. That's what you can expect from this book and the projects we'll explore together.

HAVE FUN!

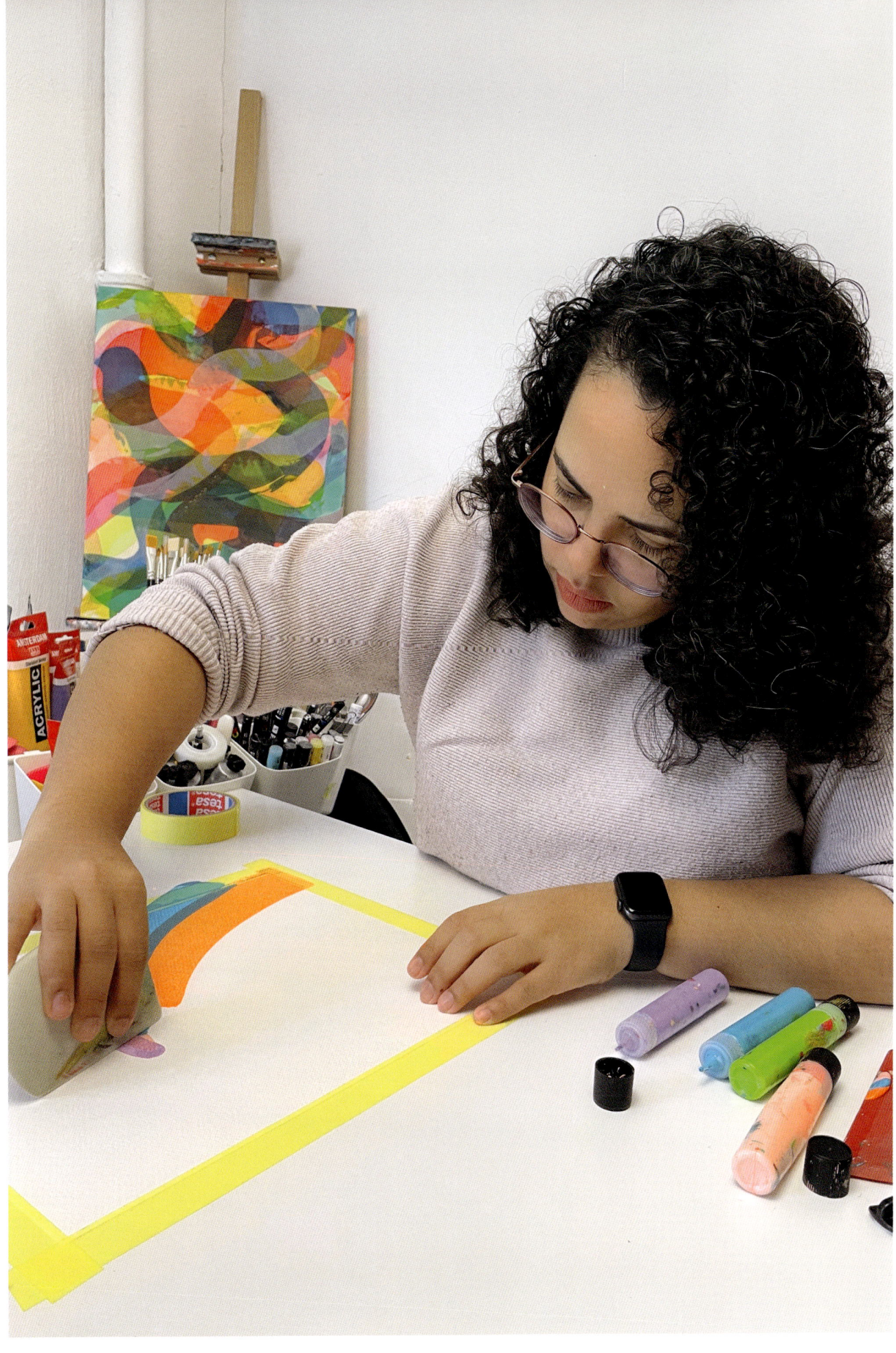

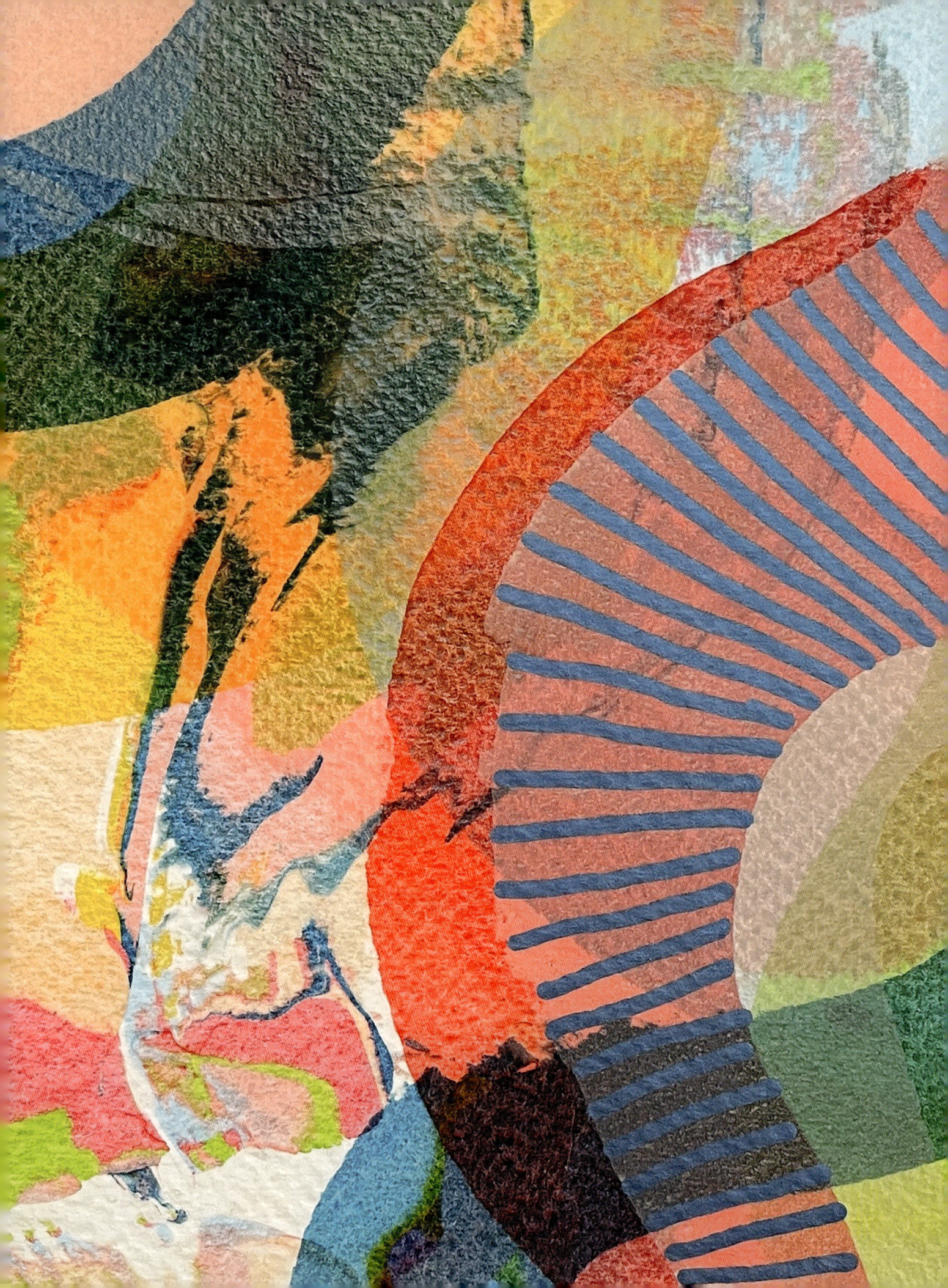

CHAPTER 1

The Basics of

SQUEEGEE ART

In this chapter, I'll show you what materials you need and how the technique works. We'll also practice using a squeegee. Before we get started, I'll tell you more about my introduction to the world of squeegee art. Your pictures probably won't match up with your expectations at the beginning, and that's okay. The same thing happened to me, and I have the pictures to prove it! Keep going: Practice makes perfect.

HOW I DISCOVERED SQUEEGEE ART

It takes more than creative talent to make beautiful things that bring you joy and happiness. Regular practice and the desire to try out new things are just as important.

One winter's day back in December 2020, I was scrolling through Instagram when I saw a video by Phoebe Gander, an artist from New Zealand. In her video, she put a few dollops of paint on a piece of paper, seemingly at random. Then, she took a large squeegee and scraped off all the paint in one go. In the span of a second, right before my very eyes, those dollops of paint had transformed into a landscape of the sun setting over the mountains. It was love at first sight. I felt inspired to try it out for myself.

I rushed to my nearest art supplies store and started looking for squeegees, paint, paper, and tape. I then went home and got stuck. To my surprise, the process wasn't quite as easy as Phoebe had made it look, no doubt a sign of her experience. The edges of her pictures were well-defined, the paints didn't smudge, and the texture was much smoother than mine. I posted my attempt on Instagram, writing, "I enjoyed the process so much, but it's quite difficult to get a decent result."

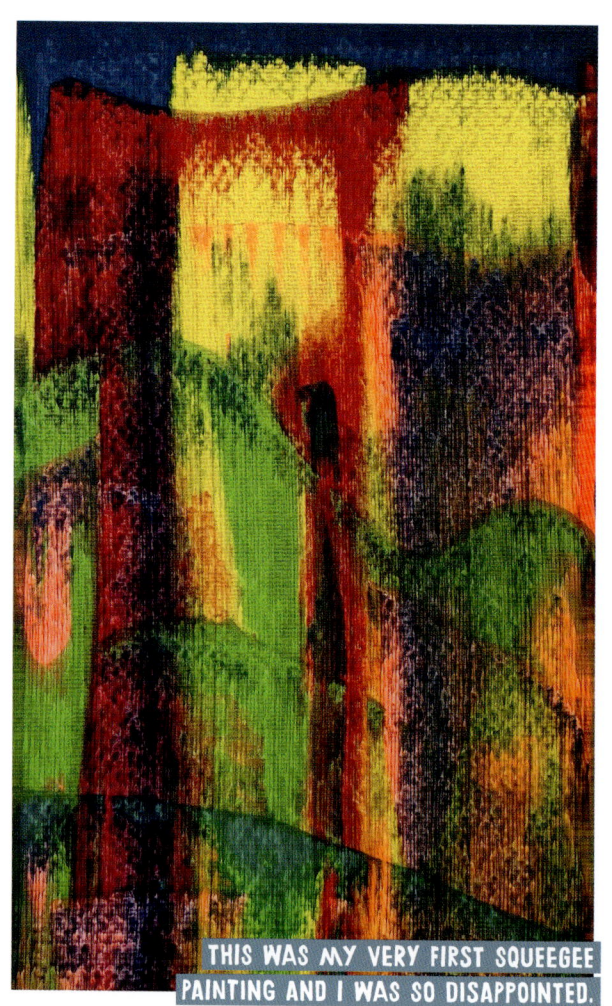

THIS WAS MY VERY FIRST SQUEEGEE PAINTING AND I WAS SO DISAPPOINTED.

The paints mixed together in a way that I didn't like. They looked really smudged and the colors along the paper's bottom edge didn't look good at all. I know it could happen to anyone, and that's perfectly okay, but when I compared the image I had in my head with the result I had in front of me, I just wanted to give up. Nevertheless, I tried again, picking up the squeegee and a fresh sheet of paper. As far as I could tell, this attempt was even worse.

I have to admit: I'd given up on the technique so hadn't touched my painting materials for a few days. Nevertheless, I was feeling restless.

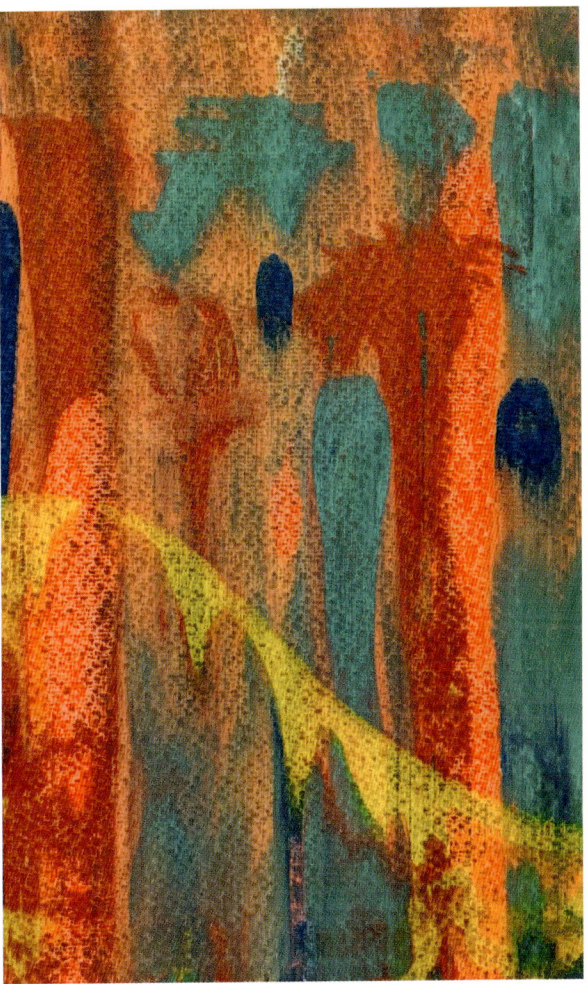

I couldn't stop thinking about getting the technique "right." So I went back to the art supplies store and bought a different variety of paper and another squeegee in preparation for the next round. In one session, I painted more than twenty-five pictures. Most of them weren't very great, but after a while, some of them looked all right. There were even a few that I reckoned looked . . . good! That spurred me on: I was hooked.

I like to have control over what I create and a clear idea of the result. With squeegee art, that's impossible. I still have an element of control—now more than when I started—but it's nothing compared to drawing. I've since learned how to deal with the lack of control. Somewhere along the line, I accepted it and let go. It was very liberating.

Squeegee art is a great activity for kids. I often get pictures from teachers who are exploring squeegee art with their kindergarten classes. These pictures bring me so much joy, especially when the teachers tell me how much fun they're having. This technique isn't just for kids, though. After two intense years of learning and experimentation, I can tell you that squeegee art is a great creative outlet for people whose job doesn't give them space to embrace their creativity. This style of painting is also great for getting rid of the day's stress, for meditating, and for relaxing when you're in the flow.

The most important thing is to focus on what's good for you and what brings you joy.

MATERIALS: BASIC EQUIPMENT

These are the basic materials you need for your first squeegee painting.

ACRYLIC PAINT

The most important thing to bear in mind when choosing which acrylic paint to use is its opacity. Opaque paints are best because they give the most effective results. Semi-opaque paint sometimes works, but not always. That's mostly because semi-transparent or transparent paints look less intense on paper. If that doesn't bother you too much, you can use semi-opaque paints. I don't recommend transparent paints, though. They generally make a painting look a bit jarring, as they don't add much color to the paper. They don't have as much contrast or presence as other paints either. Of course, you're welcome to experiment and find out for yourself what works best for the result you have in mind.

Regardless of whether you're buying new paint or using what you have at home, I recommend paints with a black square (see image). This symbol means that the paint is opaque. This is perfect for the squeegee technique.

I've tried out many different sorts of acrylic paint, from heavy body paint to soft body paint. I've come to the conclusion that all of them work. The difference is how easily the paint can be applied to the paper and how much paint is needed for each layer.

Soft body paints are very fluid, so less paint is needed to draw a long line across the paper. If you use ordinary acrylic paint to make an even, uninterrupted stroke, you'll probably need a lot more paint than you would with soft body paint. You'll probably have more paint left over too. The type of acrylic paint has no impact on the transparency of the layers.

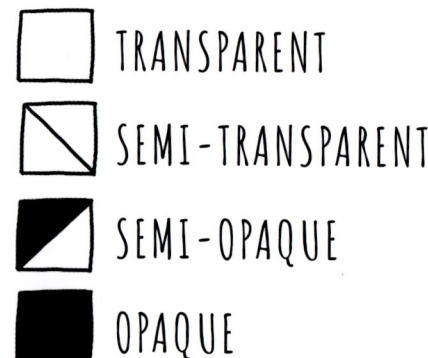

TRANSPARENT

SEMI-TRANSPARENT

SEMI-OPAQUE

OPAQUE

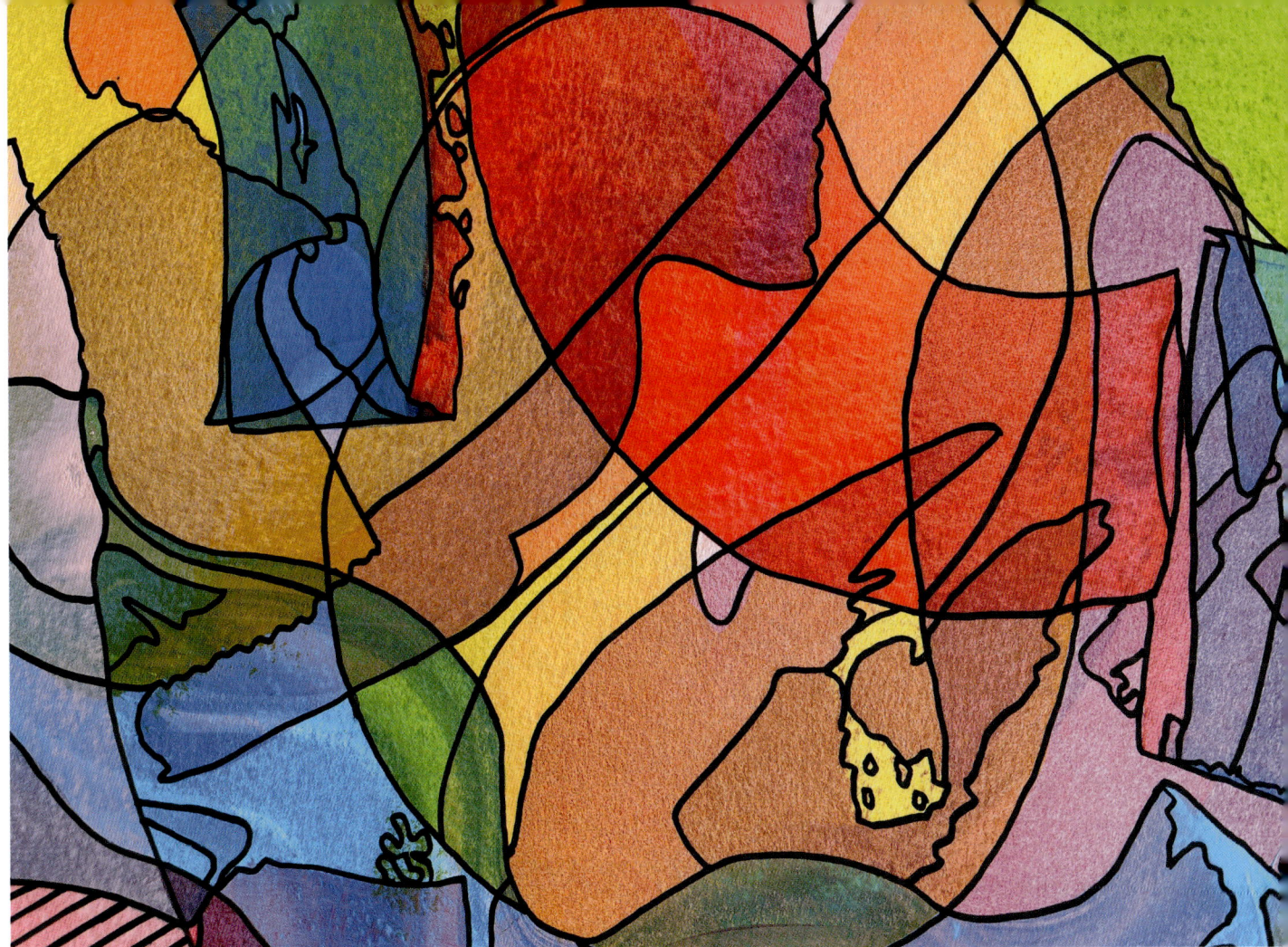

In this book, the acrylics I usually use are thinner than heavy body paints and thicker than soft body paints. This viscosity gives you more control, makes your painting neater, and reduces the amount of paint left over. You can use whichever paint you feel most comfortable with.

I'm often asked what brand of paint I use. I think most people are under the impression that the brand has a bearing on the result. To a degree,

it does. A higher-quality paint generally produces a more vibrant result, and cheap paints might not look as good. In this case too, however, it all depends on your budget and what your objectives are. I started out with cheaper paints until I was feeling more confident. I then increased the quality. My favorite brand of acrylic paint is now Amsterdam Acrylics. I get just the result I'm expecting every single time, and I love that.

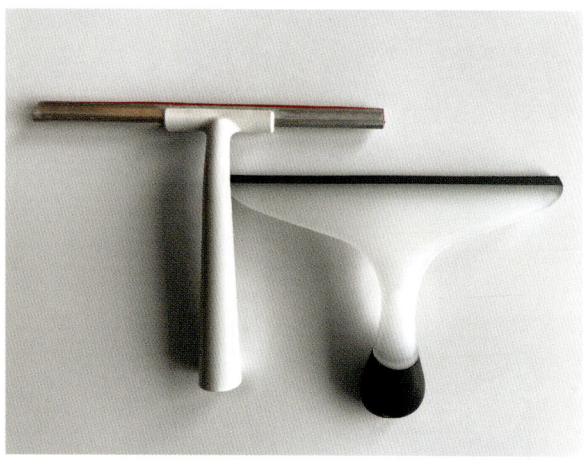

PAINTING WEDGE OR SQUEEGEE

For my first squeegee paintings, I used a conventional squeegee, just like the ones you'd use in the bathroom for removing water from the shower doors. It was interesting and the result wasn't bad, but I had a feeling it wasn't the right tool for me.

I didn't have a clear idea of what I was looking for yet, but I started testing out different tools for applying the paint.

I didn't limit my search to the bathroom or art supplies store. I also went to the DIY store, where I found plastic squeegees. These are usually used for applying plastic film to glass windows. I went to cookware stores as well. Here I found dough scrapers that could also be used for painting. Everywhere I went, I asked myself: Could I use this tool for painting? Sometimes it worked well. Other times, it was a disaster, but I'm glad to have learned something in the process.

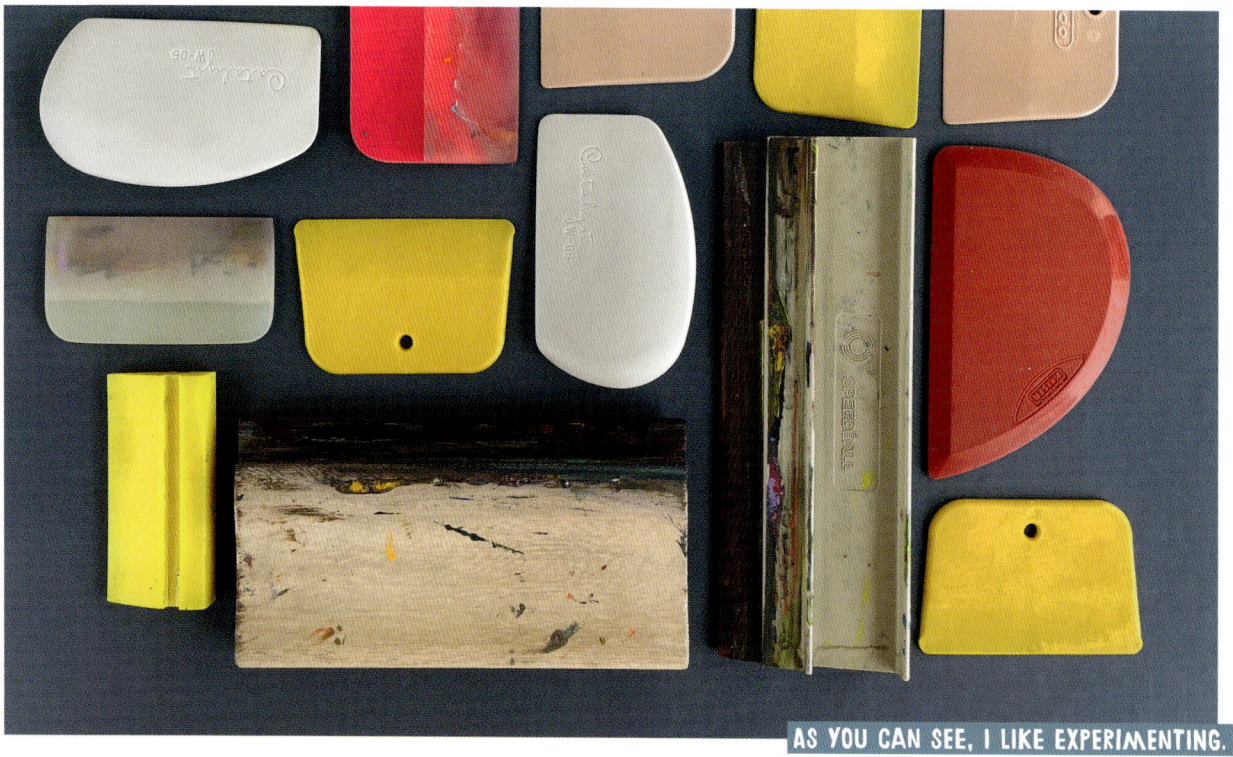

AS YOU CAN SEE, I LIKE EXPERIMENTING.

On a practical note, if you just want to give this technique a go, you can apply the paint with a piece of hard cardboard, a ruler, or the squeegee from your bathroom. One of those might be enough to get what you want from your painting session. On the other hand, you might try something out, only to discover that the result isn't what you wanted after all. If that's the case, I have a few tips:

After trying out all the various painting wedges and squeegees I could lay my hands on, I finally found my favorite: the Catalyst Wedge W-06 by Princeton Brushes. It gives me the most consistent results, so I use it as my main tool. When I want to experiment or try something new, I opt for a different tool: In this situation, the tool's unpredictability can be really helpful.

Here are some of the things to bear in mind when searching for your perfect tool: If the material is too soft or the edge is too round, your pictures will probably smudge a lot. If the material is too hard, it will remove too much paint from your paper unless you're able to control the pressure consistently. I recommend choosing a tool that is medium-soft and, when in doubt, a little harder. Thin plastic squeegees also work well, but finding one with a smooth edge is like winning the lottery. Most of the ones I've bought had a slightly uneven edge, and when you scrape your paint off the paper, they can leave behind scratch marks or even damage the paper.

Whichever tool you choose, before investing time and materials in a bigger painting, I recommend a trial run with your painting wedge or squeegee so you can find out how the paint behaves on paper, what texture it creates, and whether the tool causes any irregularities.

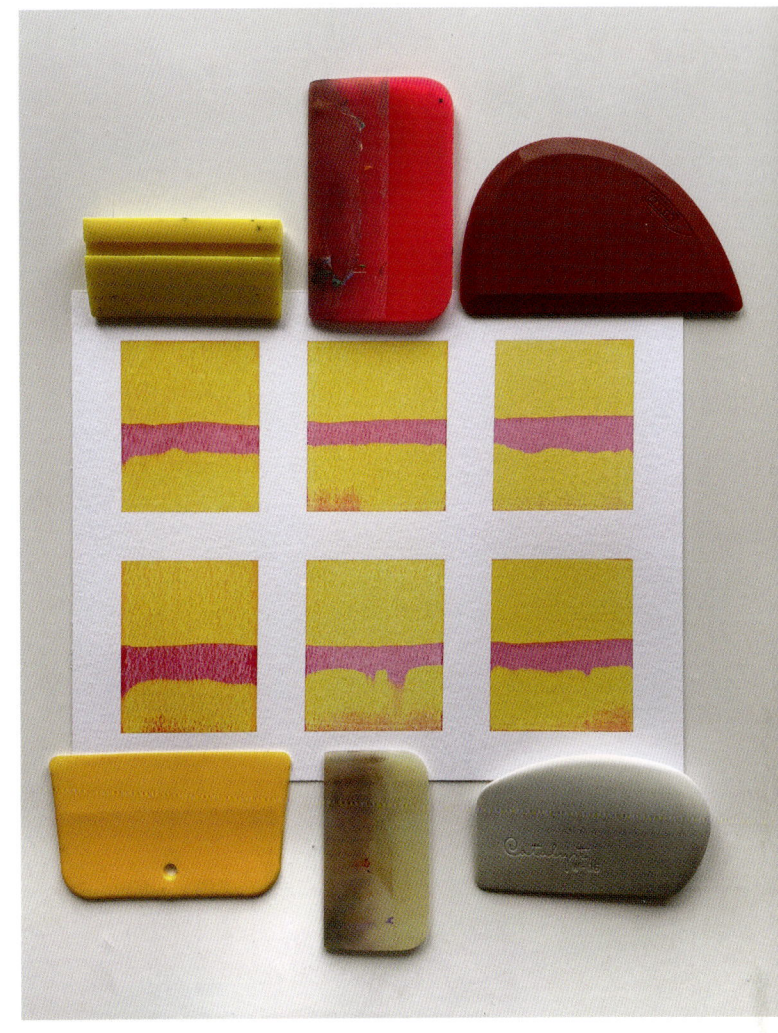

PAPER

The most important feature of the paper I use is the grammage. The grammage gives you a rough idea of the paper's thickness. Low grammage paper, such as printer paper, may buckle or even tear when the paint is scraped off, since squeegee art uses so much paint. I recommend a paper with a minimum weight of 200 lb (300 g/m²).

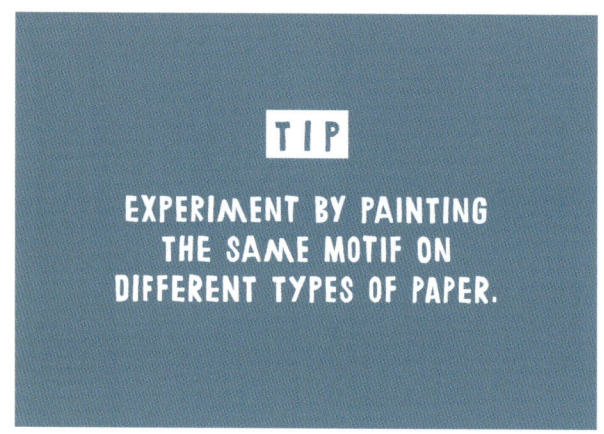

TIP

EXPERIMENT BY PAINTING THE SAME MOTIF ON DIFFERENT TYPES OF PAPER.

I recommend watercolor or acrylic paper. Cold press paper, hot press paper, fine grain, or coarse: The choice is yours. Just bear in mind that textured paper may have an impact on your final result, as the paint will not be applied as evenly as on smooth paper.

I like all sorts of textures. However, if you're looking for the easiest place to start, I recommend fine-grain paper.

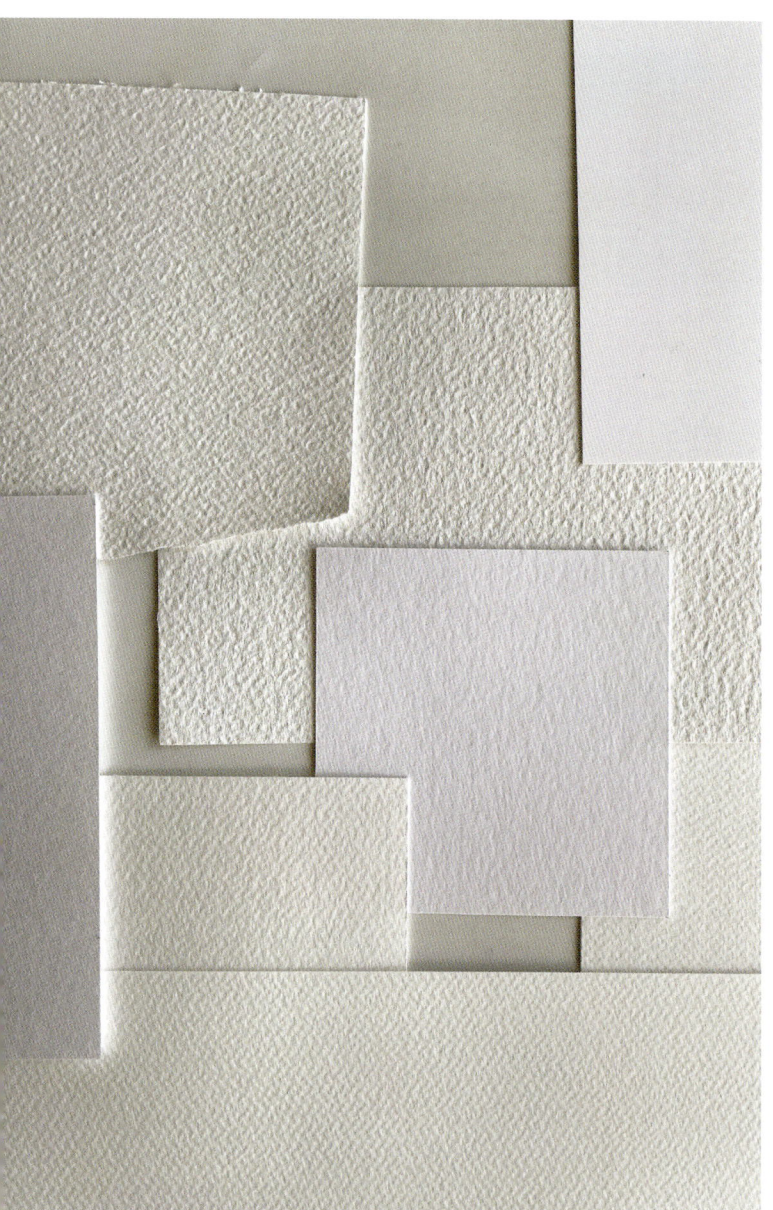

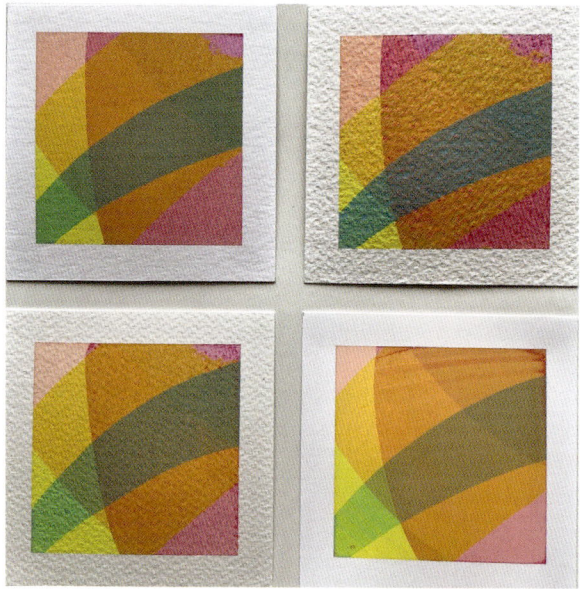

The paper that you choose will determine the sort of tape that you use to secure the picture. Some of the paper I've bought over the years didn't work with any of the tape I bought. It ripped the minute I removed it, no matter how careful I was. If this happens, it means either the paper or the tape is unsuitable for squeegee art, as I've found the paper needs to be secured with tape to a surface to stop it from slipping. I also recommend testing out the tape with the paper before you start painting so your work doesn't get damaged at the last minute.

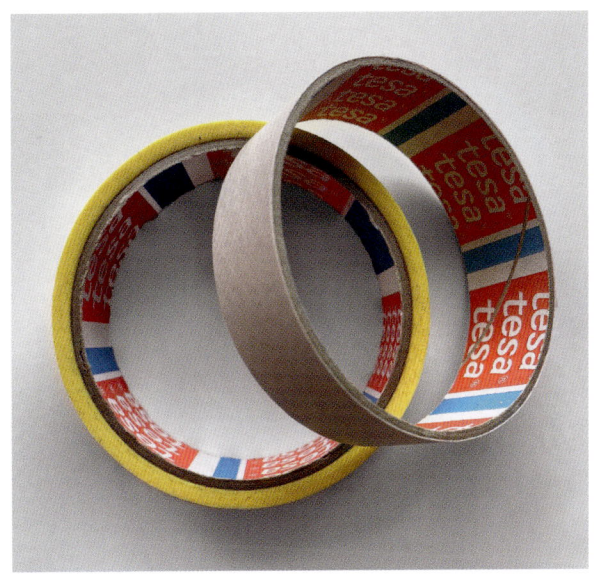

TAPE

When working on the projects in this book, a low adhesive tape is your best option. I recommend masking tape or Goldband rice paper tape, but washi tape works as well. I had lots of problems with tape in the past, so I've tried out lots of different brands and varieties of masking tape. My current favorites are by Tesa and are used on delicate surfaces. They're more expensive than the basic masking tapes I found in DIY stores, though, so I recommend trying the more affordable tape to see whether it works first before buying a more expensive type.

I use different sorts of masking tape for the projects in this book (you'll be able to tell from the colors). The results are the same, though.

TIP

IF YOUR TAPE RIPS YOUR PAPER, STICK THE TAPE TO A SMOOTH SURFACE OR YOUR CLOTHES BEFORE APPLYING IT TO THE PAPER YOU'LL BE PAINTING ON. THAT WAY, THE ADHESIVE IS WEAKER. THIS CAN BE ENOUGH TO PROTECT THE EDGES OF THE PAGE AND KEEP YOUR PAPER IN ONE PIECE.

OPTIONAL MATERIALS

The following materials are not essential. However, they make some of the projects in this book easier to paint.

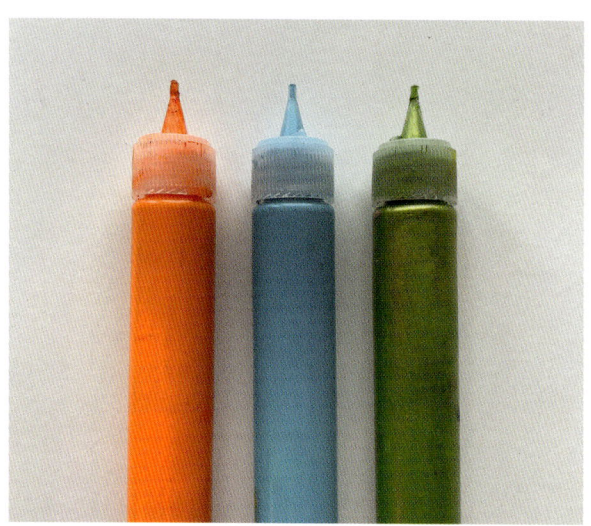

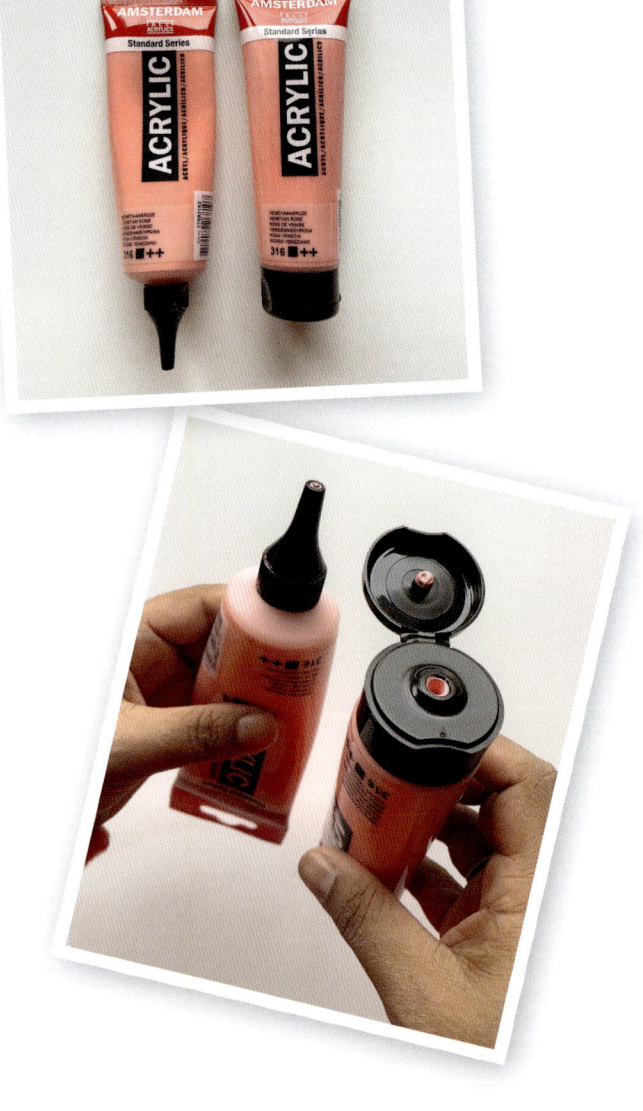

PAINT BOTTLES

When I started using squeegees to paint fonts, I needed to find a paint bottle that gave me more control over the amount of paint I applied to the paper. I found the containers I use today in my local art supplies store. They're empty bottles of Marabu Kids Window Color; all the ones I found online were full. Of course, you can also use plastic tubes or bottles with a pointed nozzle.

Amsterdam Acrylics, for example, sells nozzles that make writing in paint a lot easier. They're easy to clean and can also be attached to another bottle once the paint is finished.

MARKERS

Acrylic markers are great for adding another dimension to your squeegee art creations. A black or white marker will make the outlines of your picture look really sharp. If you add lots of details, you can even create a pop-art style. Drawing faces, animals, and plants in marker on painted shapes is especially fun. Experiment with different options and find out where your "sweet spot" is. You'll either fall in love with this technique or decide it's not for you.

Metallic markers can add an extra element of magic to your pictures when the light shines on them. I recommend branching out beyond the usual gold and silver and trying out a metallic purple or blue. The contrast of metallic blue against orange, complemented by a touch of yellow, looks stunning: I think you'll like it too.

You can use different nib sizes according to the size of your picture. I prefer 0.7 mm, 0.9 mm, and 1.8 mm markers with a round nib. The bigger the picture, the bigger the nib size. I do this because I don't like covering small paintings in thick marker: It steals the show. The marker should enhance the painting, not overpower it.

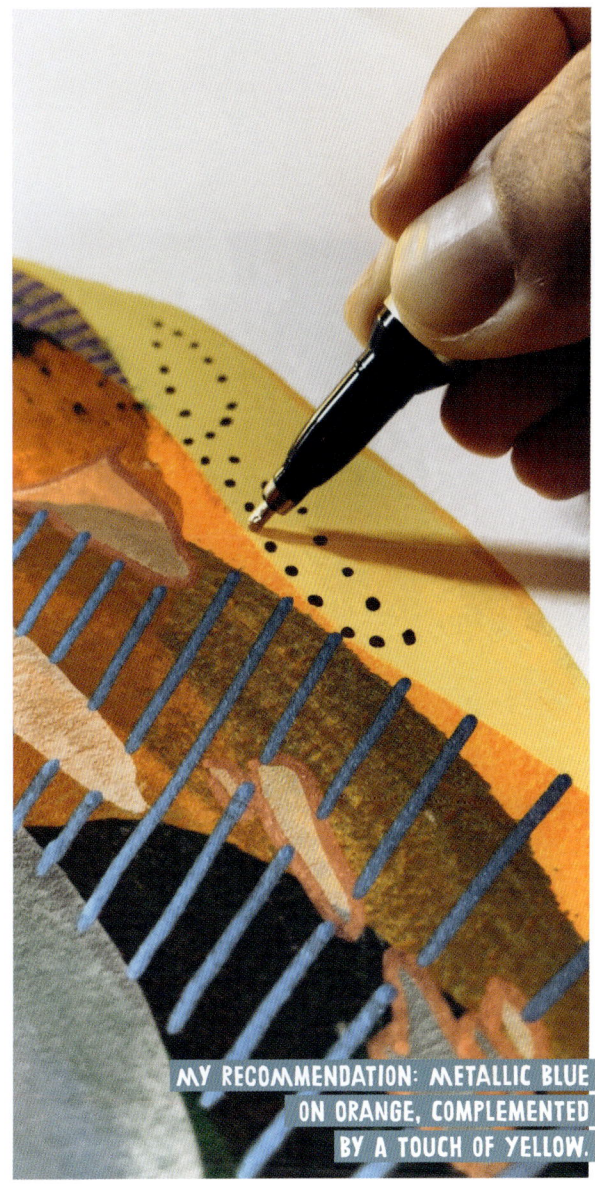

MY RECOMMENDATION: METALLIC BLUE ON ORANGE, COMPLEMENTED BY A TOUCH OF YELLOW.

Another reason I like adding marker to my picture is the meditative aspect. It's a time when I can take a deep breath, watch pen meet paper, admire every corner of my work, and find the beauty not only in the whole, but in the smaller elements making up the bigger picture. I like the surprises that are revealed when one paint overlaps another or a few lucky accidents happen along the way.

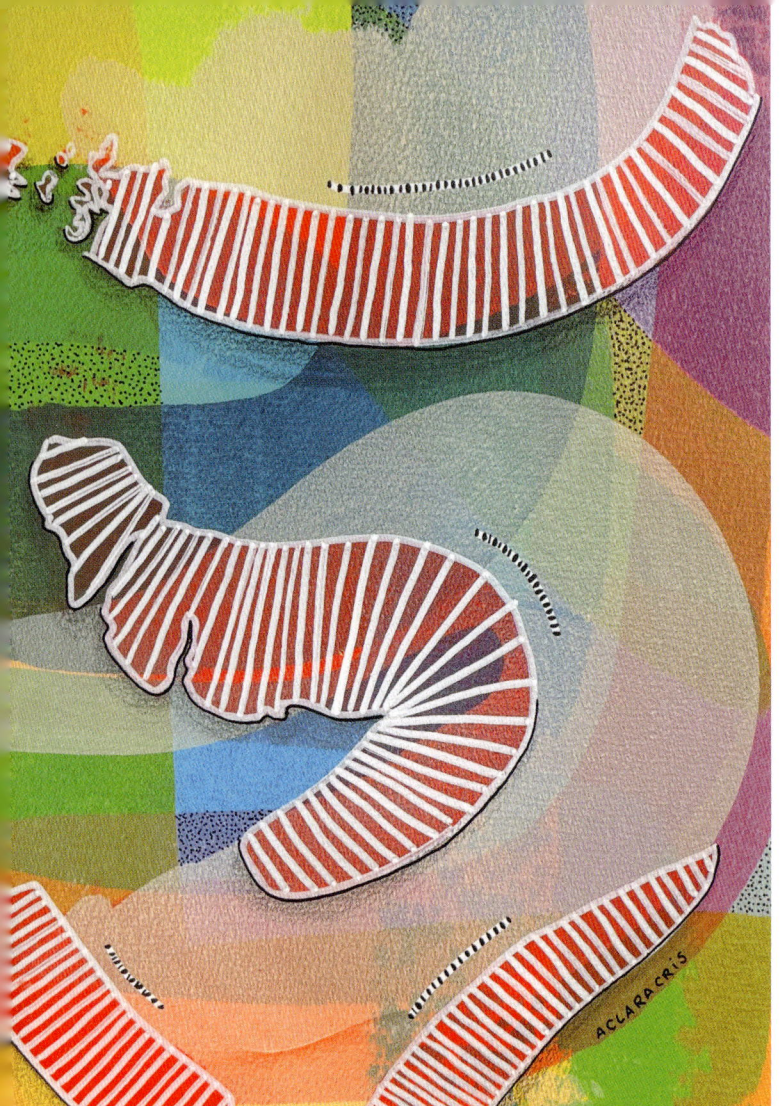

PALETTE KNIVES

Palette knives are a helpful, versatile tool in almost all my painting sessions. I use them to transfer paint from the squeegee back to the paper, to mix a specific shade, or to apply a second coat of paint over the paint I've already applied with the squeegee. I don't have a specific recommendation for palette knives, but in the photo, you can see the ones I use most often.

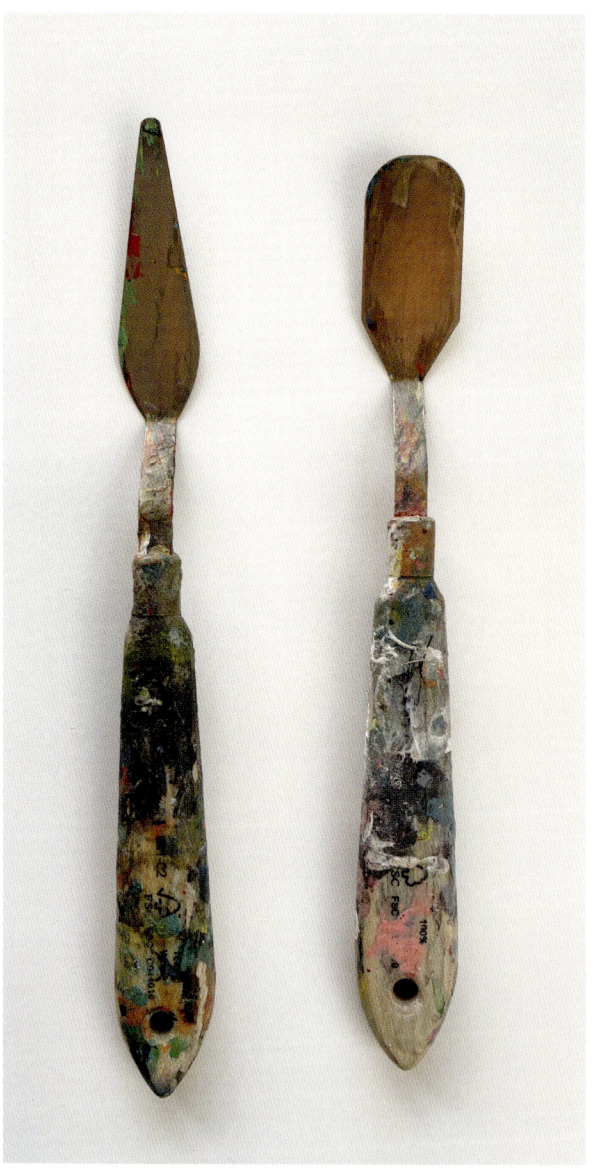

BLACK COLORED PENCIL

You can use a dark-colored pencil to create an interesting effect in addition to your outlining. By adding shadow in pencil, you create the illusion of depth so it looks like your paint layers have been added in different levels.

You can create a similar effect with acrylic paint and a brush; however, depending on how much shadow you want to add, the result can look boring and mechanical.

PAINTBRUSHES

In general, I use paintbrushes to create a black foreground or background for the colored part of my painting. Unless you're using high-quality metallic paints, if you paint squeegee art on black paper, your colors will look dull. Even then, the painting might not turn out how you imagined. That's why I apply my chosen paint on white paper, then paint the background black. I like how dramatic it looks and also enjoy the delicate task of outlining the central element in black paint.

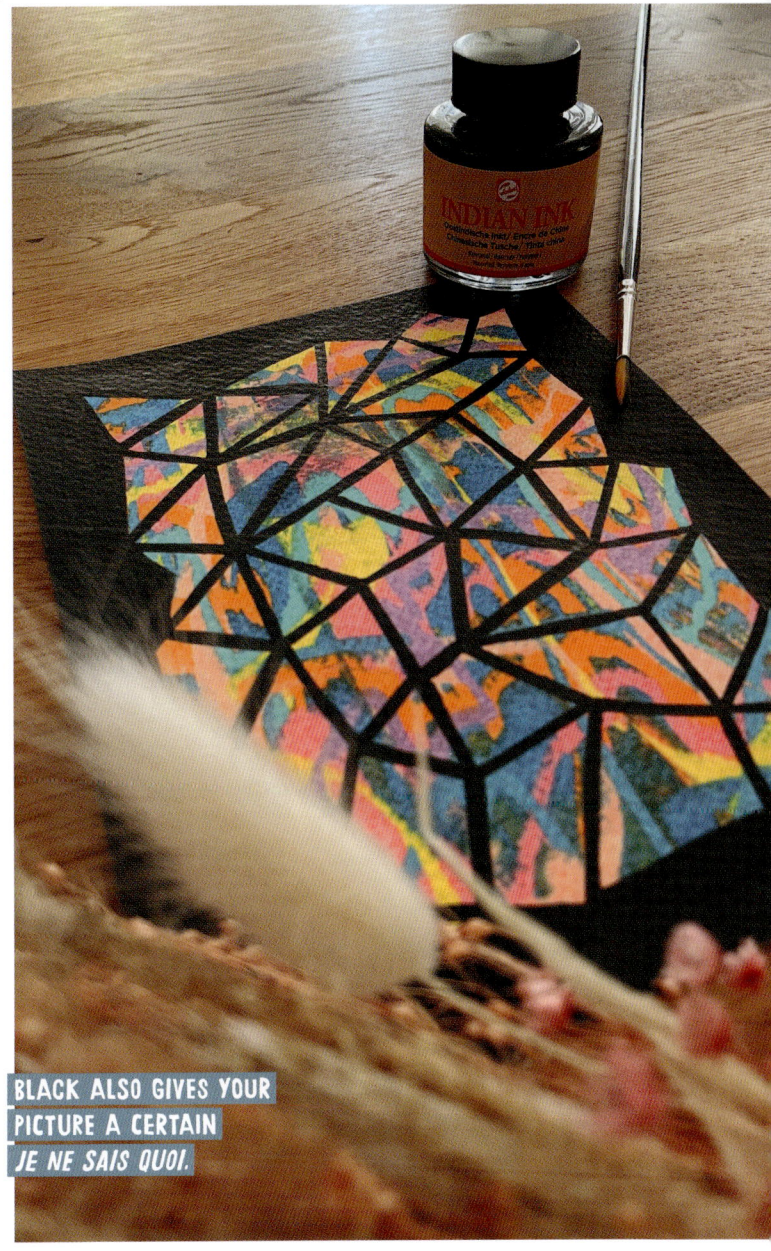

BLACK ALSO GIVES YOUR PICTURE A CERTAIN *JE NE SAIS QUOI*.

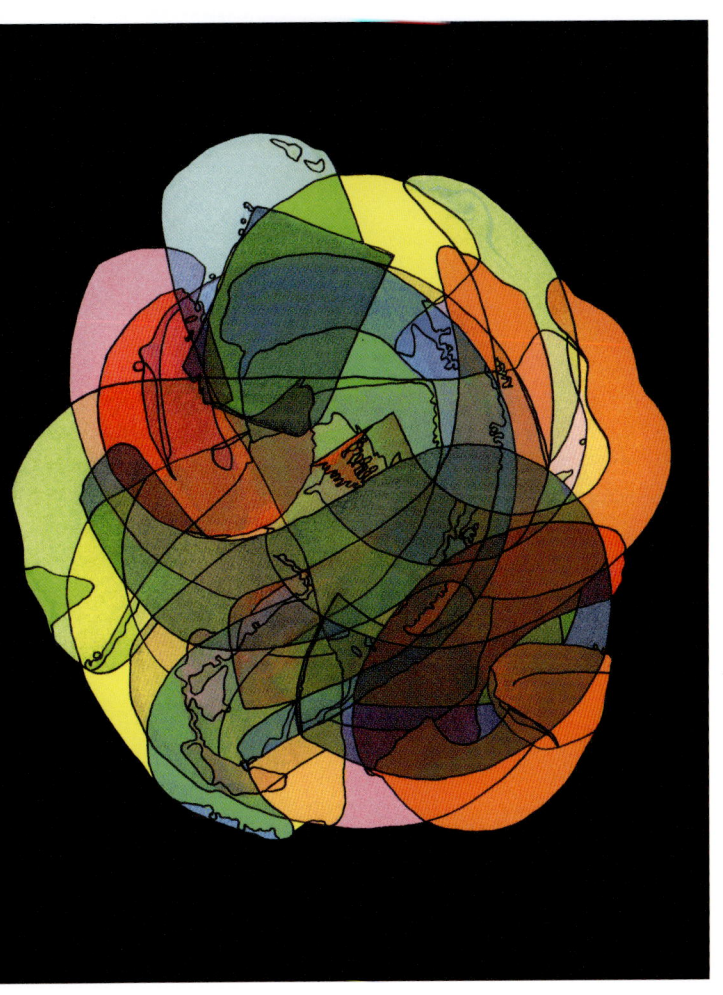

The size of your brush depends on the size of the pictures you usually paint. If you paint on smaller paper, I recommend a size 12 flat brush and a size 8 round brush. If the picture is bigger, perhaps use a larger brush so you can paint more quickly.

THE TECHNIQUE

Now we've come to the exciting part: I'm going to share my experiences of squeegee painting with you. That way, you can avoid some of the mistakes I made and get off to a flying start.

SQUEEGEE SIZE

The type of picture you can create depends on the size of your squeegee. This is important because when you scrape off the paint—once on the left half and once on the right half of your paper—the point where the two sides overlap may be patchy, smudged, or oversaturated. This might be okay, though, depending on what you're going to do next—if you're going to paint over areas of the picture in black or outline them in marker, for example.

So make sure your squeegee is wide enough for your picture. Bear in mind, however, that large squeegees can be more difficult to handle. If you opt for a smaller squeegee, you can divide your paper into smaller, more convenient sections with masking tape, as demonstrated in the picture on the right. Here you can see that I've divided my 13" × 17" (42 × 32 cm) painting into twelve squares so I can use a small squeegee. I've then painted each section individually.

Another option is to cut your paper into smaller pieces and make smaller paintings. You can also use masking tape to make the page borders wider and the painting area narrower than your squeegee.

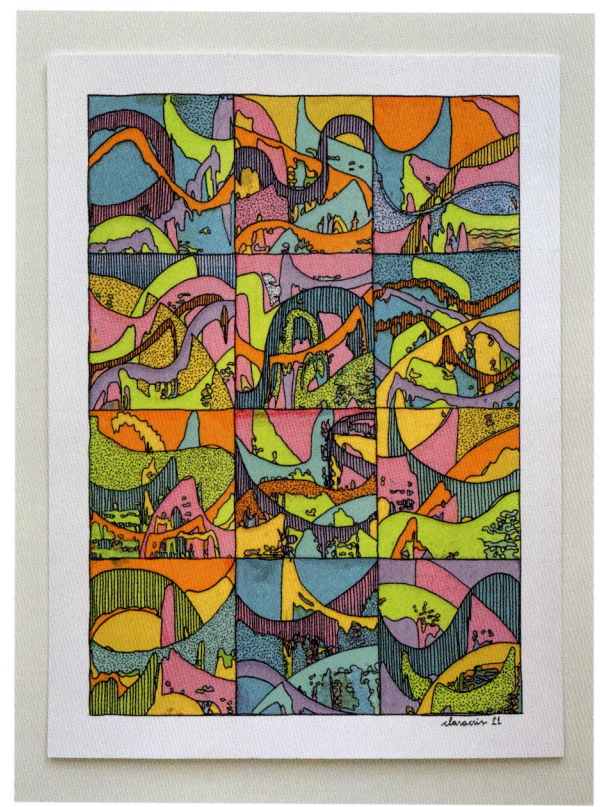

HOW TO USE TAPE

I've already shared a few tips about tape on page 17, however here are a few more recommendations to consider when applying and removing it from your paper.

I usually stick down all four edges of the paper. In some pictures, I make the border really narrow and in others, I make it thicker. If the border is really narrow, I recommend running the back of your nail over the top of the tape a few times to make sure none of the paint seeps through while you're scraping it off.

If the border is wider, I recommend applying pressure only along the inside edge of the tape that's in direct contact with the paint. I'd also recommend sticking down only the short ends of the tape that are attached to the surface you're painting on, i.e. a table or panel. This will stop the paper from slipping while the paint is being scraped off. You don't need to press all the way along the tape: This just increases the likelihood of the paper tearing when you remove the tape after painting.

When you're finished, it's okay to remove the tape before the paint is completely dry. Just make sure to do it slowly and at a 90-degree angle (see image). This greatly reduces the risk of tearing the paper and damaging your work in the final moments of your painting session.

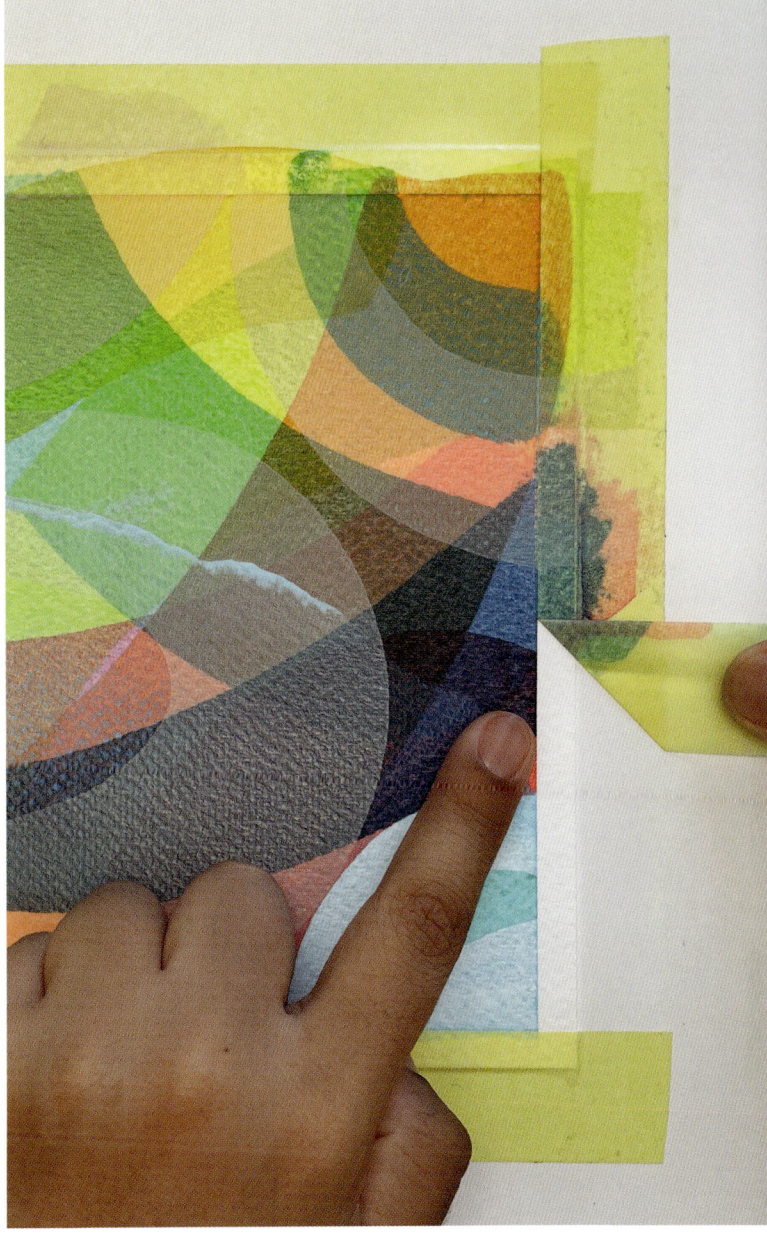

TIP

STICK THE SHEET OF PAPER TO THE TABLE SECURELY SO THAT IT DOESN'T MOVE WHEN YOU SCRAPE OFF THE PAINT.

CHOOSING YOUR COLOR PALETTE

For many people, knowing how to mix colors isn't something that comes naturally. I was fortunate to grow up in a very creative household: My dad, my granny, and my aunt celebrated my creations not just for their own sake, but because they truly appreciated my work. They also gave me tips on how to improve.

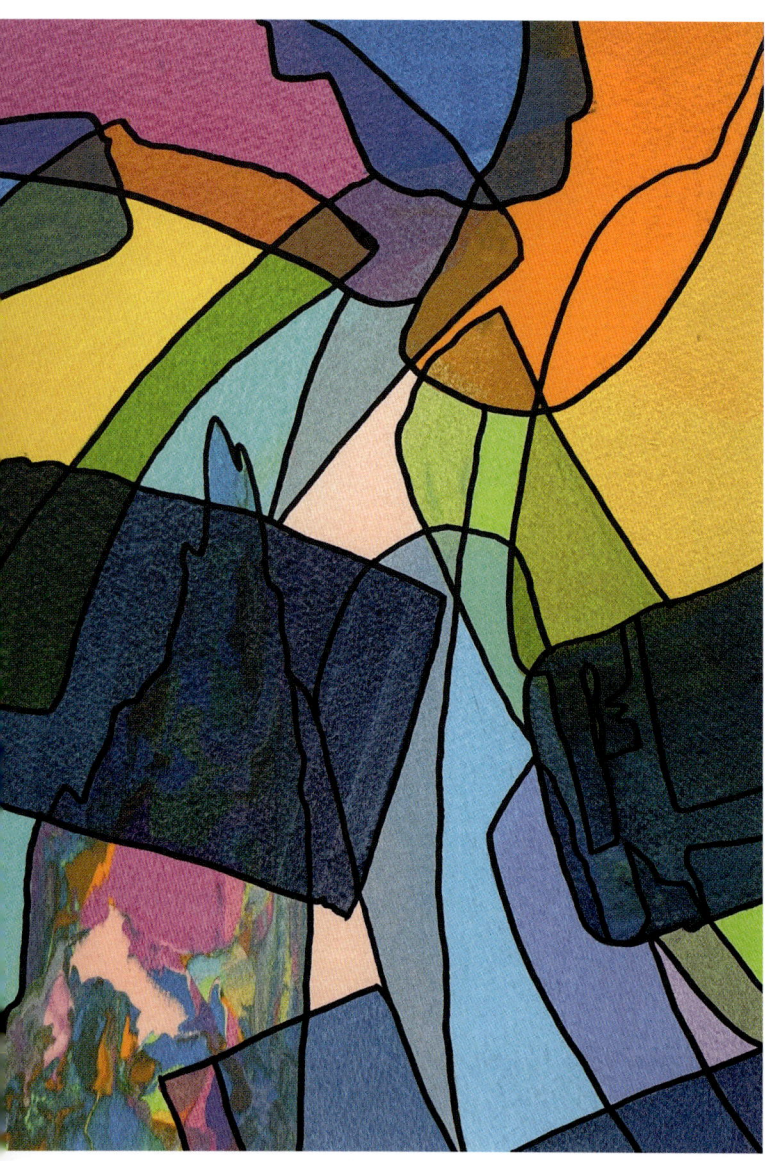

Later on in life, when I started studying design at university, there were several subjects that helped me improve my skills. Lectures about base paint, color mixing, contrast, and so on were all part of my schedule. I still made mediocre color mixes from time to time; however, I can now say, more often than not, I got it right rather than wrong. The more you practice, the better you get, and refining your color palette can help too.

There are also online tools that suggest different color palettes: Just search for a "color palette generator." Designers like me sometimes use these for inspiration when designing digital products, and they can also work well for an abstract painting. Just make sure there's enough contrast between each overlapping color or the colors you place beside one another. Otherwise, the difference between the two colors won't be obvious enough or will look like a mistake.

At the start of every project in this book, you'll find the names of the paints I've used. You don't have to use the same shades as me to get a good result, though. If you don't have the same paint, I recommend looking for it online to get an idea of the shade and perhaps using something you've got at home.

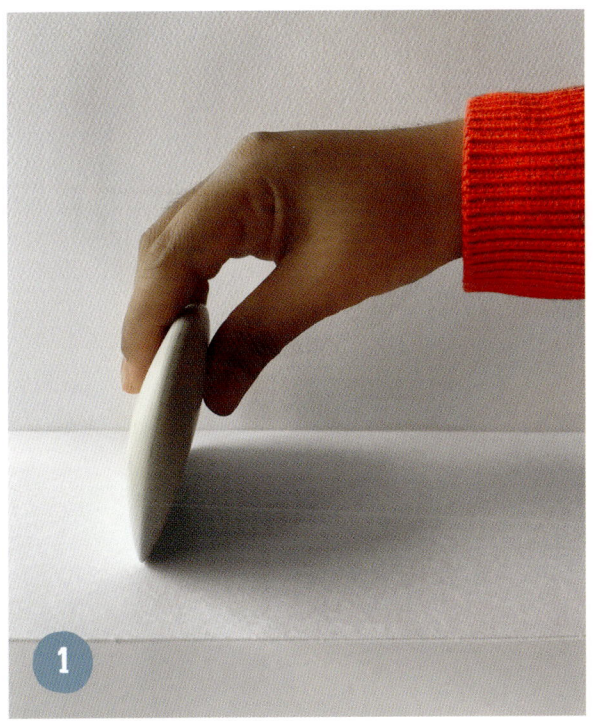

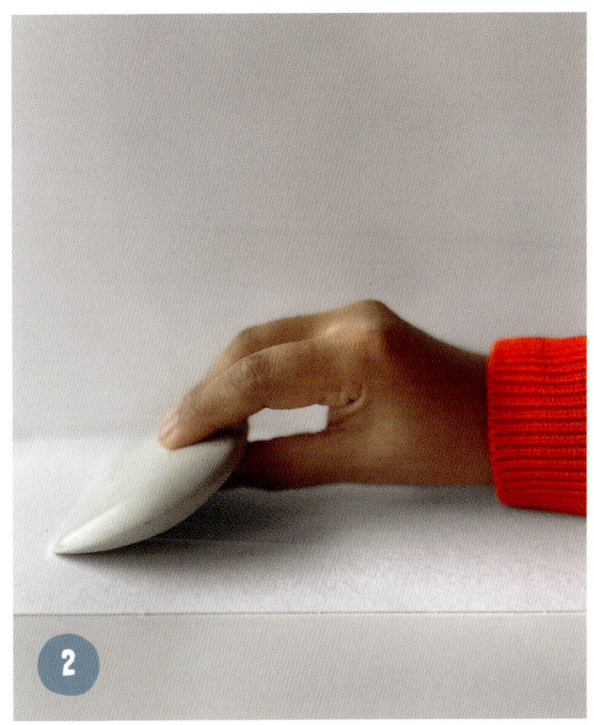

REMOVING THE PAINT

The method you use to scrape off the paint, and the tool you use to do it, will affect your result. You can experiment with different methods to find out which one best suits your process.

The first and easiest way of removing the paint is using medium to firm pressure, while holding your tool at a right angle to the paper. You'll have even more control over the paint when you move it across the paper to create your desired shapes (1).

You can also scrape off the paint by holding your squeegee or painting wedge at less of an angle, at 15 degrees or fewer, for example. Although this often produces striking, cool-looking textures, the paint can be much more difficult to control as it spreads across the squeegee (2).

A last option is to split the process into two phases. In the first phase, you hold your squeegee at an angle of 15 degrees and go over the paint using very light pressure. The paint is then distributed across the paper in a thick layer, covering it completely. In the second phase, you clean your squeegee and scrape over the same area again, this time applying firm pressure at a vertical angle. Your picture is in its final form. This technique can add real wow factor, and the end result can look really amazing.

PAINT LAYERS AND DRYING TIME

The question I get asked most often is this: "Do you wait until one layer has dried before painting the next one?" My answer is: No, I don't. The reason is simple: I apply my paint layers so thinly that they dry right away. That's the secret to using acrylic paint without having to wait for it to dry and also to maintaining its transparency.

So, while you're painting, make sure you either apply each layer thinly or wait until each layer has dried before you apply the next one. Otherwise, the paint could smudge, or the colors might not look as good as they otherwise would.

If any paint oozes out the sides of your squeegee and gathers on the paper, you can finish the line you're on, clean your squeegee, and quickly go over the residue to remove the excess. It's important to do this as soon as possible so paint doesn't stain the paper.

A CERTAIN SOMETHING

When my painting has lots of overlapping shapes and colors, there often comes a point when I feel like a certain something is missing—contrast, for example. Something that catches the eye and makes the picture look more balanced. On the other hand, when I'm adding more weight to a picture, I can sometimes add a little too much or part of the picture can become unbalanced. In either case, here's what to do:

If your paint is lacking contrast or weight, it could be because there's nothing to anchor the observer's gaze. This is more likely to happen when painting shorter stripes and lots of colors, with minimal contrast, one underneath the other. To balance out your picture, you can take a darker color, adding dots of it here and there to try and anchor your picture (1).

If your picture then becomes too dark, I recommend going back over the dark color with a lighter one. This ought to conceal the darker color so you can tone it down a little. I like to use an opaque Titanium Buff Light. I try to avoid pure white as the result is too cold and sterile for my tastes (2).

Squeegee art can sometimes be a bit unpredictable, as you have less control than with a brush. You can try out what works for you until you've found your groove. There's no right or wrong way: The main thing is to have fun.

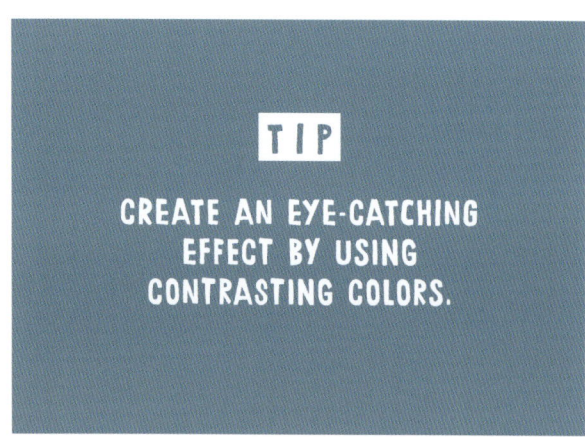

TIP

CREATE AN EYE-CATCHING EFFECT BY USING CONTRASTING COLORS.

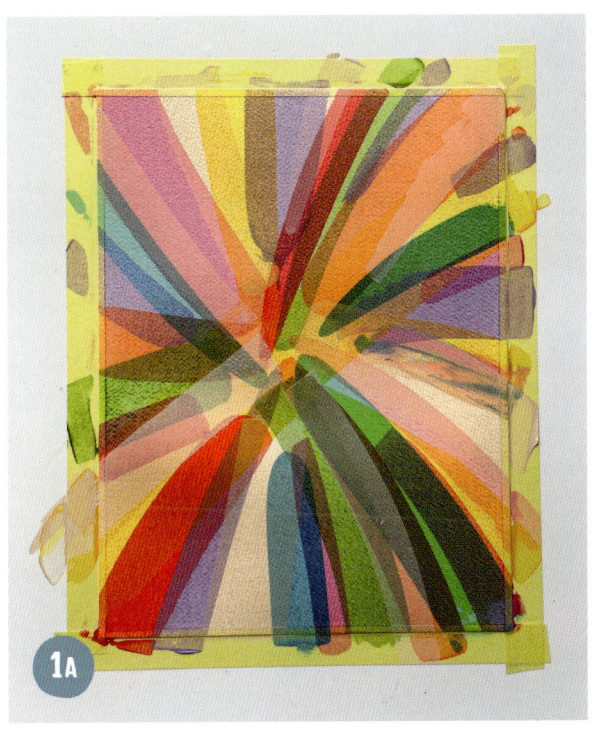

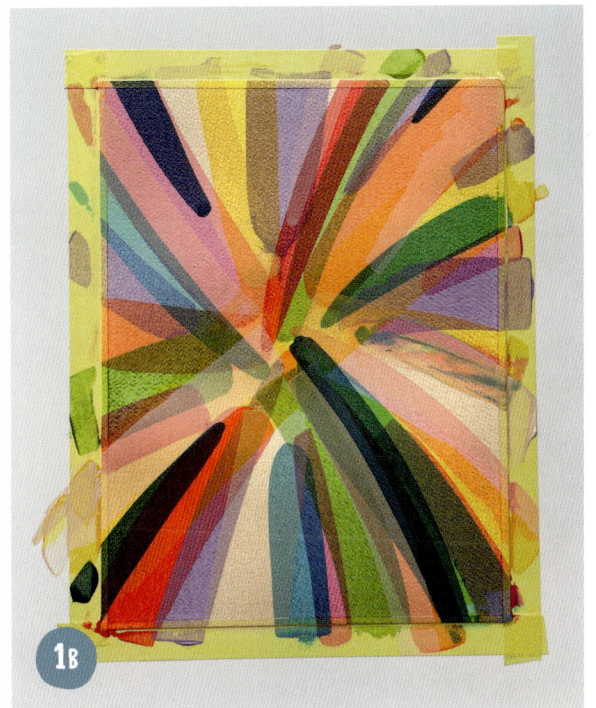

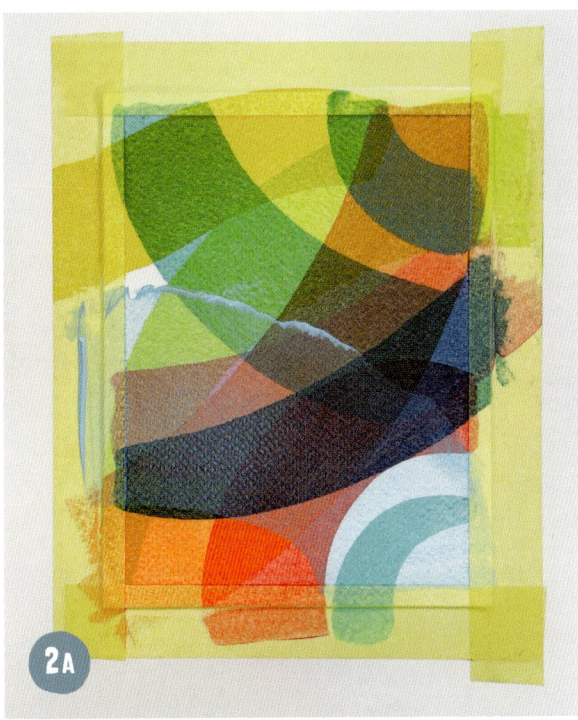

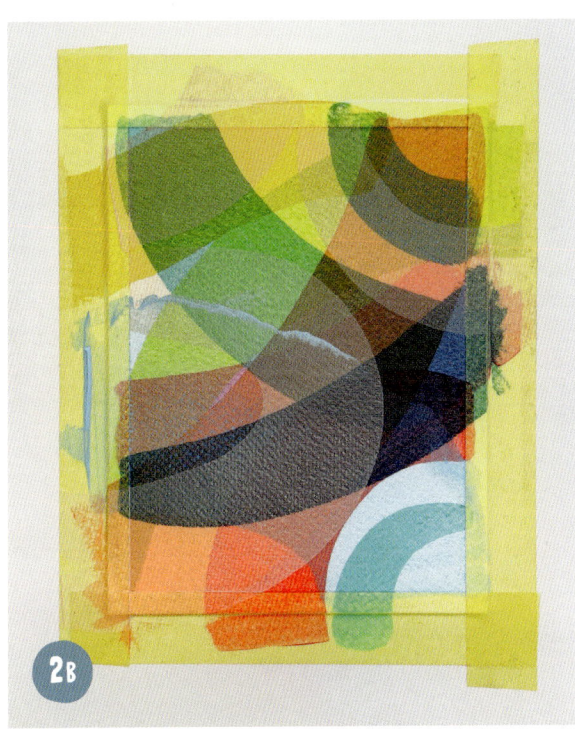

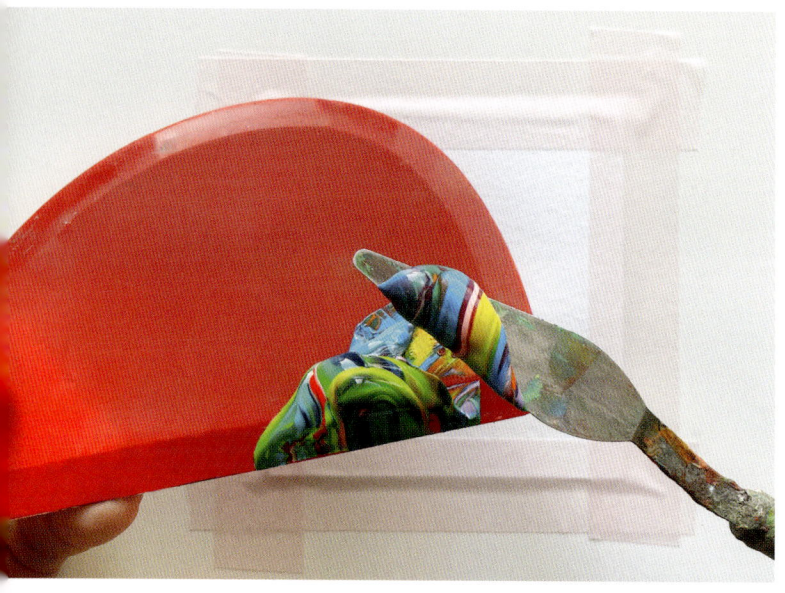

This becomes difficult, however, once you start mixing colors. How can you use this paint later? After a bit of experimentation, I discovered the "marble effect." This technique is easiest if you have two squeegees, one for scraping the paint off the paper and the other for removing the paint from the other squeegee, saving the paint. You can then load the leftover paint onto a palette knife and add it to the paper.

Mountains are motifs that work really well with the marble effect: You can create a wonderful series of paintings with them. One thing to remember is that the marble effect doesn't look as good if the various colors have already mixed together into the leftover paint. If the colors and their edges are still visible, however, the result will blow your mind.

MY TIPS FOR LEFTOVER PAINT

Painting materials aren't all that cheap. If you buy high-quality materials, things can get really expensive. I think it's a shame to waste paint after a squeegee session, so I've started changing the way I work to reduce leftovers. When painting your first pictures, there'll probably be times when you use too much and others when you use too little. In time, you'll find a balance.

When working with plain layers, it's fairly obvious what you can do with the leftover paint: You can paint more layers in the same colors until all the paint has been used up. You can also store the paint in a small container and add it to the paper later with a palette knife.

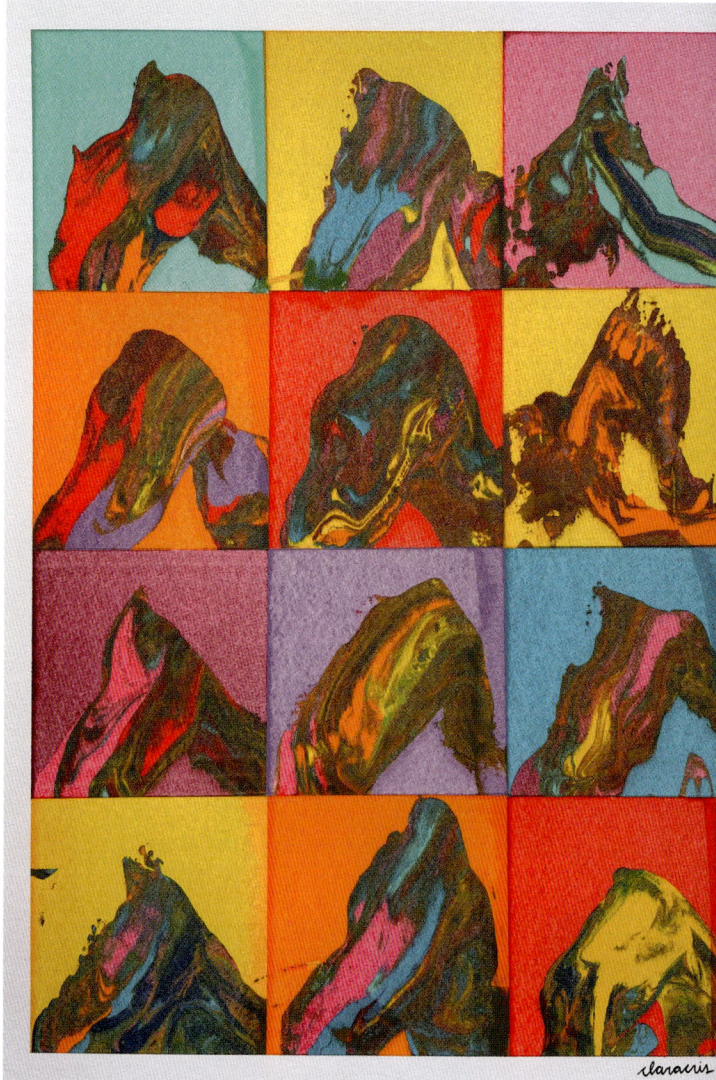

Even if you do these two things, there'll always be some paint left over. If you want to save even more, you can put the leftover paint in a container and use it later. Sometimes, brown may be the only color left; however, even it can be useful later on.

OTHER TYPES OF SUPPORT

You can try squeegee art on other surfaces too. When I was last in Brazil, I painted a 12″ × 12″ (30 × 30 cm) picture on the wall of my parents' house. I can assure you: It works really well and looks great on a smooth background that can absorb the paint. Just make sure that the background is made from a porous rather than a shiny material. If the wall is covered with a shiny material, most of the paint is likely to come off with the squeegee rather than sticking to the wall.

The technique also works well on primed wooden boards. It's a completely different experience than paper, but I loved it and can definitely recommend it. Another advantage of using wood is that you can hang your work immediately after you've finished, without having to prepare or frame it.

With canvases, you have to be a bit more careful. Depending on what you use to ground the canvas, the paint may not be absorbed as well or as quickly as on paper. This means that when you scrape off the paint, you may remove more paint than needed. The paint dries more slowly too, so the different layers may mix if you don't wait until the first layer is completely dry. The result is very different than paper. When it comes to the squeegee technique, canvas has more disadvantages than advantages, so I've stopped experimenting with it and have nothing more to say!

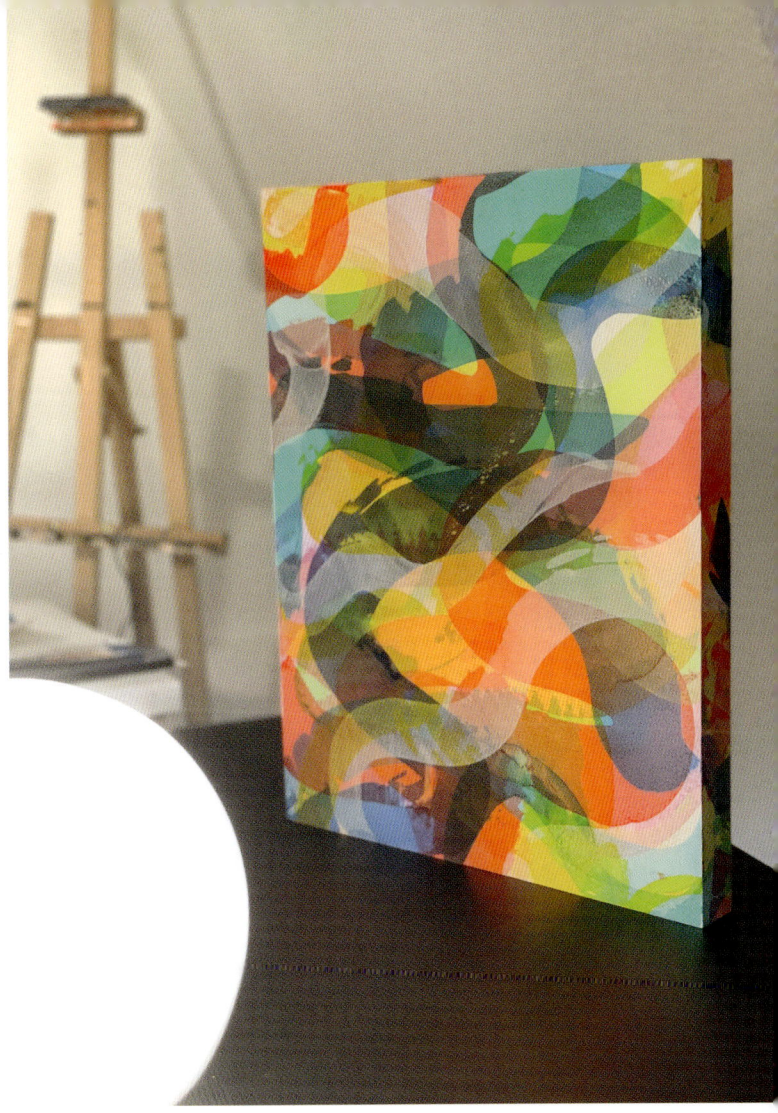

HOW TO TELL WHEN A PAINTING IS FINISHED

To make a long story short: There's no simple answer to this question. When a picture isn't finished, I get a strange feeling when I look at it. It's as if there's something missing, only I'm unsure what. This feeling starts off strong but becomes more subtle the longer I work on a piece. I've ruined so many pictures by adding one last stroke that ended up being too much. And I've also ignored the feeling, only to return to the picture the next day and finish it because I felt restless when I looked at it. Perhaps you also feel like that.

I do have one tip, though: If you're asking whether your picture is finished or not, it's either finished or missing a few details. Instead of carrying on, stop. Maybe wait until the next day so you can look at the picture again with fresh eyes and see what you couldn't see before. This tip is really helpful in my work as a designer and has been useful when painting too.

When it comes down to it, it's you who decides whether your picture is finished or not. In my opinion, it's finished when you feel good about it.

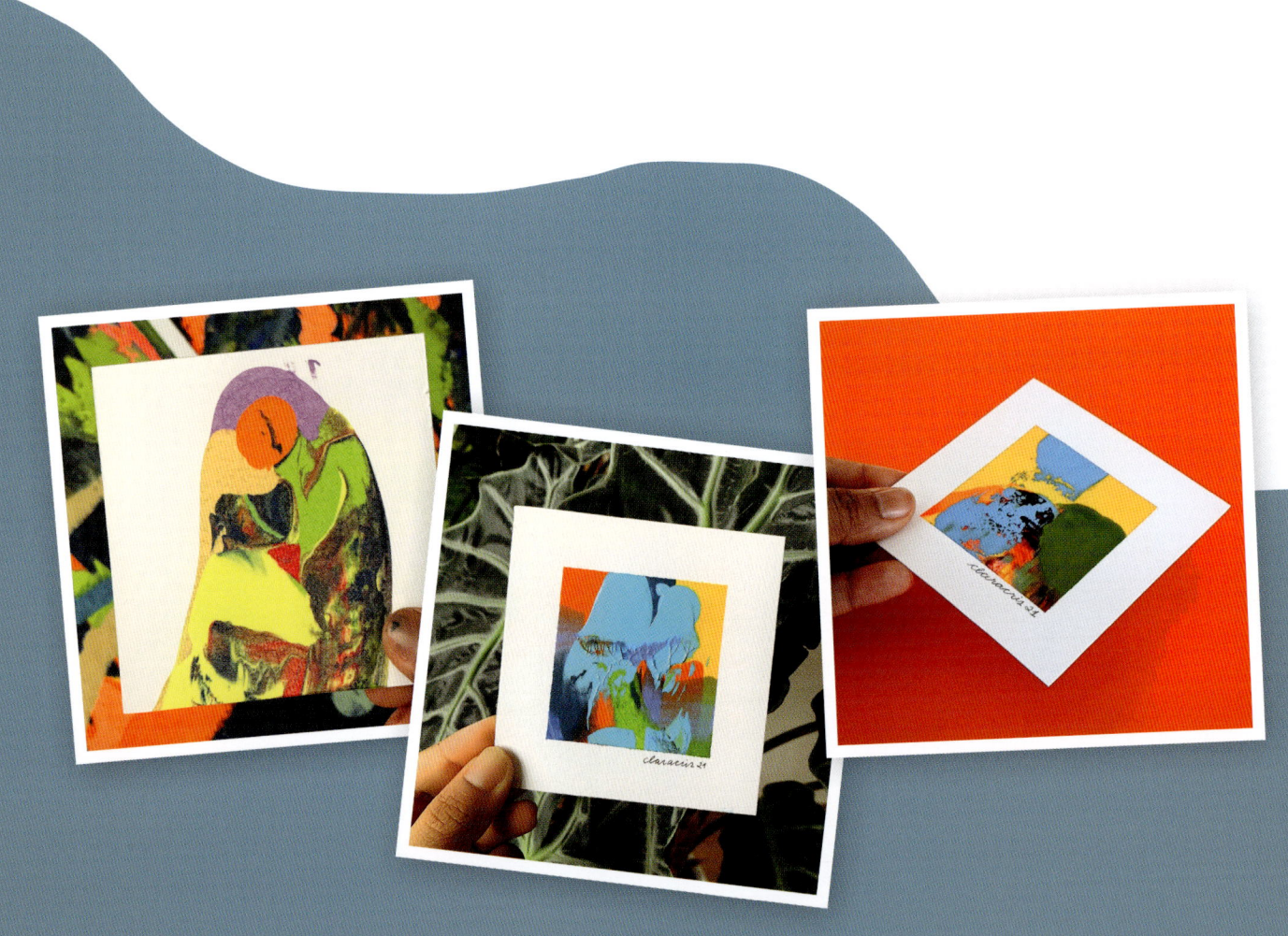

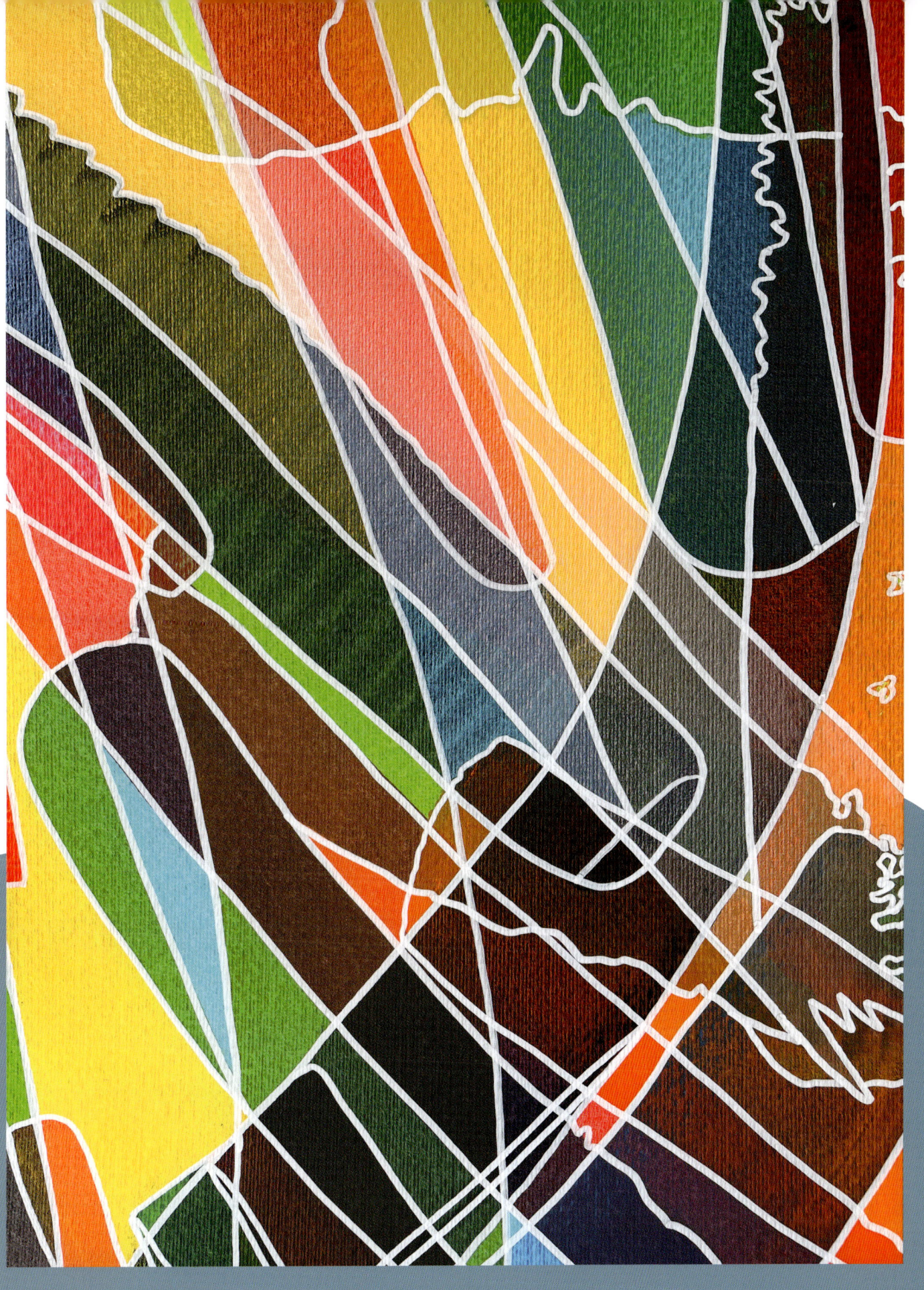

THE BASICS OF SQUEEGEE ART   31

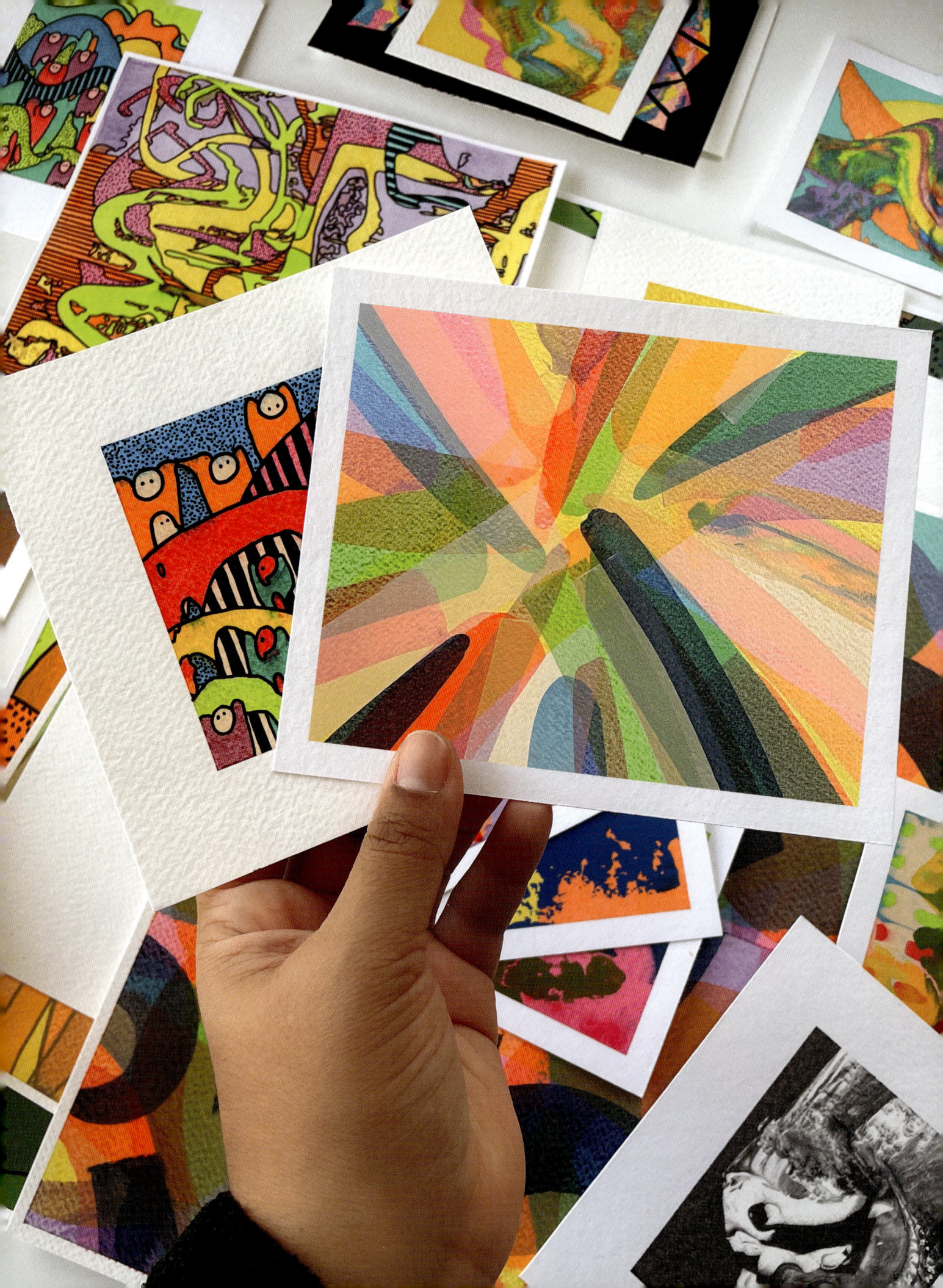

CHAPTER 2

PROJECTS

The time has come! We're now going to paint twenty-two step-by-step projects together so you can get used to the technique in practice, build on it, make it work for you, and, most importantly, have fun! In terms of the colors I've used in each project, you can use similar shades to the ones in the pictures. You don't have to use the colors I recommend, so please don't be put off if you don't have one of the colors at home. Let's get started. **I HOPE YOU HAVE FUN!**

01

JELLY

To warm up, we'll start with a small painting made from a few simple, overlapping shapes. In this project, you'll get a feel for how your paint works with the paper, how each color overlaps, and how much pressure you need to apply to spread the paint over the paper. You'll end up with a picture that I think looks like a line of jellies. Have fun!

PAPER

✖ Fine-grain 200 lb (300 g/m²) watercolor paper, 5.5" × 5.5" (13.5 × 13.5 cm)

COLORS

✖ Yellow Green
✖ Azo Yellow Medium
✖ Turquoise Blue
✖ Turquoise Green
✖ Azo Orange
✖ Permanent Red Purple
✖ Permanent Violet Opaque
✖ Quinacridone Rose
✖ Titanium Buff Light

TOOLS

✖ Squeegee
✖ Masking tape
✖ Damp cloth

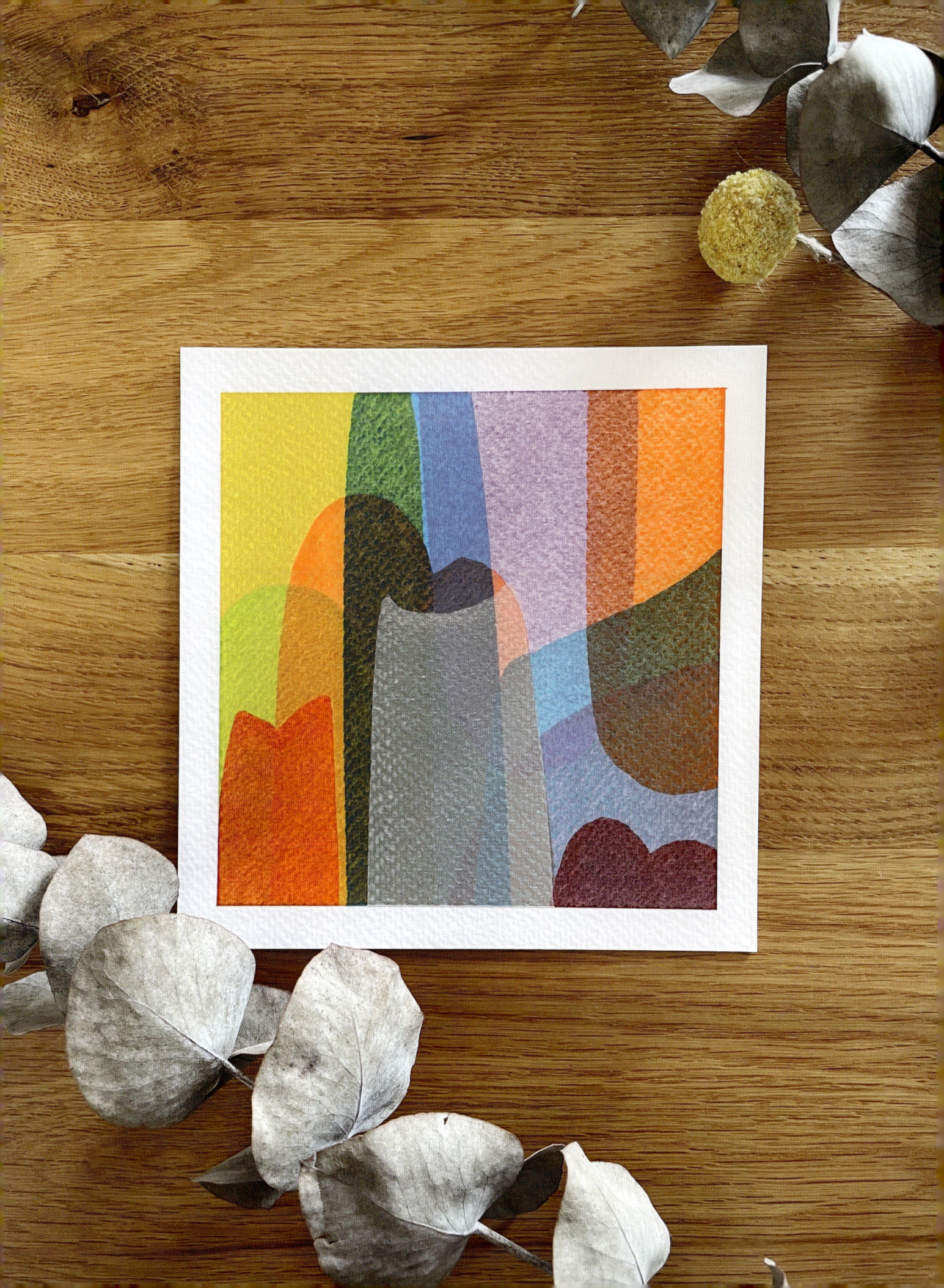

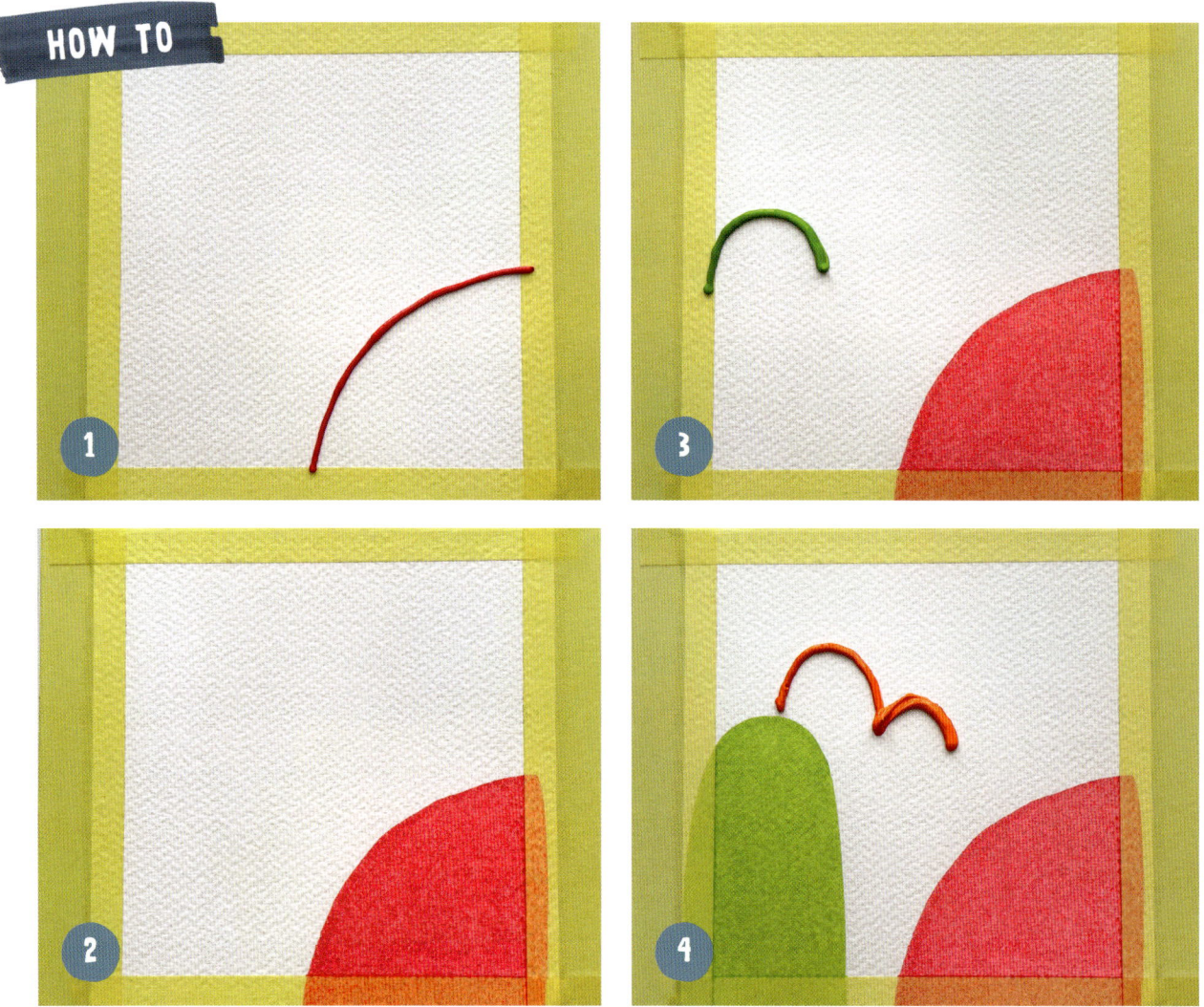

1 Tape down the four edges of your paper. Apply your paint in an arch in the bottom right-hand corner. Make sure the shape is narrower than the squeegee. If the nozzle of your paint bottle isn't narrow enough, that's okay. Just make sure you don't use too much paint or you'll end up with lots left over at the end.

2 Scrape the paint from the top down, applying moderate pressure to your squeegee and dragging it down the paper from the top. You should end up with a shape like the one shown here. After you've

scraped off the first color of paint, use your damp cloth to clean your squeegee to avoid any unwanted paint splatters or color mixing.

3 Now we're going to make a narrower arch on the left of the picture, halfway up the paper.

4 Scrape off the paint with moderate to firm pressure from the top down. Add more shapes and don't be afraid to experiment.

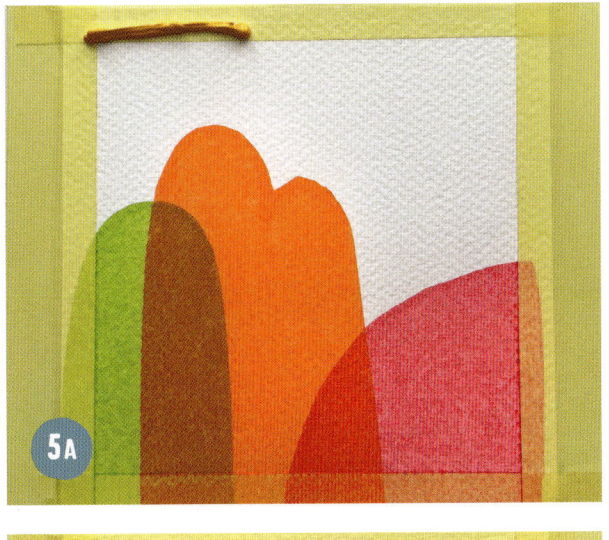

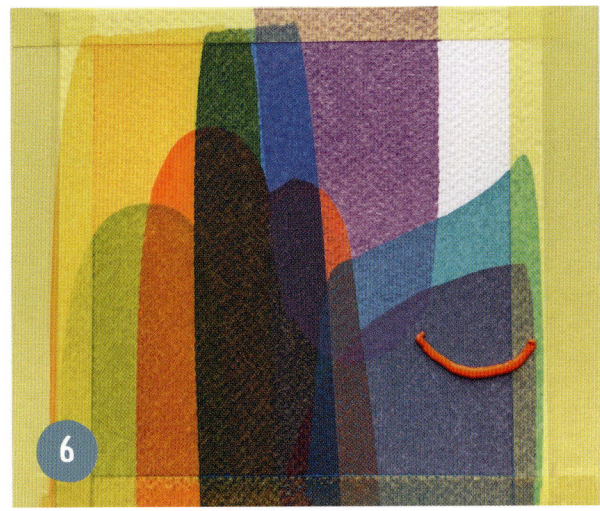

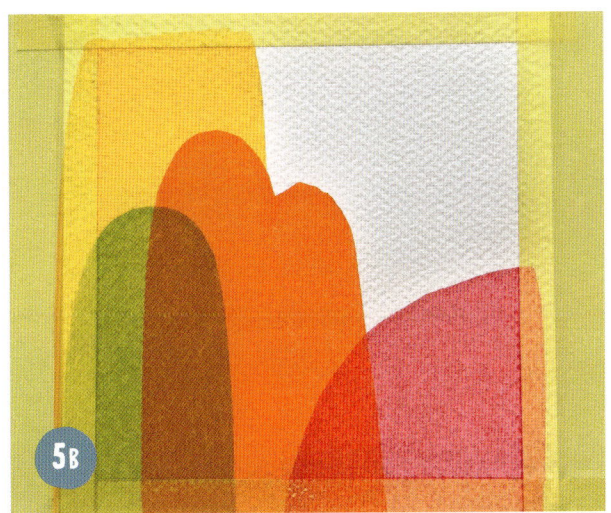

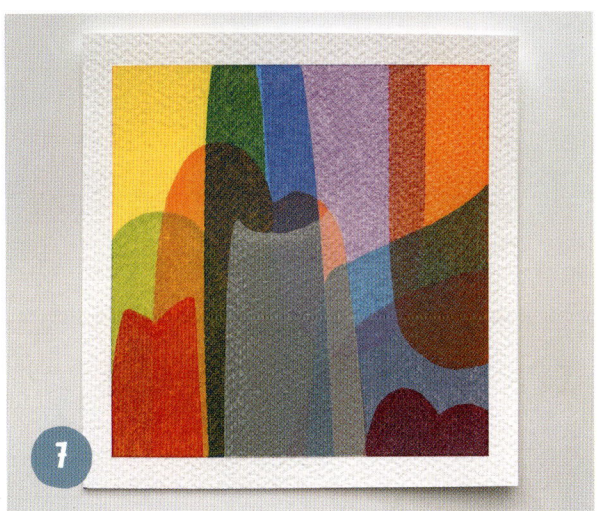

5 You can also apply some paint along the top edge of the picture and scrape it down the length of your paper. Yellow is great for this, as it adds an attractive ray of light to the picture.

6 Keep filling the paper with different shapes. You can scrape from the top down or from the bottom up, depending on the type of shape you want to create. Going from the bottom up is sometimes more difficult, as the motion is slightly less natural yet just as effective.

7 Once I'd added all my colors, I thought the picture looked a little darker than I'd intended. So I added a reversed arch in Titanium Buff Light, scraping the paint from the top down. And that's it! Don't all the overlapping colors look great?

02

JELLY x 4

Now that you've got a feel for the technique, we're going to use what you've learned in the first project to make a bigger picture. To do this, we'll divide the paper into four sections with tape so your squeegee can cover the entire width of the surface. This is really helpful if you're choosing to use one color across the whole surface.

PAPER

✖ Fine-grain 200 lb (300 g/m^2) watercolor paper, 12" × 12" (30.5 × 30.5 cm)

COLORS

✖ Azo Orange
✖ Permanent Red Purple
✖ Turquoise Blue
✖ Azo Yellow Deep
✖ Venetian Rose
✖ Yellow Green
✖ Pearl Violet
✖ Quinacridone Rose
✖ Titanium Buff Light

TOOLS

✖ Squeegee
✖ Masking tape
✖ Ruler
✖ Pencil
✖ Damp cloth

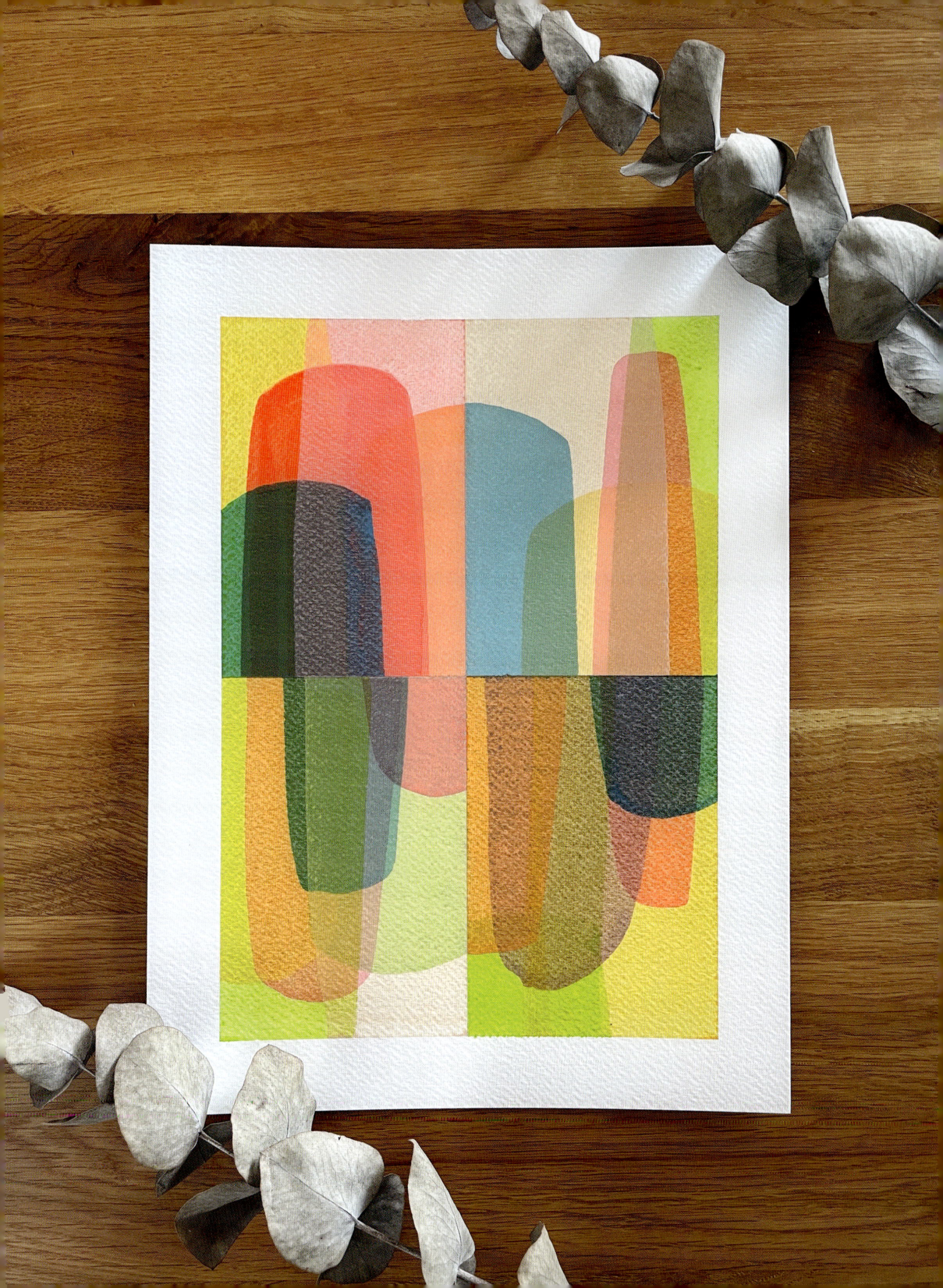

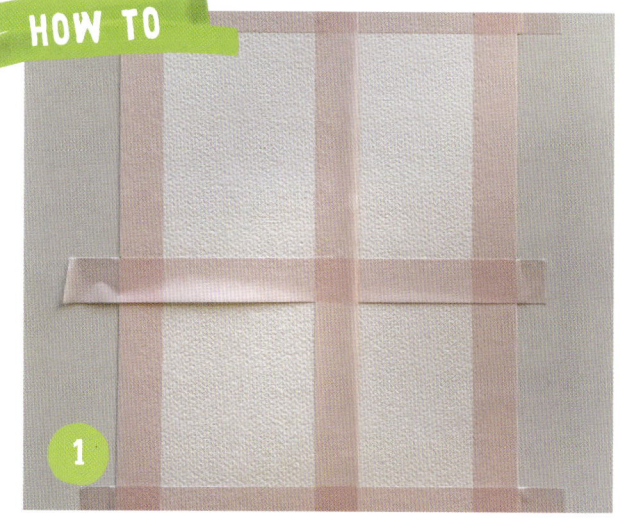

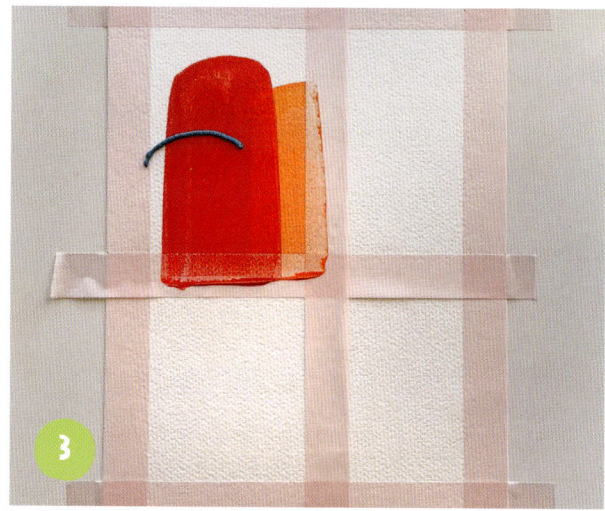

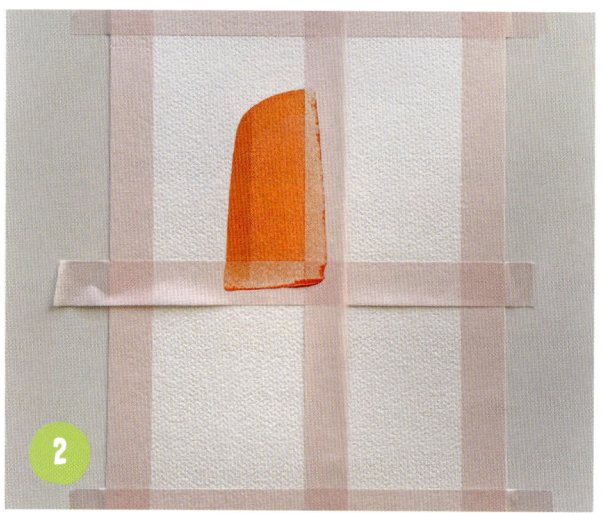

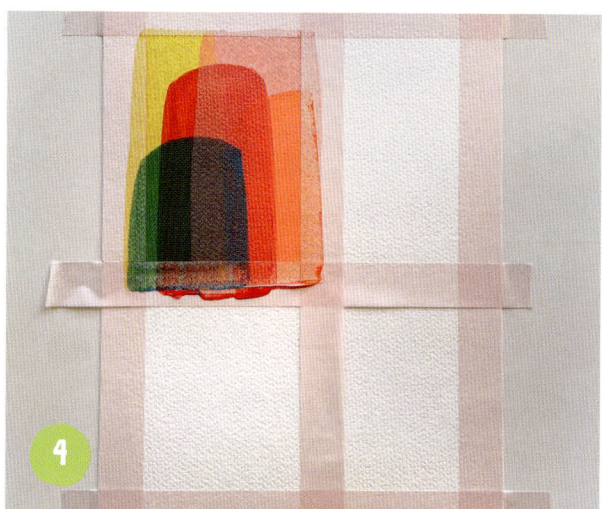

1 Tape down the four edges of your paper. Then take your ruler, measure the midpoint of each side, and mark it in pencil. We're going to paint the top left of the picture now, so take some more tape and isolate this area using the pencil marks to guide you.

2 Start adding different colors in different shapes to this section and scrape the paint across it.

3 Try to vary the height and width of your shapes to make them look more dynamic.

4 Once you're happy with your shapes, you can add a little paint along the top edge of the paper and scrape it across the surface to create an interplay of background and foreground. You can also change the tone of the colors by overlapping them.

5 After letting the paint dry a little, move the tape on the vertical side of the paper so that the right edge of the tape is in line with the center of your paper. Then paint the section in the top right, following the above steps, this time using different colors and shapes. I try to reuse my tape as often as

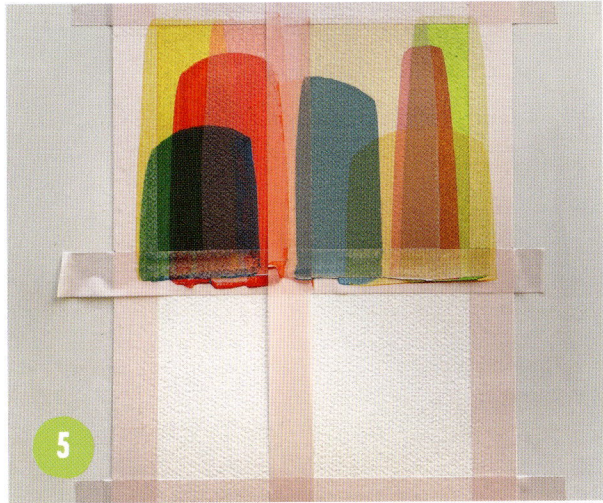

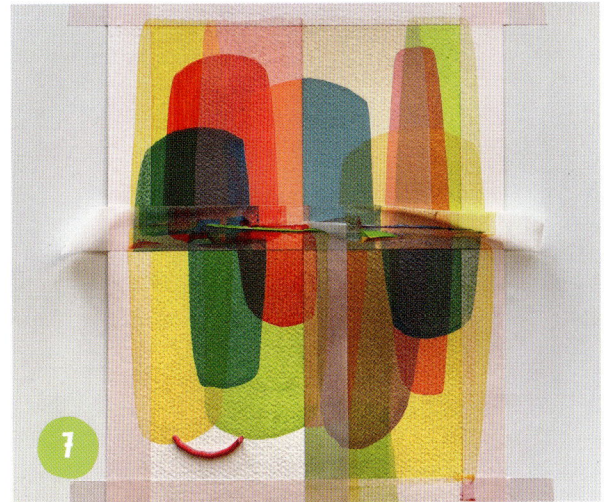

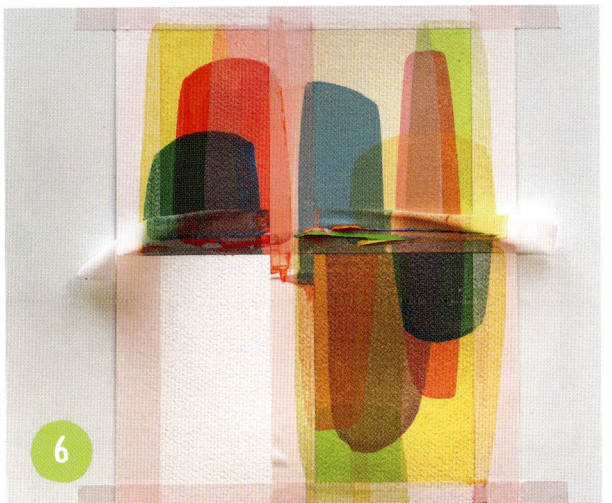

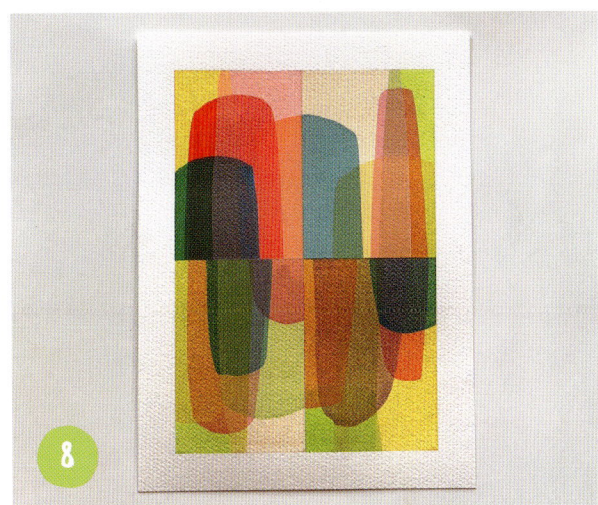

I can, but if it gets smeared with wet paint, I recommend replacing it to avoid any unwanted paint splatters.

6 Once you've finished, move the tape on the horizontal edge of the paper upwards so that the bottom edge of the tape is now in line with the center of your paper. Continue by painting the section in the bottom right of your paper. For a cooler-looking result, I recommend turning the arch upside down and scraping from the bottom up.

7 You can then move the vertical tape again to isolate the last section and continue adding upside-down shapes. Add a few background layers to give your picture that final touch.

8 Now you just need to remove the tape and that's it: You're done! For a style that's completely different but just as cool, you can follow the same steps but leave out the layers that cover the length of each section.

03

DYNAMIC SHAPES

Small, colorful paintings add a bit of sunshine to a room. With organic shapes and overlapping layers, you can create a dance of color on the page. I hope you can relax a little as you paint, enjoying the surprising colors you'll discover when you overlap each individual layer. This lively painting will hopefully bring a smile to your face.

PAPER

✖ Fine-grain 200 lb (300 g/m²) watercolor paper, 5.5" × 7" (17.5 × 13.5 cm)

COLORS

✖ Sky Blue Light
✖ Light Rose
✖ Turquoise Blue
✖ Venetian Rose
✖ Quinacridone Rose
✖ Yellow Green
✖ Azo Yellow Deep
✖ Titanium Buff Light

TOOLS

✖ Squeegee
✖ Masking tape
✖ Damp cloth

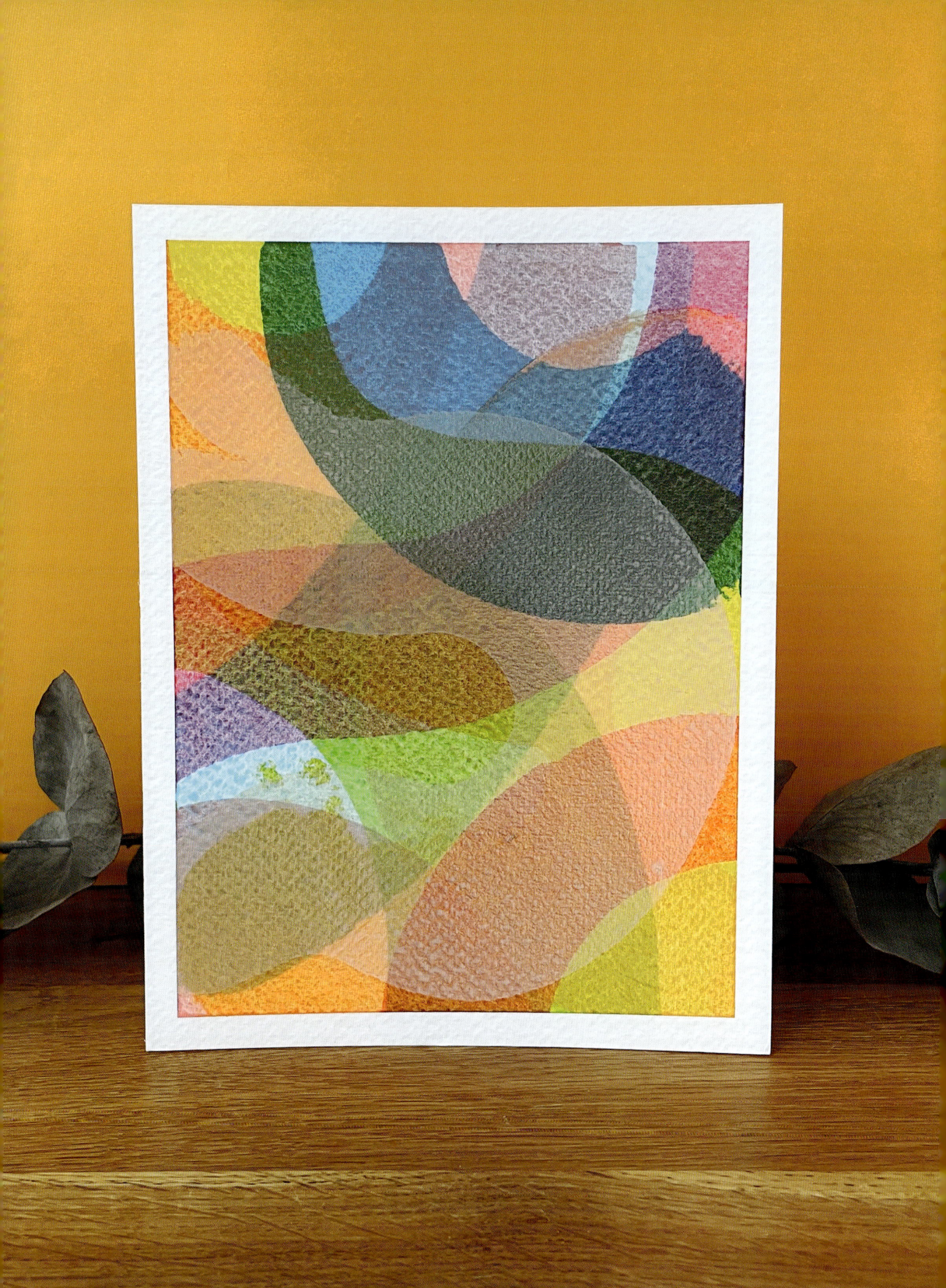

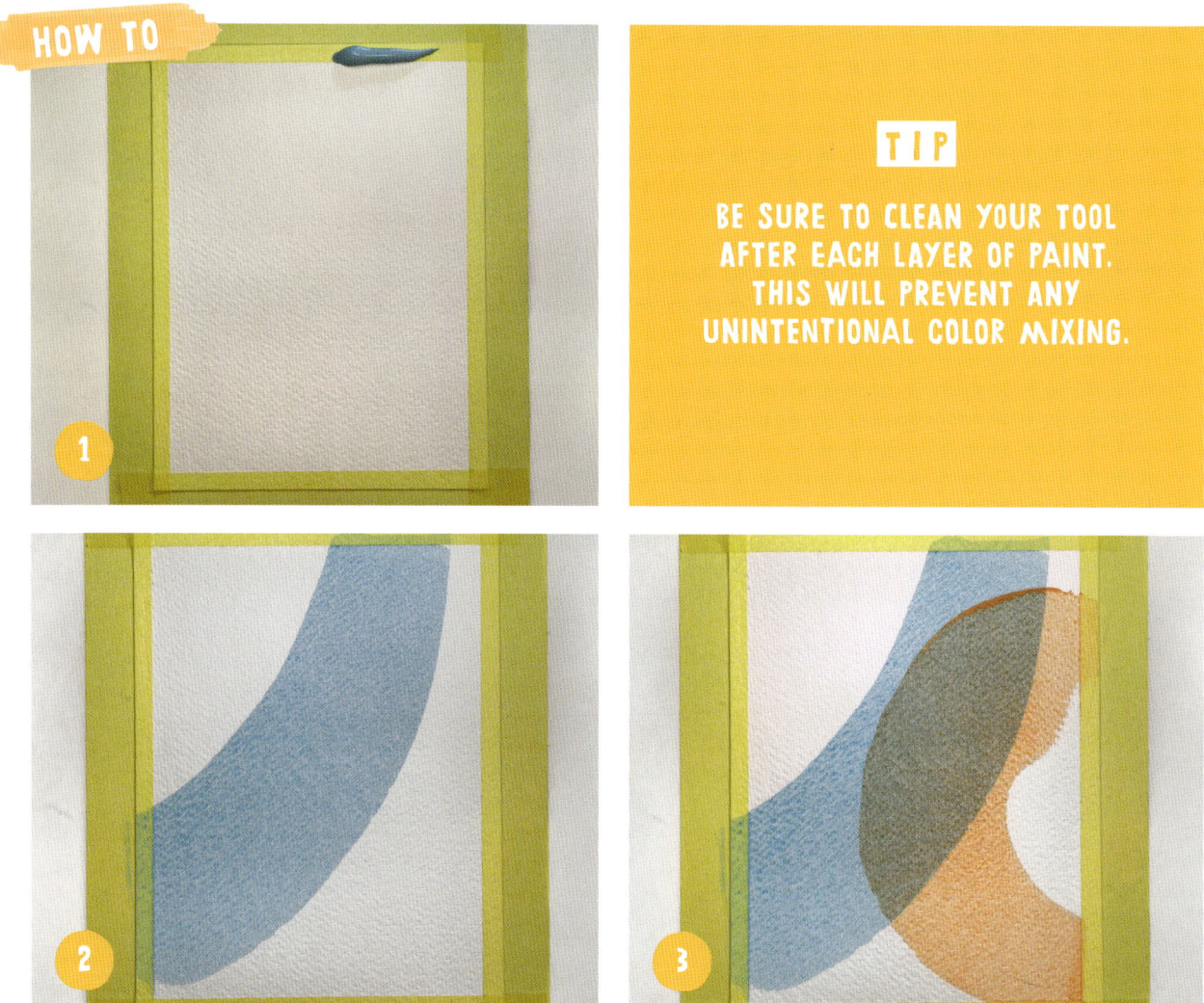

TIP

BE SURE TO CLEAN YOUR TOOL AFTER EACH LAYER OF PAINT. THIS WILL PREVENT ANY UNINTENTIONAL COLOR MIXING.

1 Tape down all four sides of your paper. You can decide how narrow or wide you want the borders to be. Start by applying some blue paint to the top right of your paper, preferably on the tape.

2 Now scrape the paint across your paper and make an open curve toward the bottom left corner. Make sure you hold your squeegee at a vertical angle to the paper, using moderate to firm pressure to create a very thin layer.

3 Apply paint on the top right side of your tape and scrape, following the instructions in the previous step. This time, though, try making the arch narrower. When I did it, I removed more paint from one part of the curve than the other. If this happens, go over it again with your squeegee and remove the excess paint so it doesn't accidentally mix with the next layer.

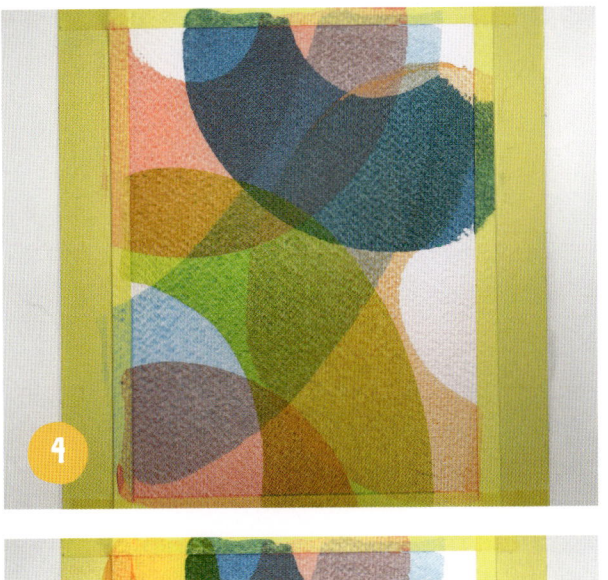

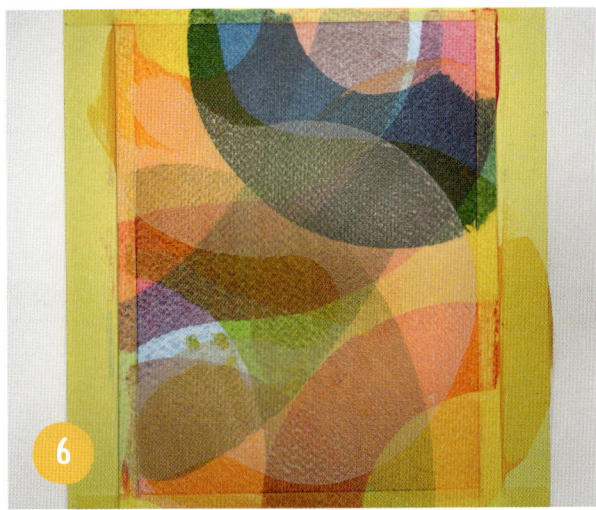

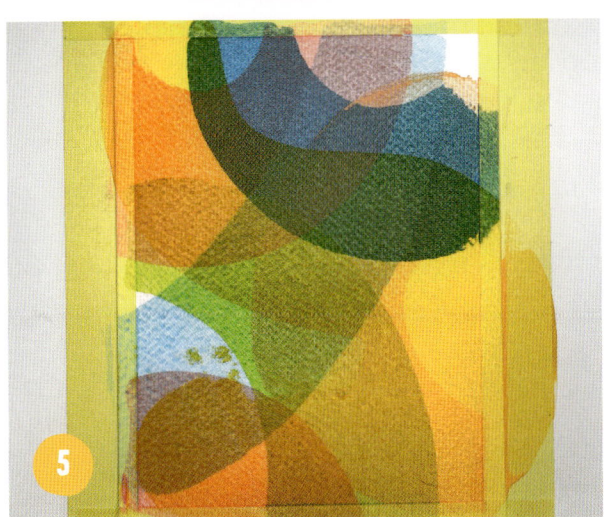

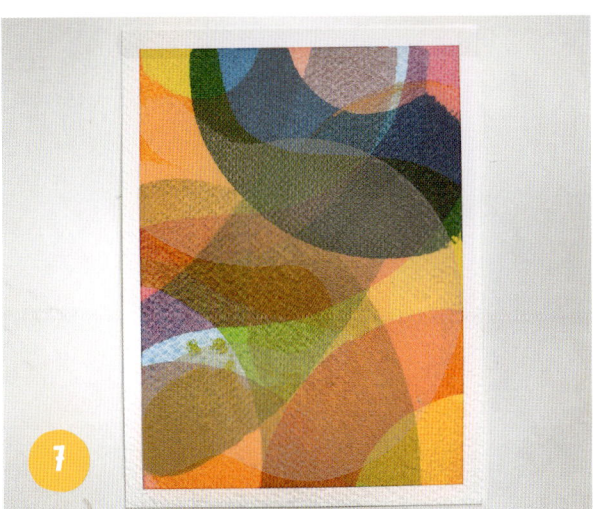

4 Keep using different colors to make wider and narrower arches, transitioning from lighter to darker shades and gradually overlapping them.

5 If you apply too much paint along one edge (like I did with the yellow), just go over the paper again with an organic motion until you've covered a larger area and used up more of the paint. If there's too much paint for the size of the paper, try to reach the next edge and then remove the excess with your squeegee.

6 Keep applying your paint until the white paper is no longer visible.

7 Once you've decided the picture is finished, you can remove the tape and admire your new work of art.

04

A DANCE OF COLOR

How about painting the picture on the cover of this book? You've practiced the technique a little in the previous project, so now all you have to do is find the right colors. One thing you might find hard to copy is the "happy accident" in the middle of the painting where a light-blue stripe formed on the paper. Perhaps you can re-create it, accidentally on purpose?

PAPER

✖ Fine-grain 200 lb (300 g/m²) watercolor paper, 5.5" × 7" (17.5 × 13.5 cm)

COLORS

✖ Quinacridone Rose
✖ Turquoise Blue
✖ Azo Orange
✖ Yellow Green
✖ Sky Blue Light
✖ Turquoise Green
✖ Azo Yellow Deep
✖ Permanent Red Purple
✖ Cobalt Blue
✖ Titanium Buff Light

TOOLS

✖ Squeegee
✖ Masking tape
✖ Damp cloth

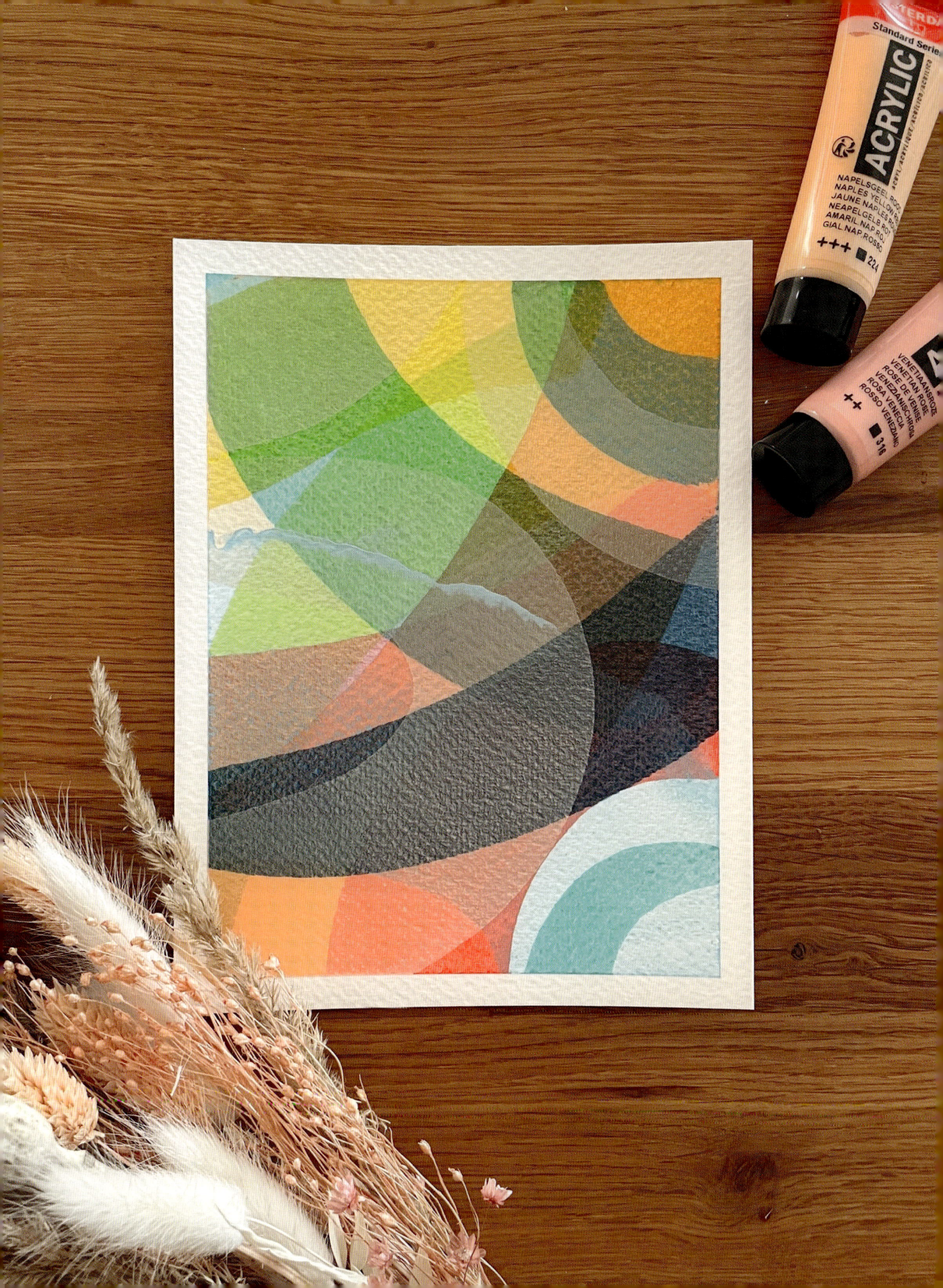

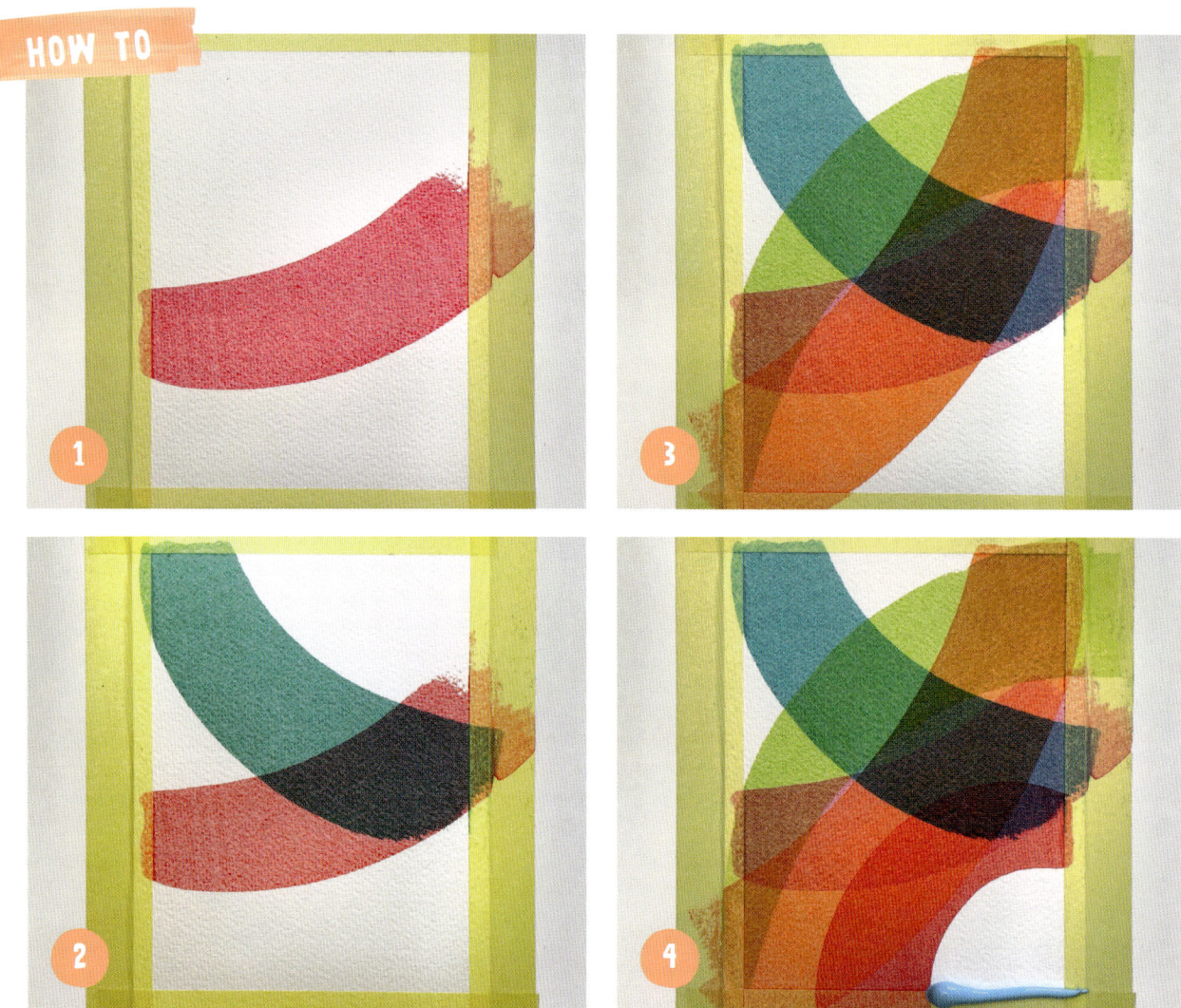

1 Tape down the four edges of your paper. Then apply some paint on the left side of your paper over the tape and scrape it to the right with a curved, upward motion.

2 Then apply some paint to the top left edge of your paper and scrape it across with a curved, downward motion.

3 Keep adding different colors over the edges of the tape and scraping them in a sweeping curve across the picture, sometimes going up, sometimes down. Try to fill the center of your paper first.

4 When you reach the bottom right-hand corner, you can create a gorgeous contrast by making the arch narrower, as you can see with the red paint. You can also reduce the width of the arch by using less paint. As you can see, I've already applied the blue paint on the bottom right. I'm going to scrape it off next. I used more paint than I actually needed but didn't notice at the time.

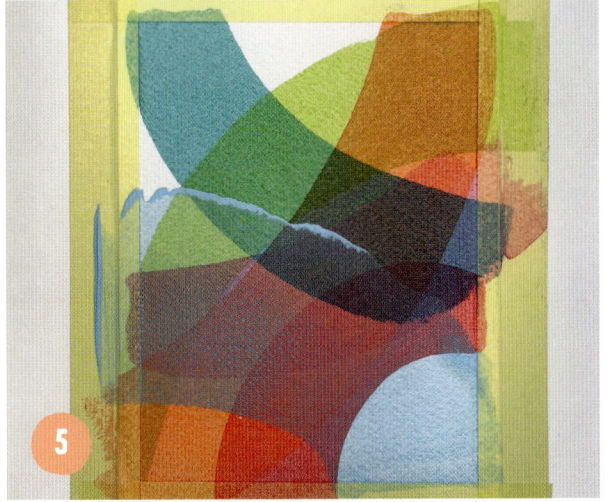

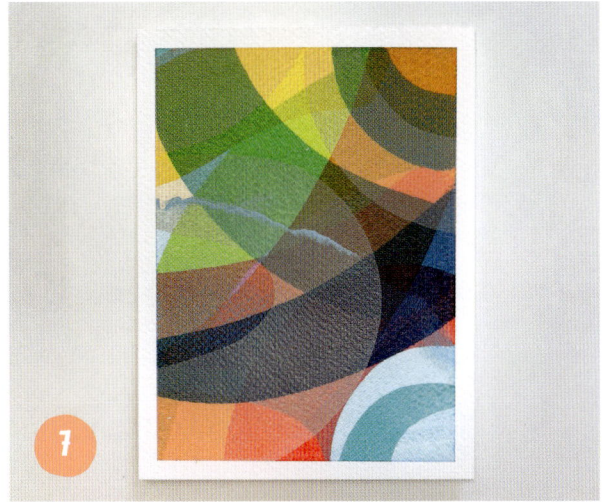

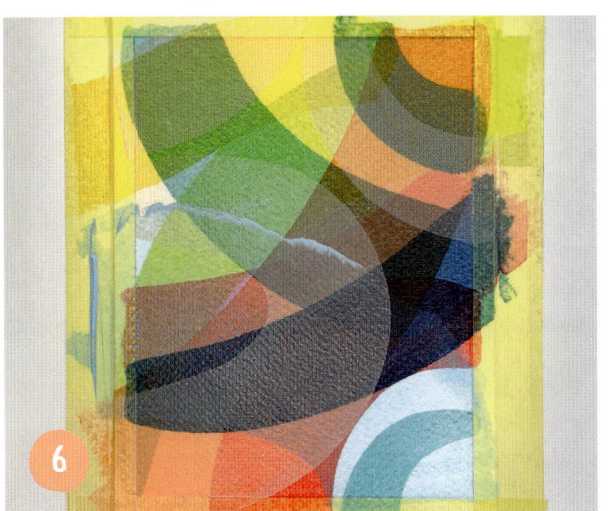

TIP

IF YOU FEEL YOUR COMPOSITION NEEDS A BIT MORE WEIGHT, ADD A LITTLE DARK PAINT.

5 While scraping, the blue paint oozed out over the sides of my squeegee, leaving behind a trail of paint on the paper. I could have gone over it again, but actually, I liked how this "happy accident" looked. If the same happens to you, you need to decide whether or not to remove the excess paint. If you decide to leave it, you need to wait until it's dried before adding any other layers.

6 After my "happy accident" had dried, I moved on to my picture's final layers. I added a little dark blue to give everything a bit more weight, but I had the feeling that it was too much, so I layered a little Titanium Buff Light over the top.

7 Remove the tape and enjoy the colorful dance in all its glory.

05

POP-ART-PARTY 1

This is a really fun project. We're going to use the squeegee technique to create the background of the painting. We'll outline the creatures that we discover in marker and add a few patterns to the plain areas.

PAPER

- ✘ Fine-grain 200 lb (300 g/m²) watercolor paper, 5.5" × 5.5" (13.5 × 13.5 cm)

COLORS

- ✘ Permanent Red Purple
- ✘ Quinacridone Rose
- ✘ Azo Yellow Deep
- ✘ Titanium Buff Light
- ✘ Azo Orange
- ✘ Yellow Green
- ✘ Turquoise Blue
- ✘ Permanent Madder Lake
- ✘ Permanent Green Deep

TOOLS

- ✘ Squeegee
- ✘ 0.7 marker (black)
- ✘ Masking tape
- ✘ Damp cloth

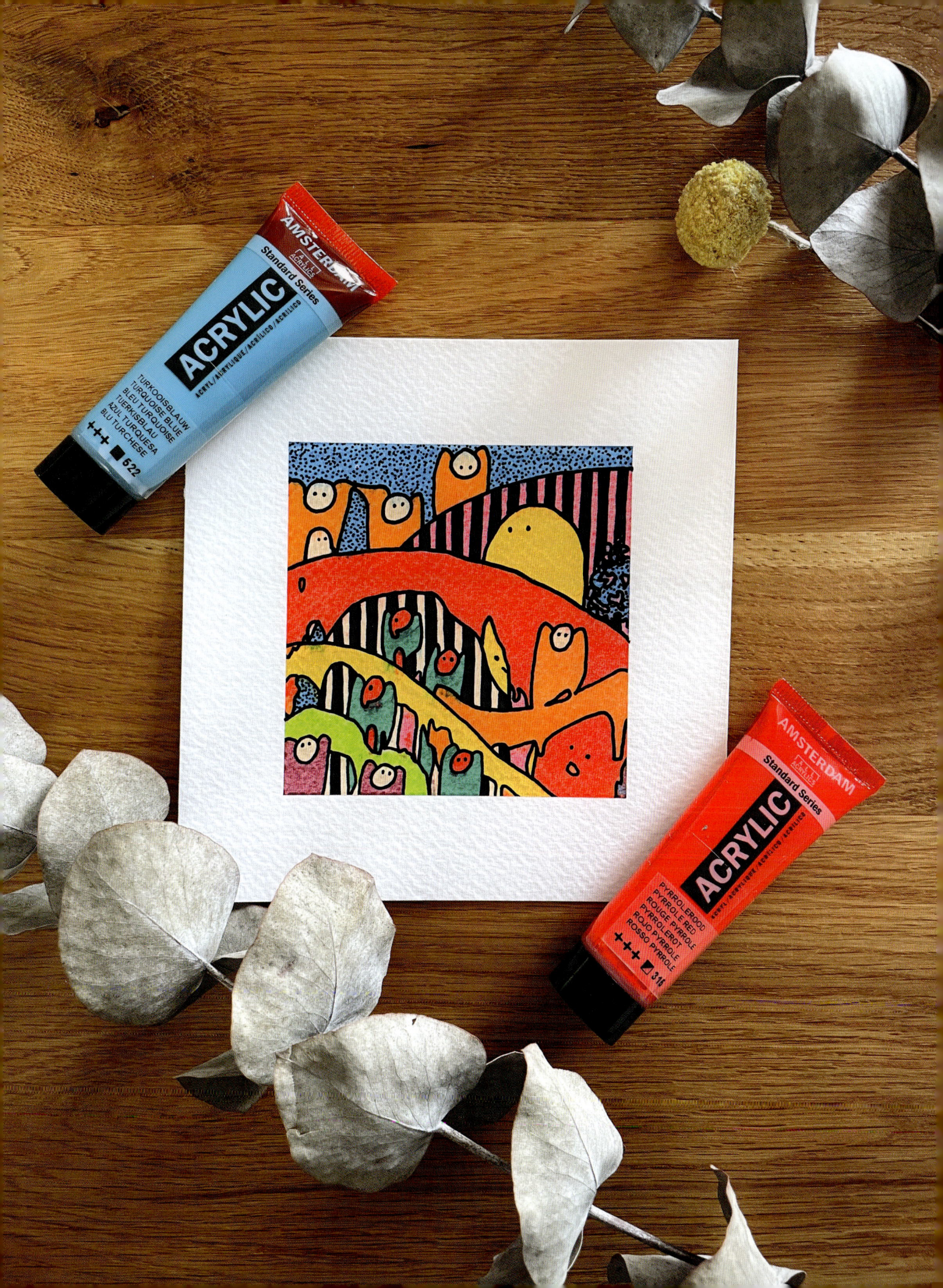

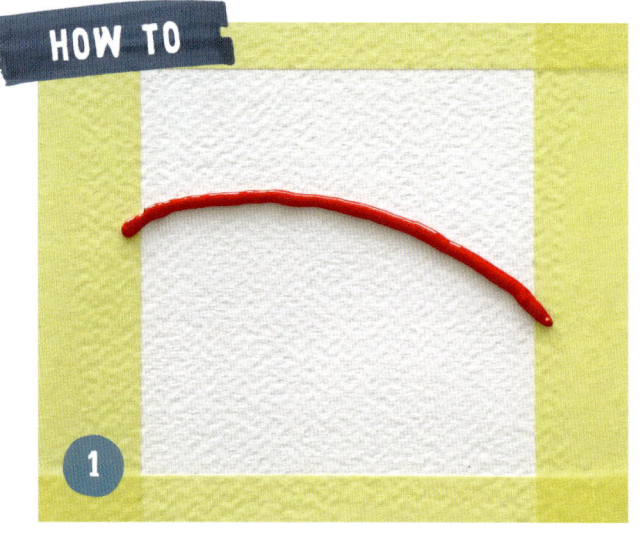

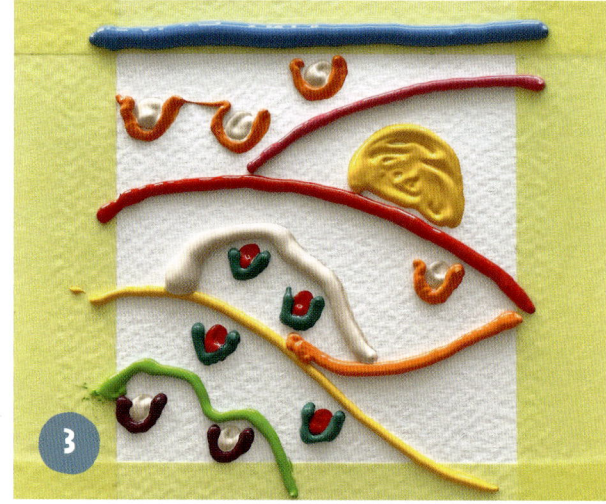

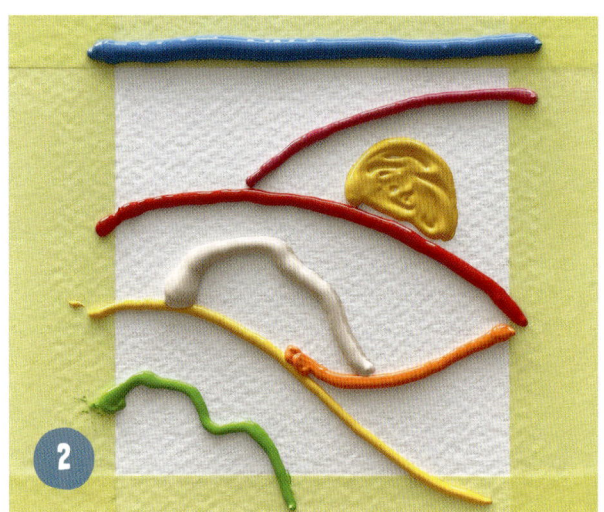

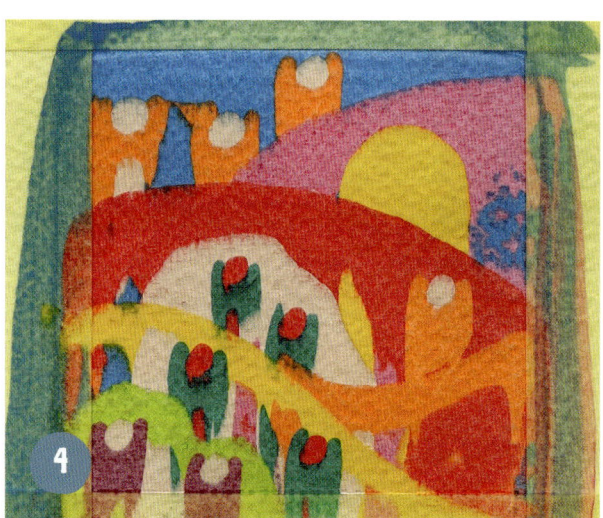

1 Tape down the four edges of your paper. Make sure the paper is narrower than your squeegee or painting wedge. In this project, we'll add all the paints to the paper first, then scrape them all off at the same time.

2 Apply the paints to the paper. This is our first time trying this sort of project, so I recommend applying the paints as shown in this picture. Apply the paint as thinly as you can: It's more likely to keep its shape and less paint will be left over.

3 In this step, you can add a few dots to the paper and a contrasting color below them.

4 Scrape off all the paint at the same time, from the top down, by placing your squeegee at a right angle and applying moderate to firm pressure.

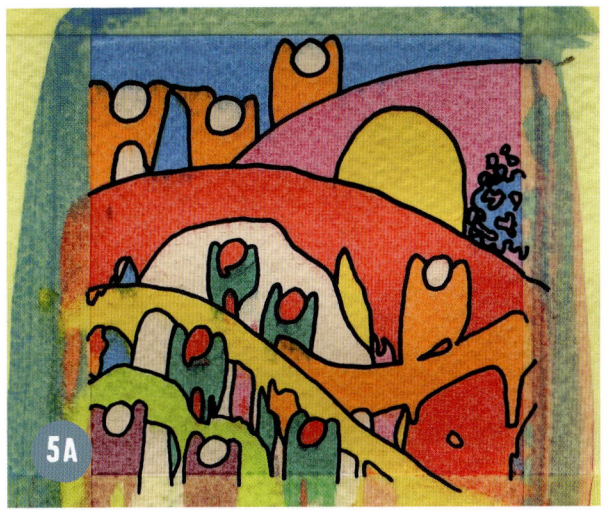

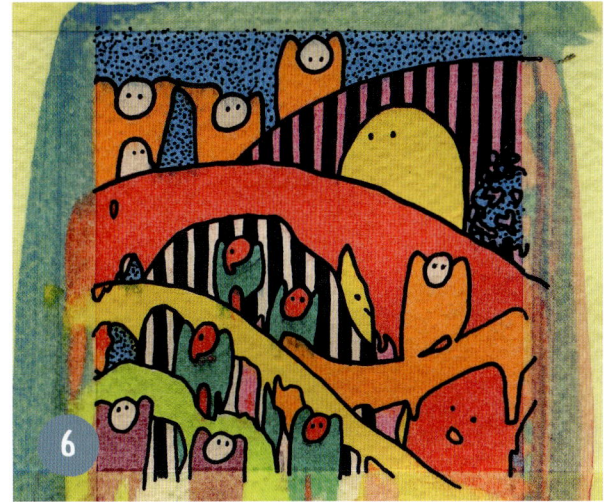

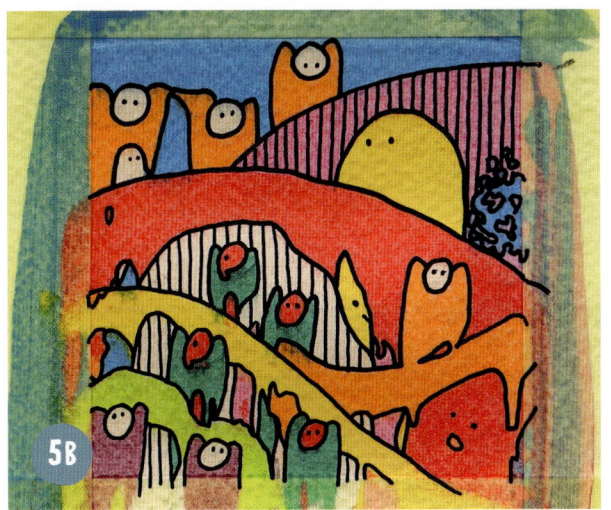

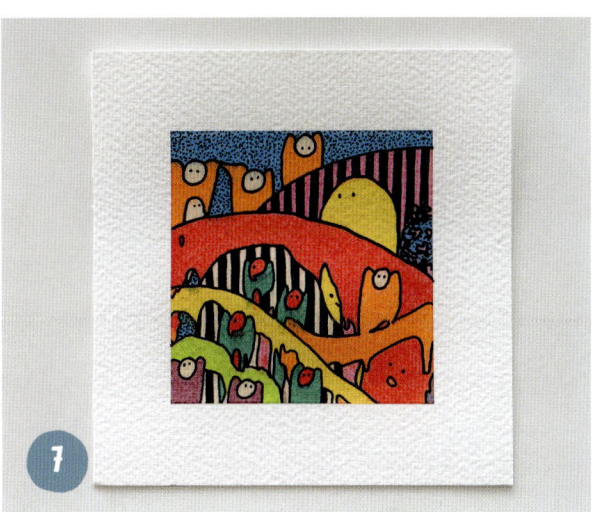

5 In this step, take a marker and draw an outline around all the shapes you can find in the picture. They can be the sun, small figures, animals . . . Let your imagination run wild! Perhaps you'd like to add some eyes, hair, clothes, or animal ears . . . The options are endless!

6 You can also make the plain areas look more interesting by adding a pattern. Stripes and polka dots are my favorites, as you can see here.

7 Remove the tape and your new pop-art-style squeegee painting is done!

06

POP-ART-PARTY II

This project uses the same style as the previous project but with a different color palette. What shapes do you think you'll discover this time?

PAPER

- ✖ Fine-grain 200 lb (300 g/m²) watercolor paper, 5.5" × 5.5" (13.5 × 13.5 cm)

COLORS

- ✖ Permanent Red Purple
- ✖ Quinacridone Rose
- ✖ Azo Yellow Deep
- ✖ Titanium Buff Light
- ✖ Azo Orange
- ✖ Yellow Green
- ✖ Turquoise Blue
- ✖ Permanent Madder Lake
- ✖ Permanent Green Deep

TOOLS

- ✖ Squeegee
- ✖ 0.7 marker (black)
- ✖ Masking tape
- ✖ Damp cloth

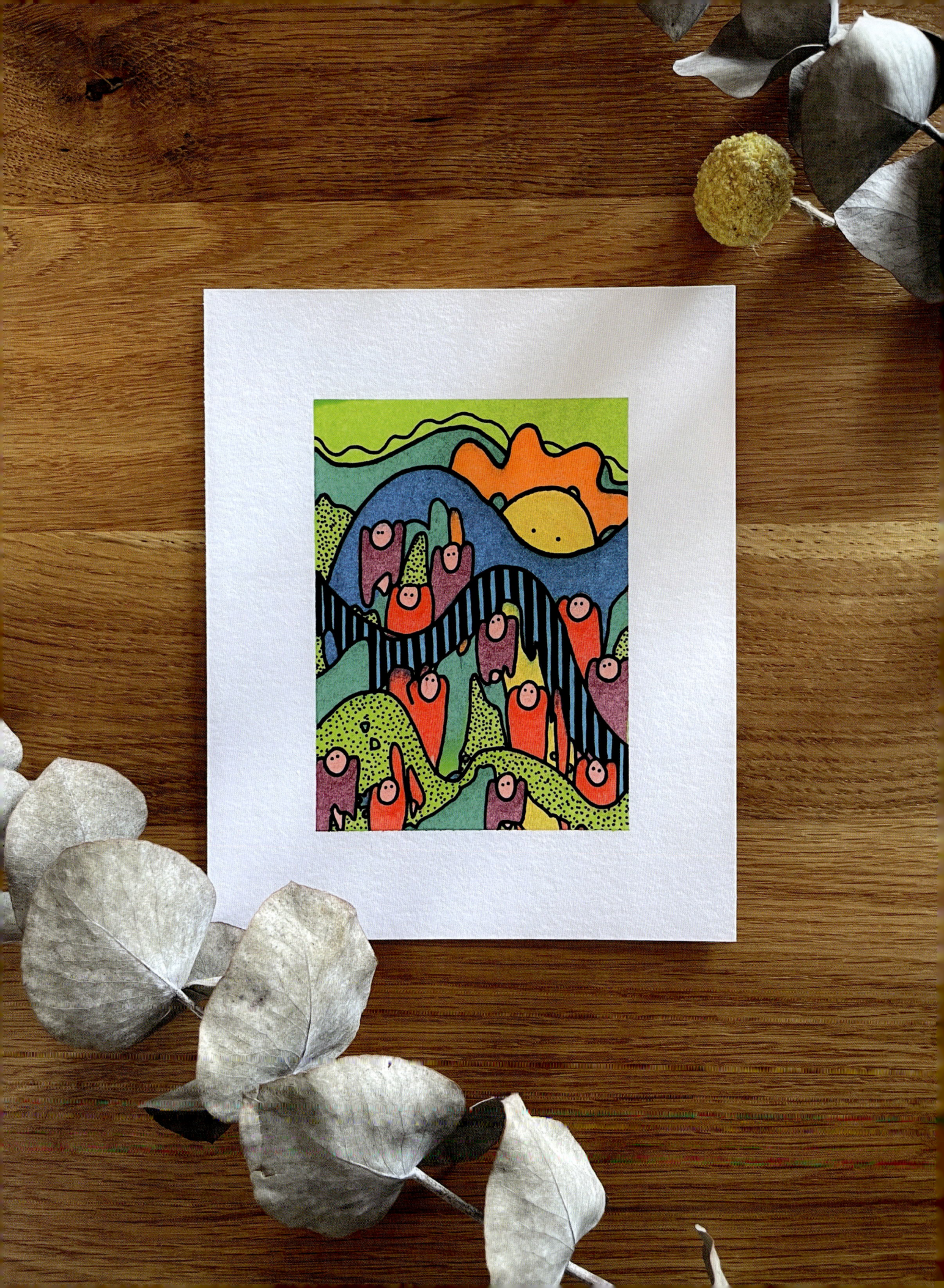

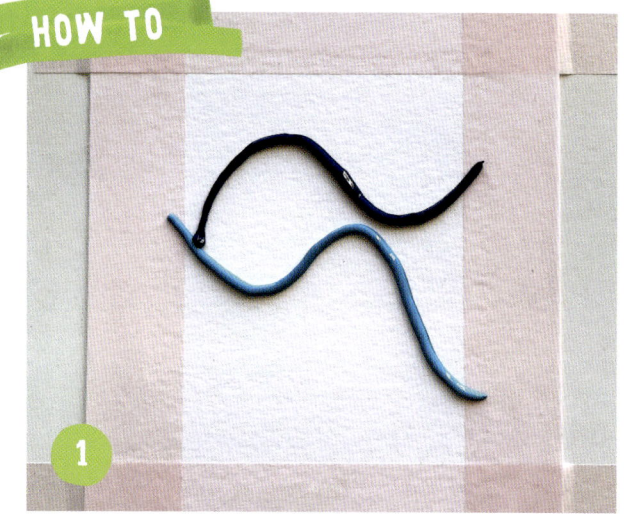

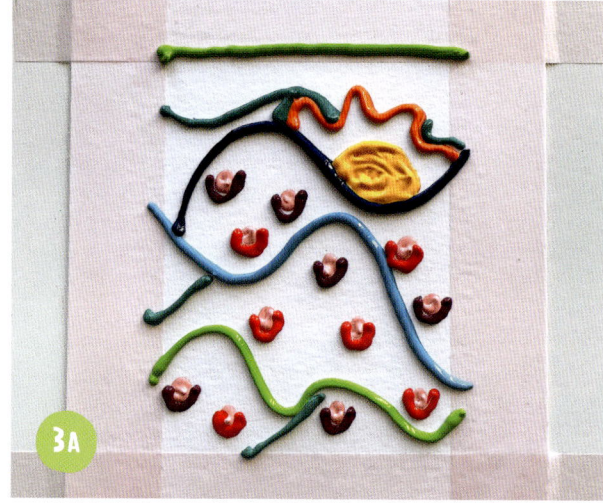

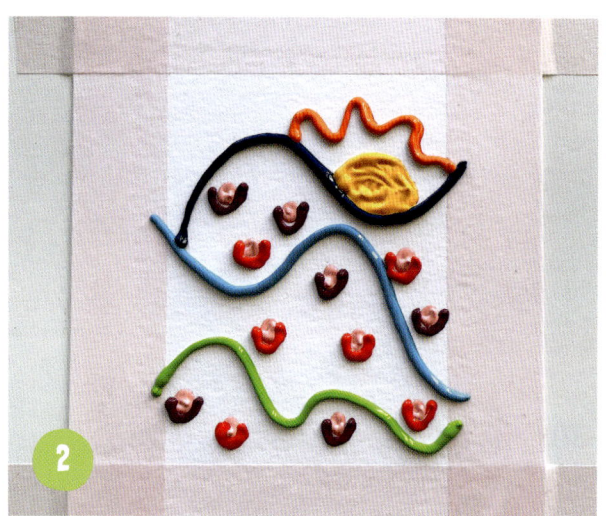

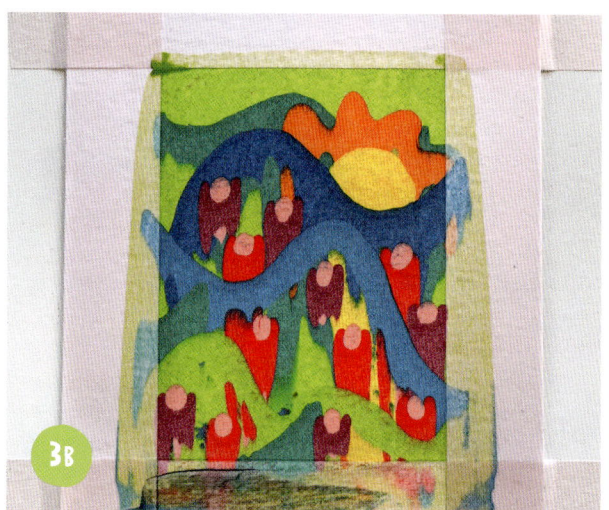

1 Let's make another pop-art-style picture. The steps are similar to the previous project, only this time, we have more freedom when it comes to placing the paint. You'll then get a better understanding of how the paint behaves when you scrape it off. The wavy lines will look like different layers once we've finished. To start, tape down all four sides of your paper.

2 Here I've added something that I hope looks like a shining sun. I then added dots with semicircles below them, just like I did in the previous project.

3 Along the top edge, I've added a horizontal line in green paint for the background. Then I scraped off all the paint.

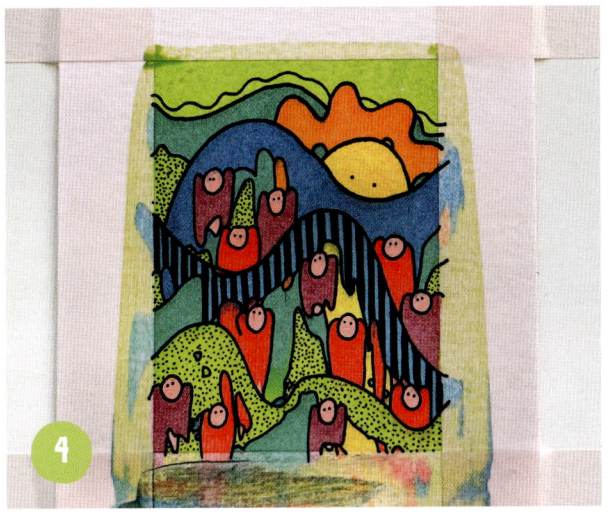

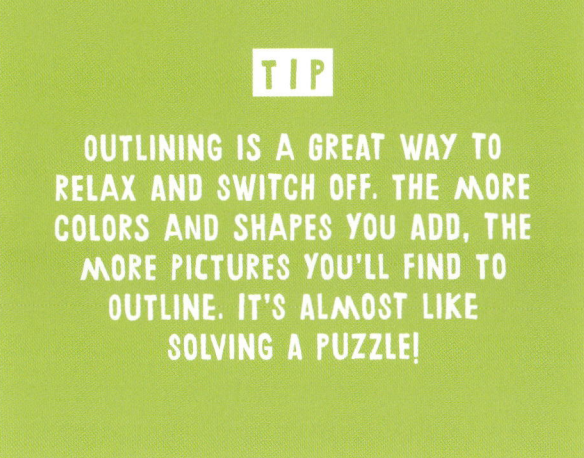

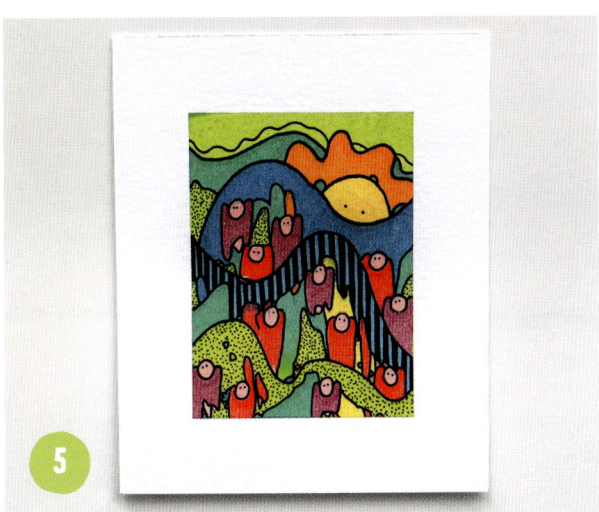

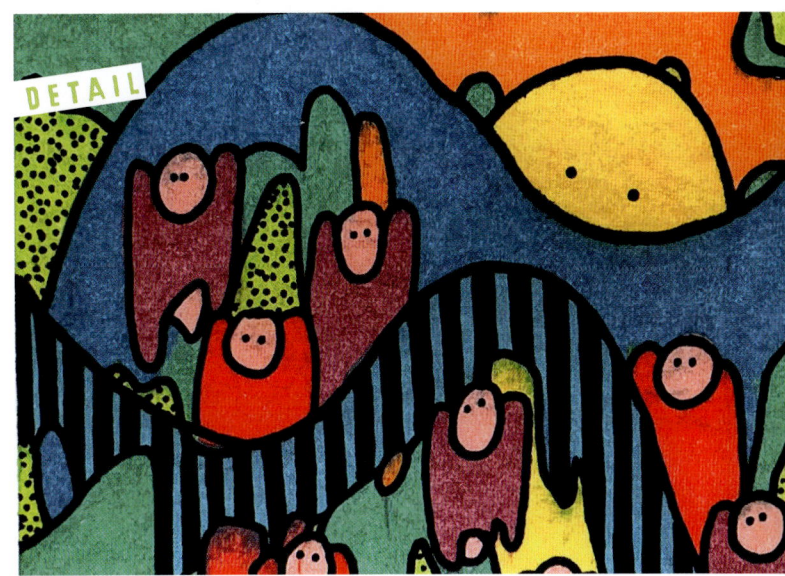

DETAIL

4 Take your marker and start by outlining everything you can find in your picture. Let it all flow and maybe take time to add some patterns.

5 The results can sometimes be surprising. This picture is no exception. I love how this color combo turned out, and the cute little sun too! I hope you feel the same about your own picture.

07

HIDDEN SURPRISES

This is one of the most interesting techniques, in my opinion. Not because of how complicated it is or how it turns out, but because of how many ways it can be interpreted. Whenever I paint a black-and-white picture, I always get lots of feedback. Why not run an experiment and ask the people around you what they see? You'll be surprised—and you're sure to get a few laughs too.

PAPER

- ✖ 245 lb (360 g/m²) acrylic paper, 6" × 5" (15 × 12.5 cm)

COLORS

- ✖ Oxide Black
- ✖ Titanium White

TOOLS

- ✖ Squeegee
- ✖ Palette knife
- ✖ Masking tape
- ✖ Damp cloth

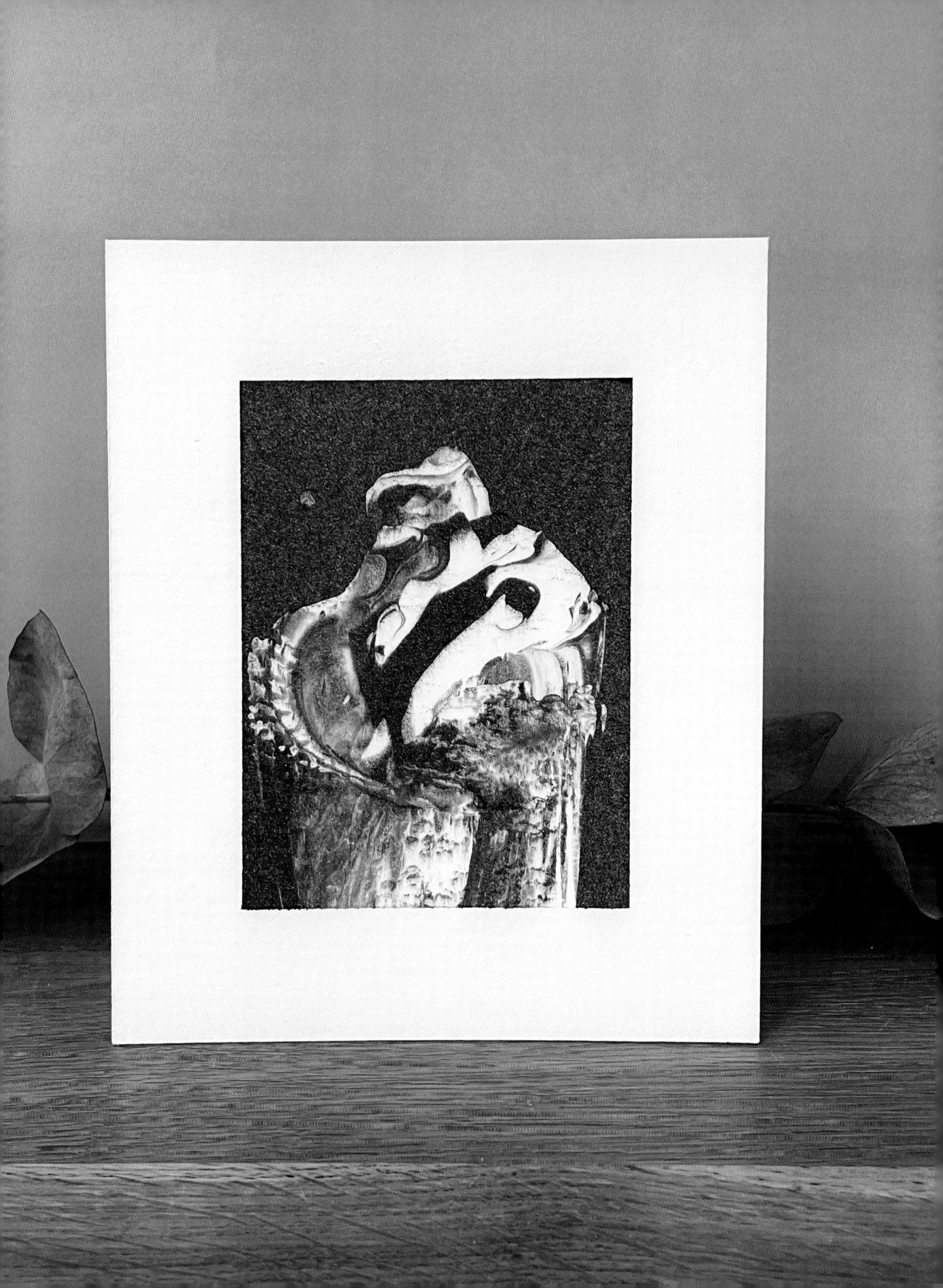

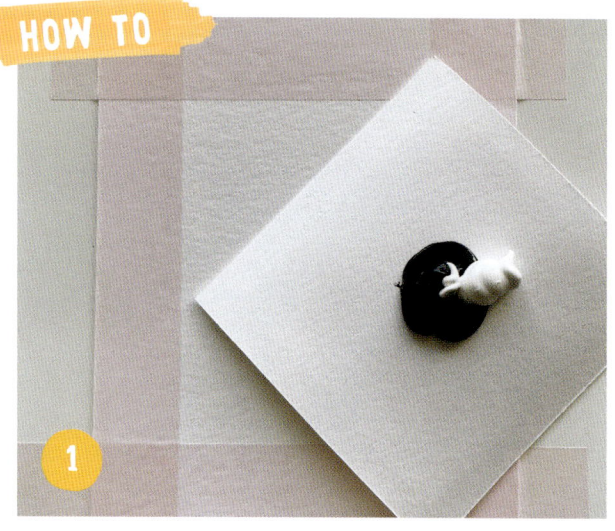

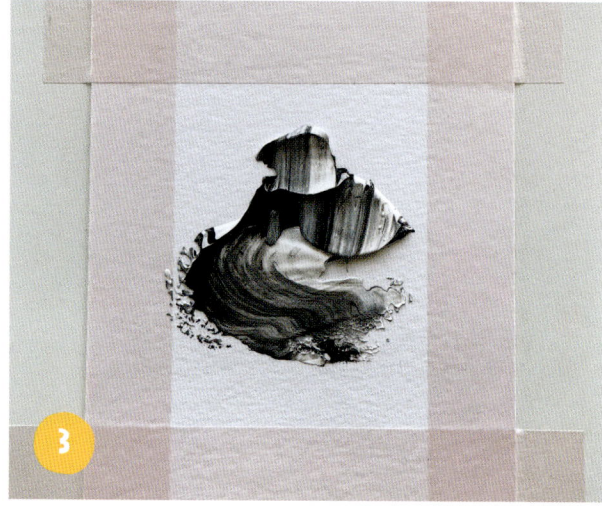

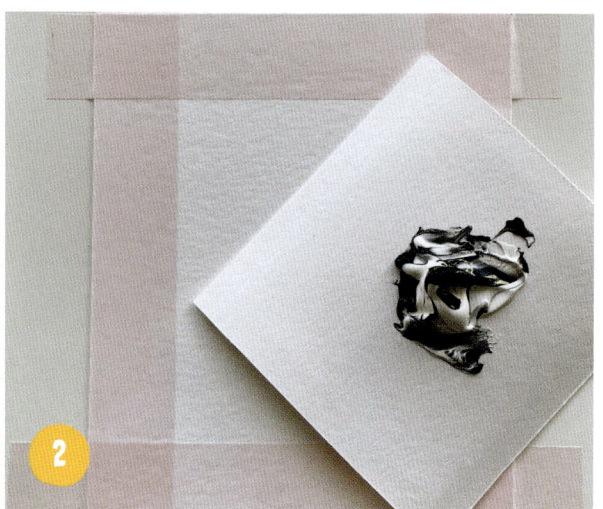

TIP

APPLY THE PAINT INTUITIVELY AND SCRAPE IT OFF TO CREATE A SURPRISING MOTIF!

1 Tape down all four edges of your paper. Then apply a little black paint to a piece of leftover paper, or in a palette if you've got one, and add a little white paint on top. Use the quantities you see in the picture.

2 Now take your palette knife and mix both colors. Make sure that you mix them slowly. The goal is to create medium-sized areas in your painting that are either empty or a combination of black and white. Don't mix the paint too much or it'll reduce the quality of your pattern and your picture will just look like a load of smudgy gray paint.

3 Load the paint onto a palette knife and add it to your paper. Spread it out, but stop if the paint layer gets too thin. Otherwise the pattern will look like a gray splodge.

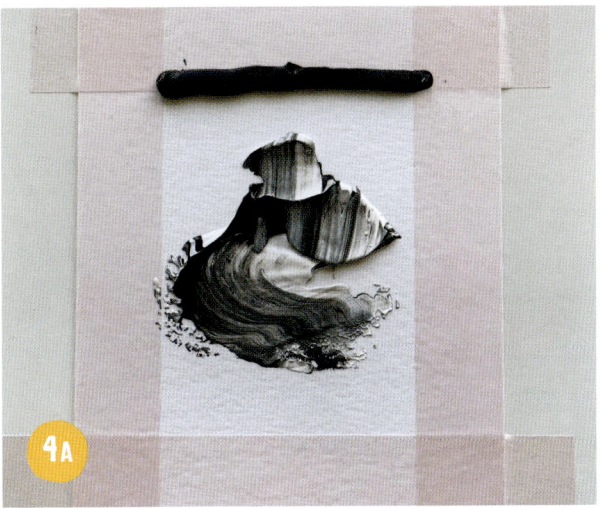

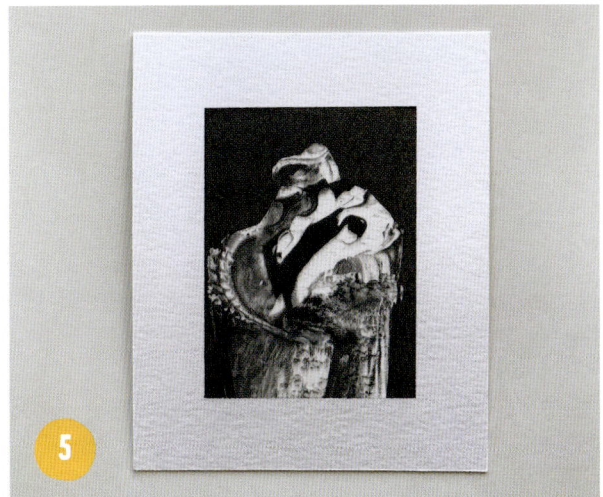

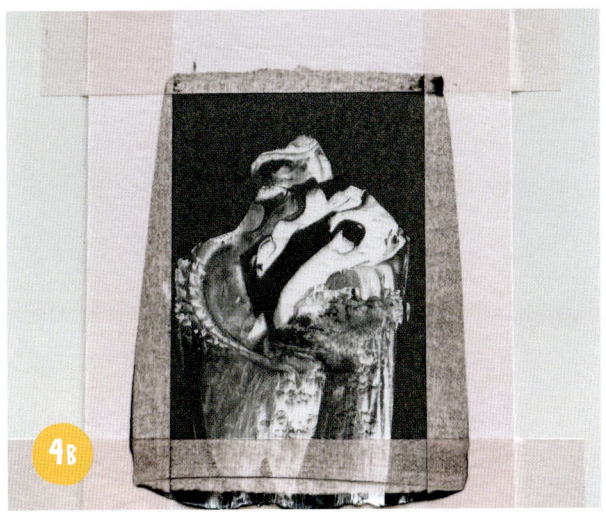

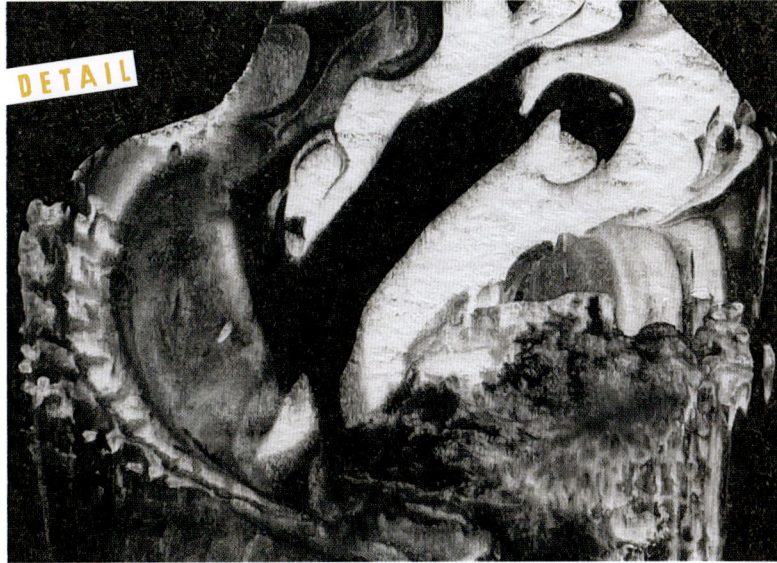

DETAIL

4 The last step is to add a black horizontal line along the top to create a black background. If you like, you can add a black line along the bottom edge of the black-and-white mixture to isolate the shape in the center of the paper when you scrape off the paint. Then scrape the paint with moderate to firm pressure from the top down.

5 What can you see? Some people have told me they can see an octopus hugging a lizard. Others see a fish. The list goes on! This is the best thing about black-and-white pictures: There's always more to see if you look for it.

08

SUNRISE MOUNTAIN

In this project and the next one, we'll be making a few mountain landscapes. The motif is simple, but the effect is impressive. If you've collected any leftover paint from earlier pictures, that'll be ideal. If you haven't, you can make a fresh blend.

PAPER

- ✘ 245 lb (360 g/m²) acrylic paper, 4" × 4" (10 × 10 cm)

COLORS

- ✘ Yellow Green
- ✘ Azo Yellow Deep
- ✘ Turquoise Green
- ✘ Azo Orange
- ✘ A blend of leftover paint

TOOLS

- ✘ Squeegee
- ✘ Palette knife
- ✘ Masking tape
- ✘ Damp cloth

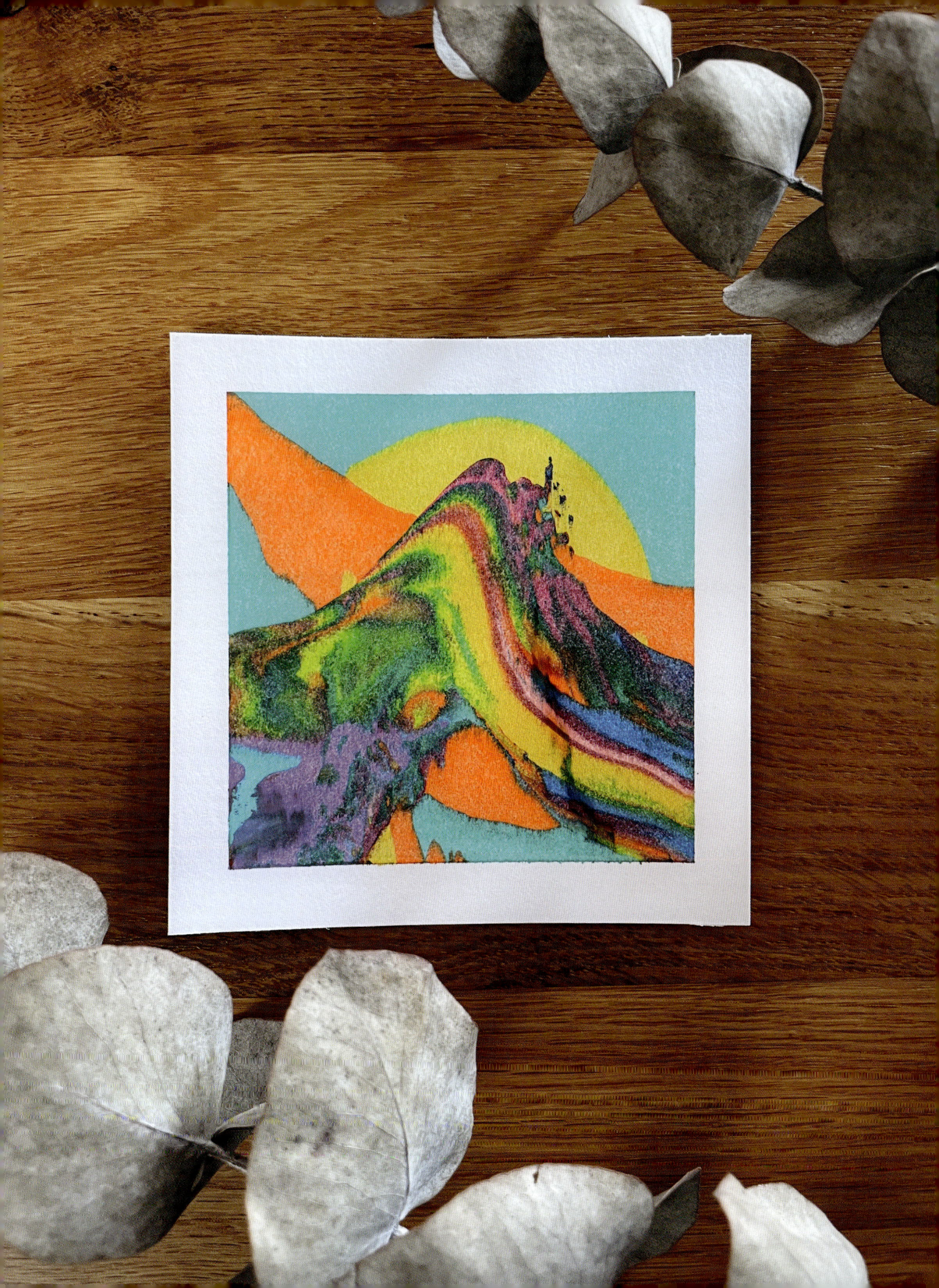

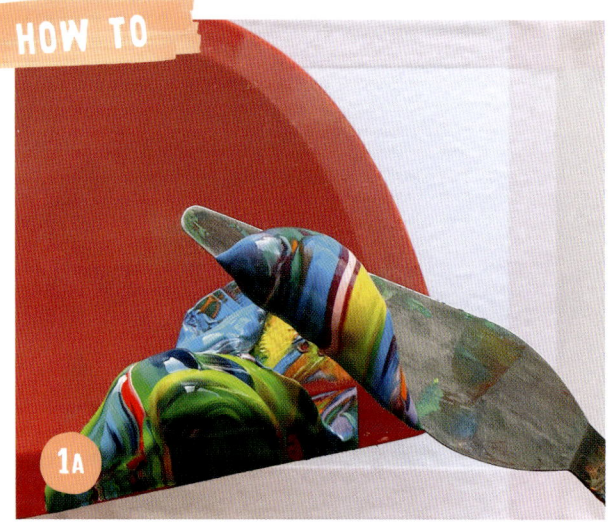

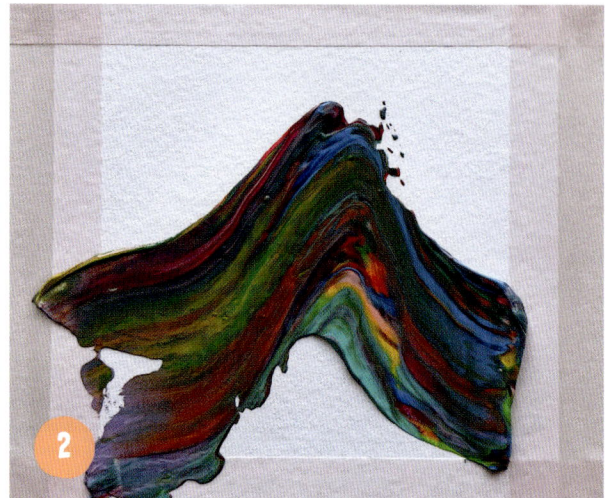

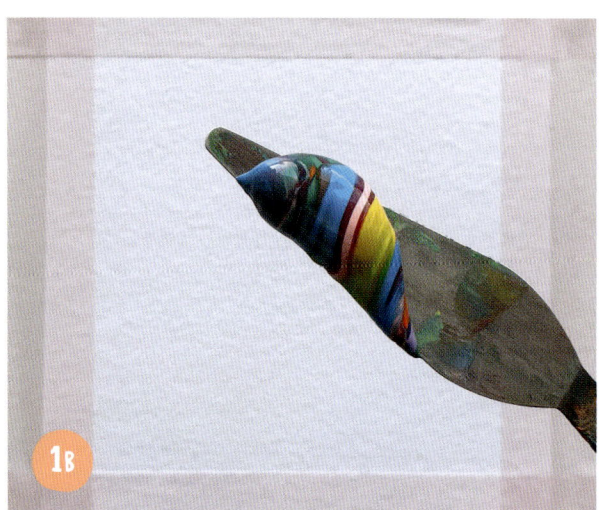

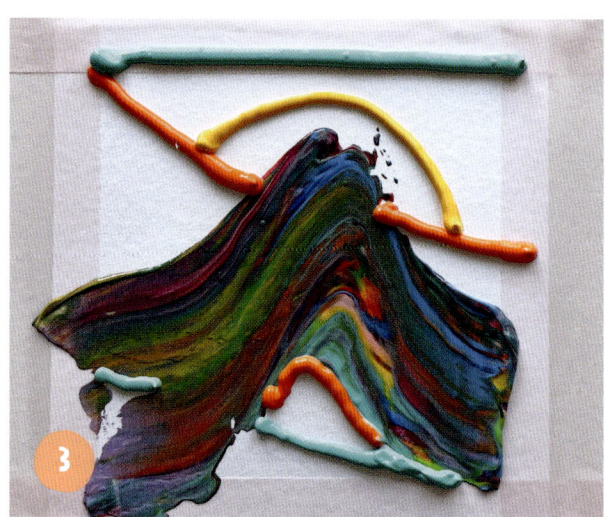

1 Tape down all four sides of your paper. Take your leftover paint. If you have more than one lot of leftovers to choose from, I recommend using the ones that best match the colors in your painting so you can create a cool marbled design.

2 Apply the paint to the paper with your palette knife, making it into a mountain shape. If you want the mountain to take up the entire bottom half of your paper, add a little more of your leftover paint.

Don't spread out the paint that's already on your paper, as that will reduce your chances of creating an attractive pattern.

3 Add a few more colors to your picture. As you can see, I've added a sun with a yellow arch and a sunset with an orange curve. For the background, I've added a turquoise horizontal line. There was still space left at the bottom, so I decided to add a bit of orange and turquoise there to see how it would turn out.

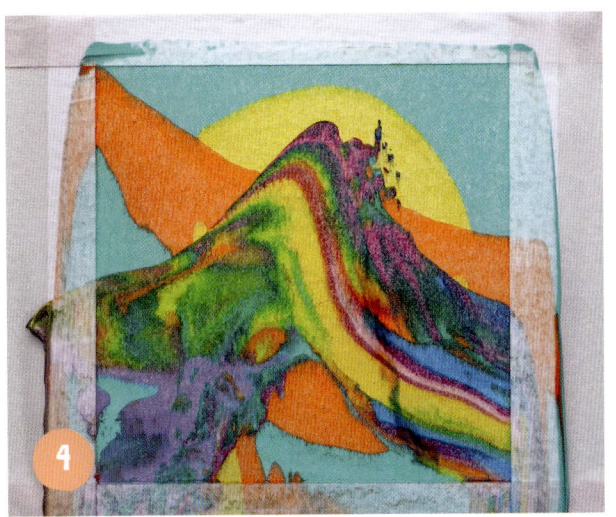

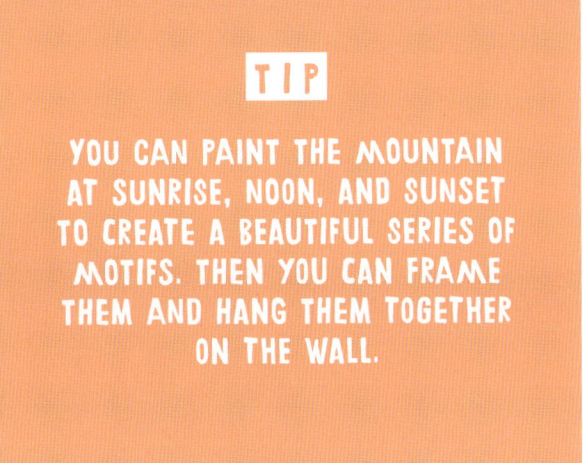

TIP

YOU CAN PAINT THE MOUNTAIN AT SUNRISE, NOON, AND SUNSET TO CREATE A BEAUTIFUL SERIES OF MOTIFS. THEN YOU CAN FRAME THEM AND HANG THEM TOGETHER ON THE WALL.

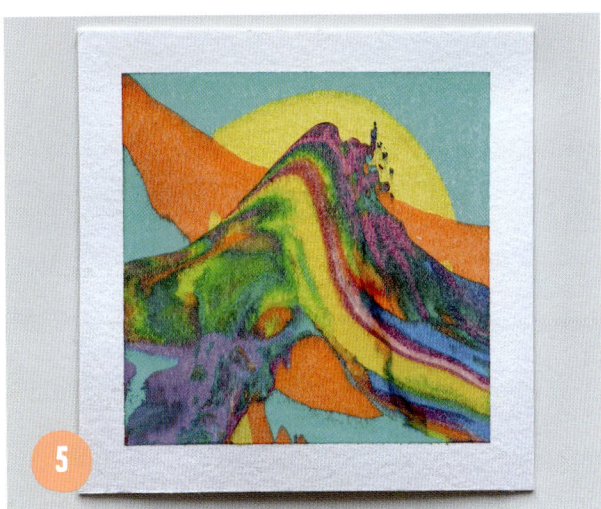

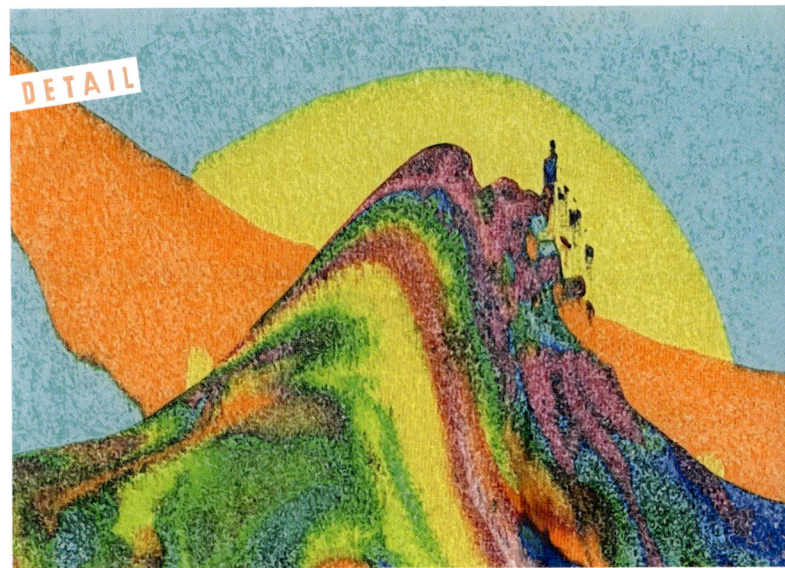

DETAIL

4 Once you've added all your desired colors, use moderate to firm pressure to scrape off all the paint in one go from the top down.

5 As you can see, the mountain and the sun work really well together. On the left, however, the turquoise paint has broken up the orange sunset. Next time, I need to add more orange so there's a better chance of it coming out as planned. I still think the painting looks great, though. I hope you like it too!

09

"NOONLIGHT" MOUNTAIN

Here's another example of how to use your leftover paint to create mountains using the squeegee technique. This time we'll add an enchanting yellow for the background to make the mountain look even more beautiful. Use a little Titanium Buff Light to create a path, adding more dimension to this afternoon landscape.

PAPER

- ✘ Coarse 245 lb (360 g/m²) watercolor paper, 5" × 7" (12.5 × 18 cm)

COLORS

- ✘ Azo Yellow Deep
- ✘ A blend of leftover paint
- ✘ Titanium Buff Light

TOOLS

- ✘ Squeegee
- ✘ Palette knife
- ✘ Masking tape
- ✘ Damp cloth

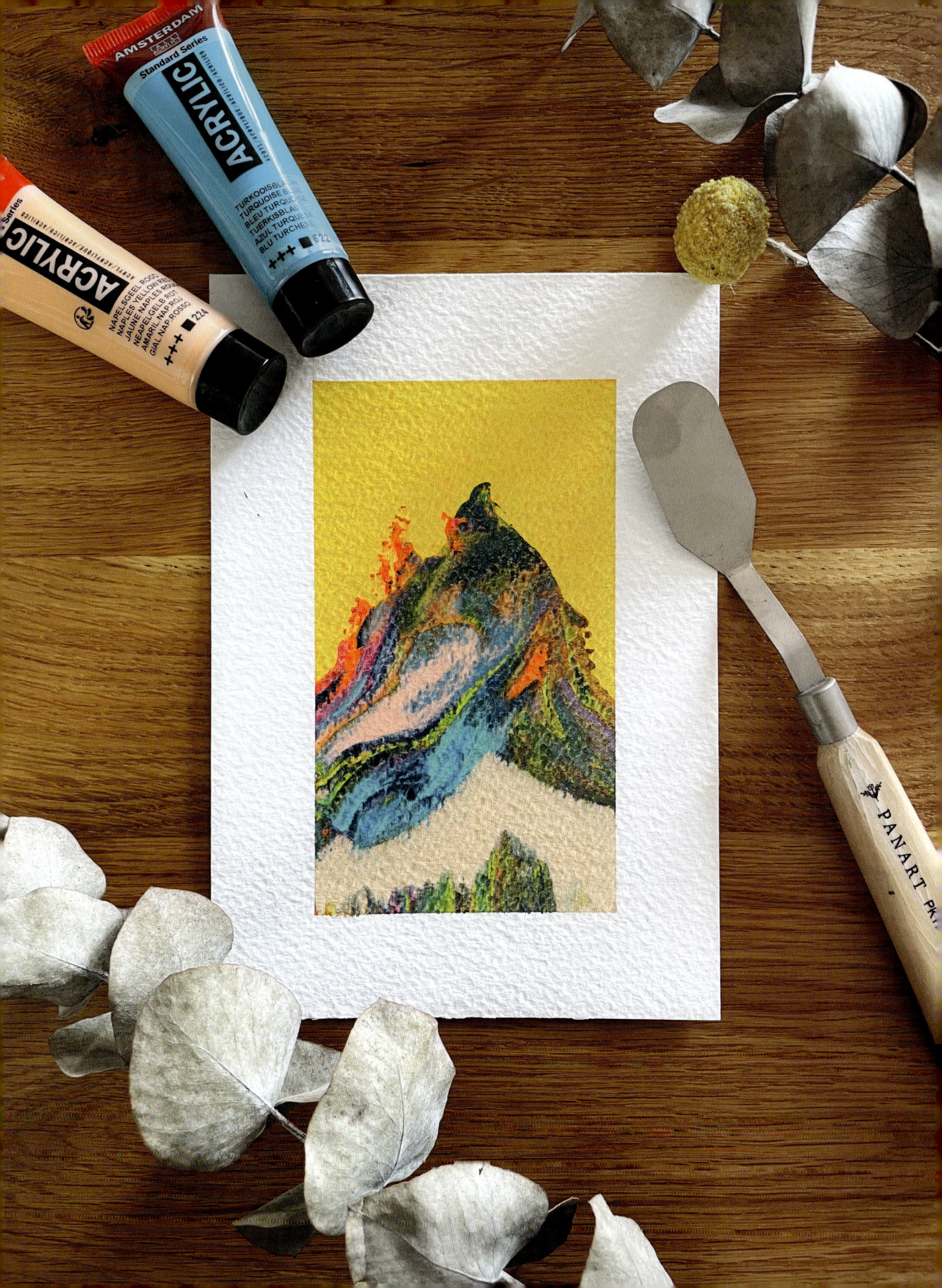

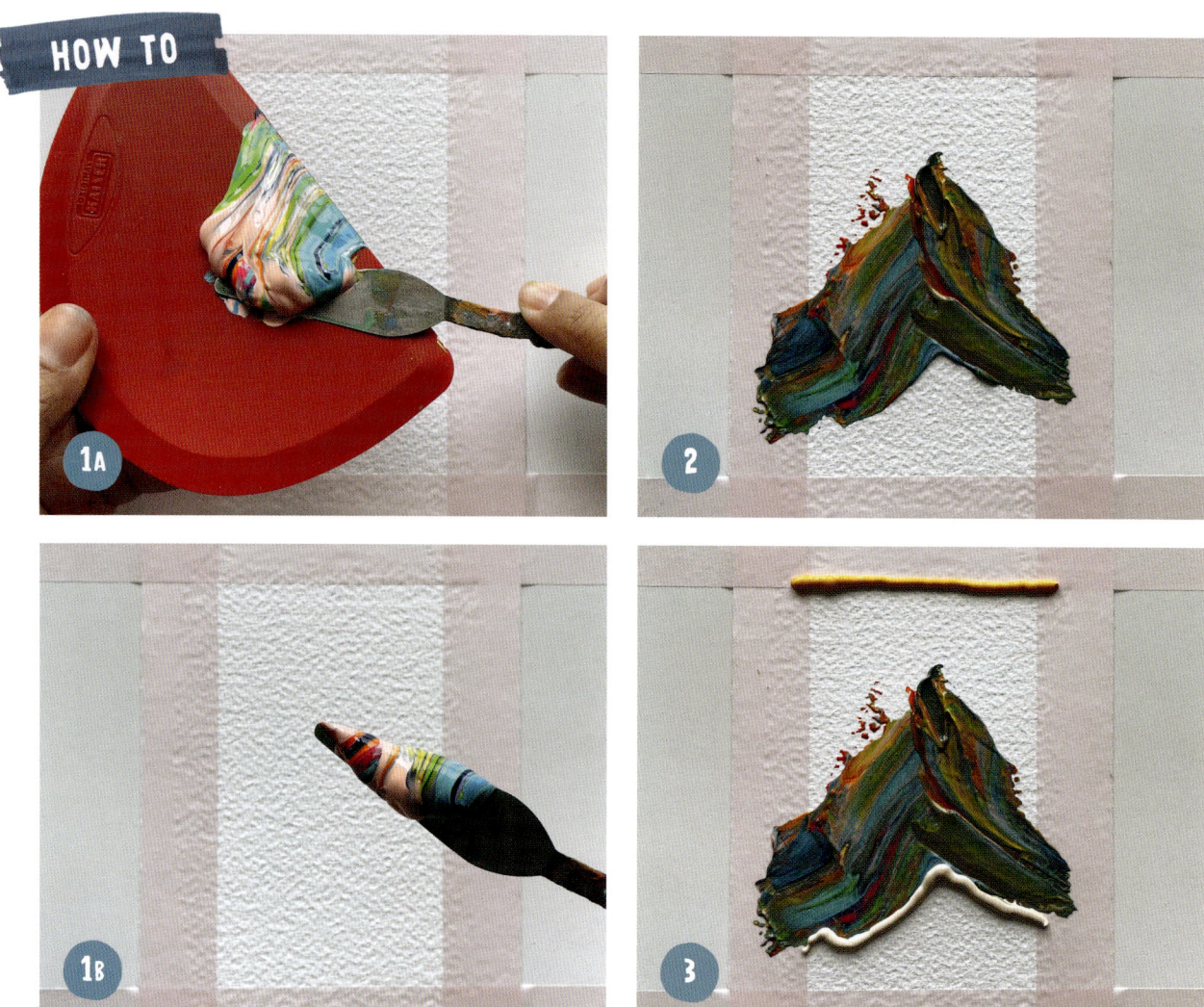

1 If you've completed the previous project, you'll already be familiar with the steps, so there won't be any great surprises here. Tape down all four sides of your paper and load some of your leftover paint onto your palette knife. Try to use the part where each individual color is still separate.

2 Using your palette knife, apply the leftover paint to the paper and form it into a mountain shape.

3 We'll make things a little easier this time around by not making any special shapes. We'll simply add a line at the top for the background color. At the bottom, we'll outline the mountain to stop the paints from smudging and losing their structure.

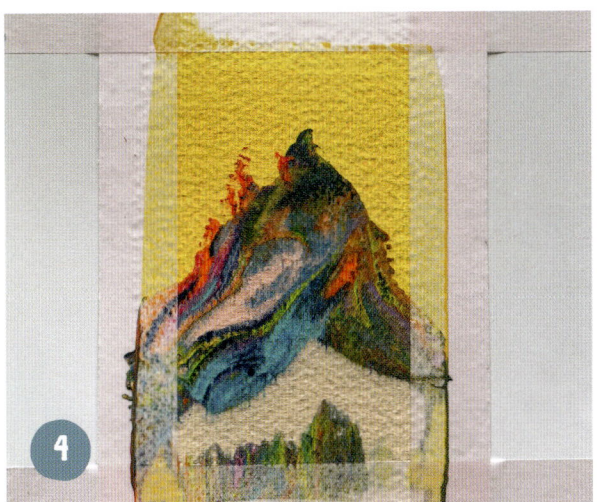

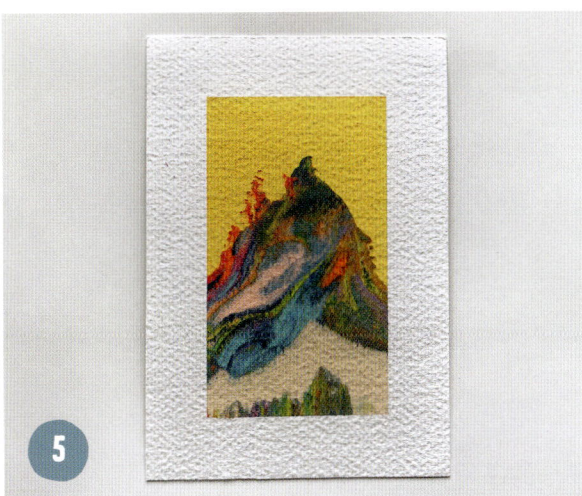

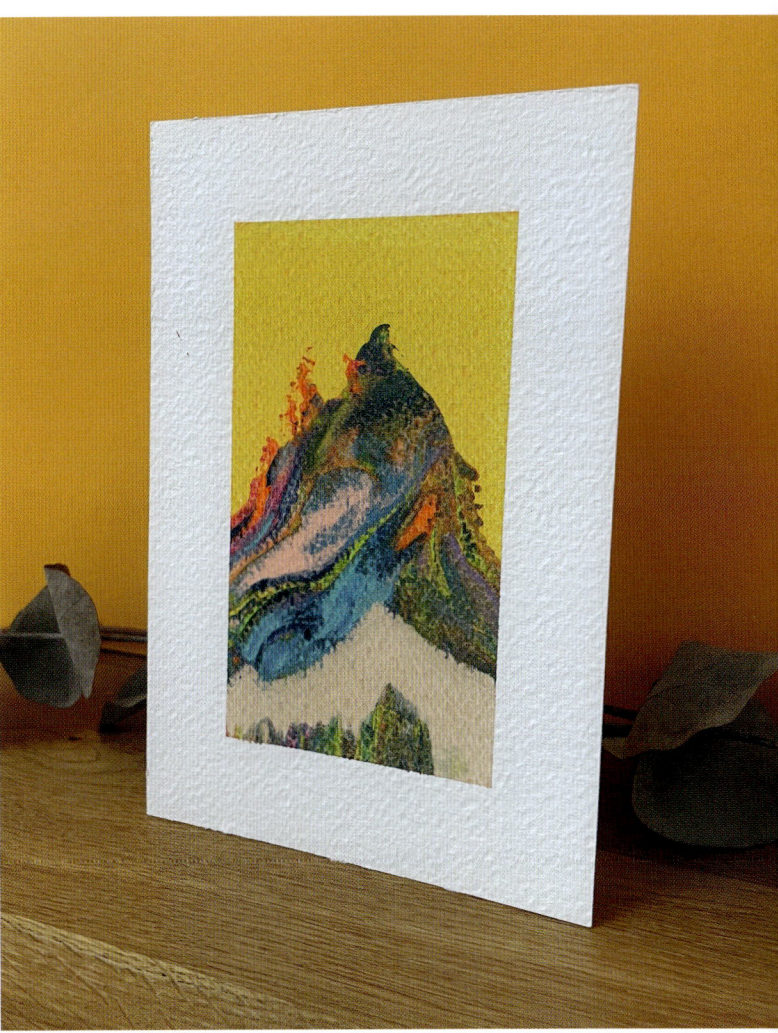

4 Reveal the result by scraping off all the paint in one go, from the top down, with moderate to firm pressure.

5 Now you have a wonderful mountain landscape with a sunny background!

10

THE MARBLE

This time, we're going to expand our options a little by making the different colors dance together in a circular shape. This technique might seem difficult in the beginning, but after a while, you'll get into the swing of things.

PAPER

- ✖ 160 lb (240 g/m²) double-sided matte paper, 8″ × 11″ (21 × 30 cm)

COLORS

- ✖ Sky Blue
- ✖ Permanent Orange
- ✖ Reflex Green
- ✖ Azo Yellow Lemon
- ✖ Turquoise Green
- ✖ Primary Magenta
- ✖ Light Rose

TOOLS

- ✖ Squeegee
- ✖ Masking tape
- ✖ Damp cloth

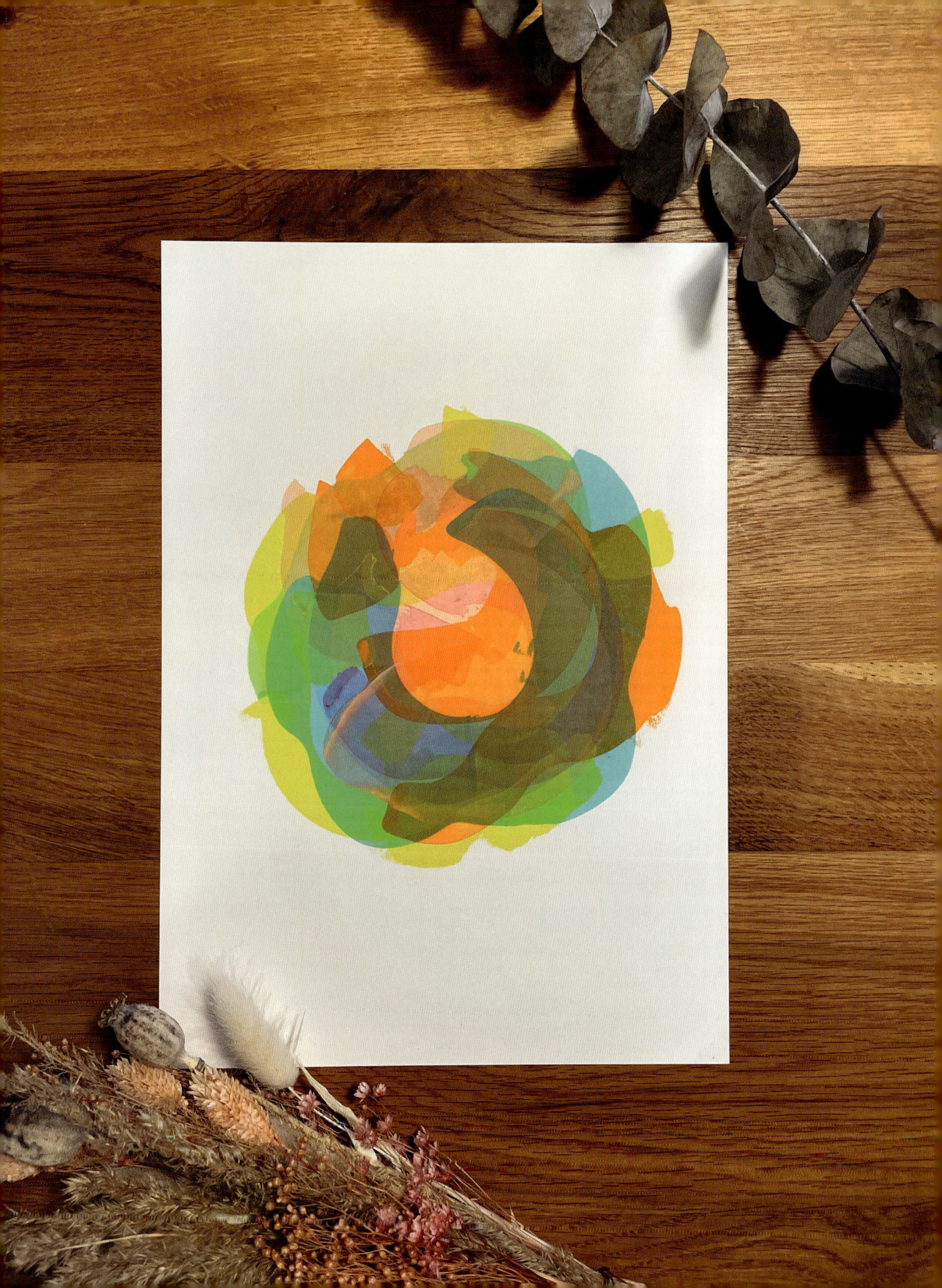

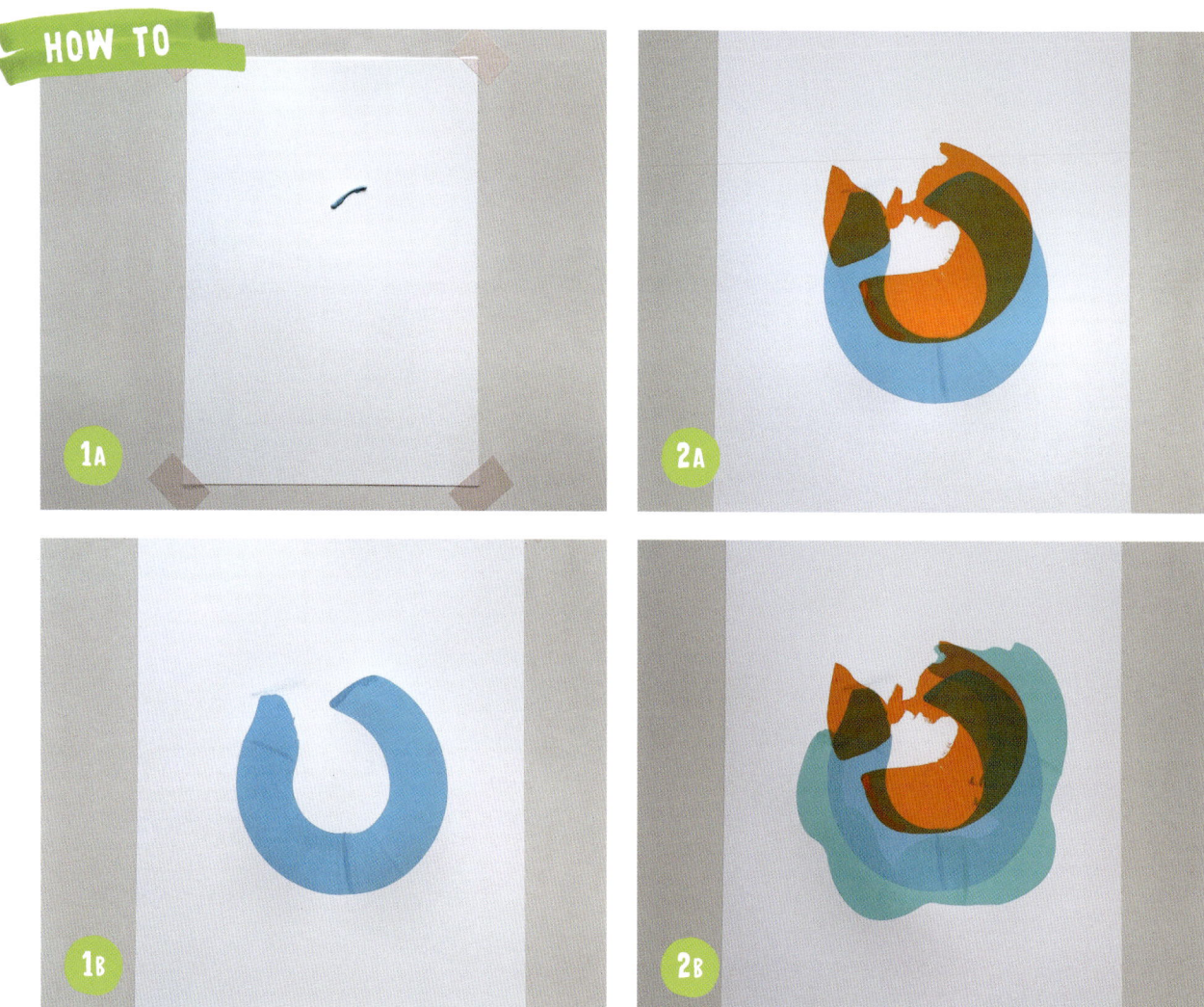

1 For this project, you don't have to tape down every side of your paper, as we're mostly going to be painting in the center of the paper. Tape the paper to the table, though, to stop it from slipping as you work. You can either measure the center of your paper or estimate the measurements, adding a light pencil mark for reference. Take a little paint and apply it to the paper to create a circle shape. Don't close up the circle. This will make the picture look more dynamic.

2 Then apply the other colors in concentric circles until they cover the mark in the center of the paper.

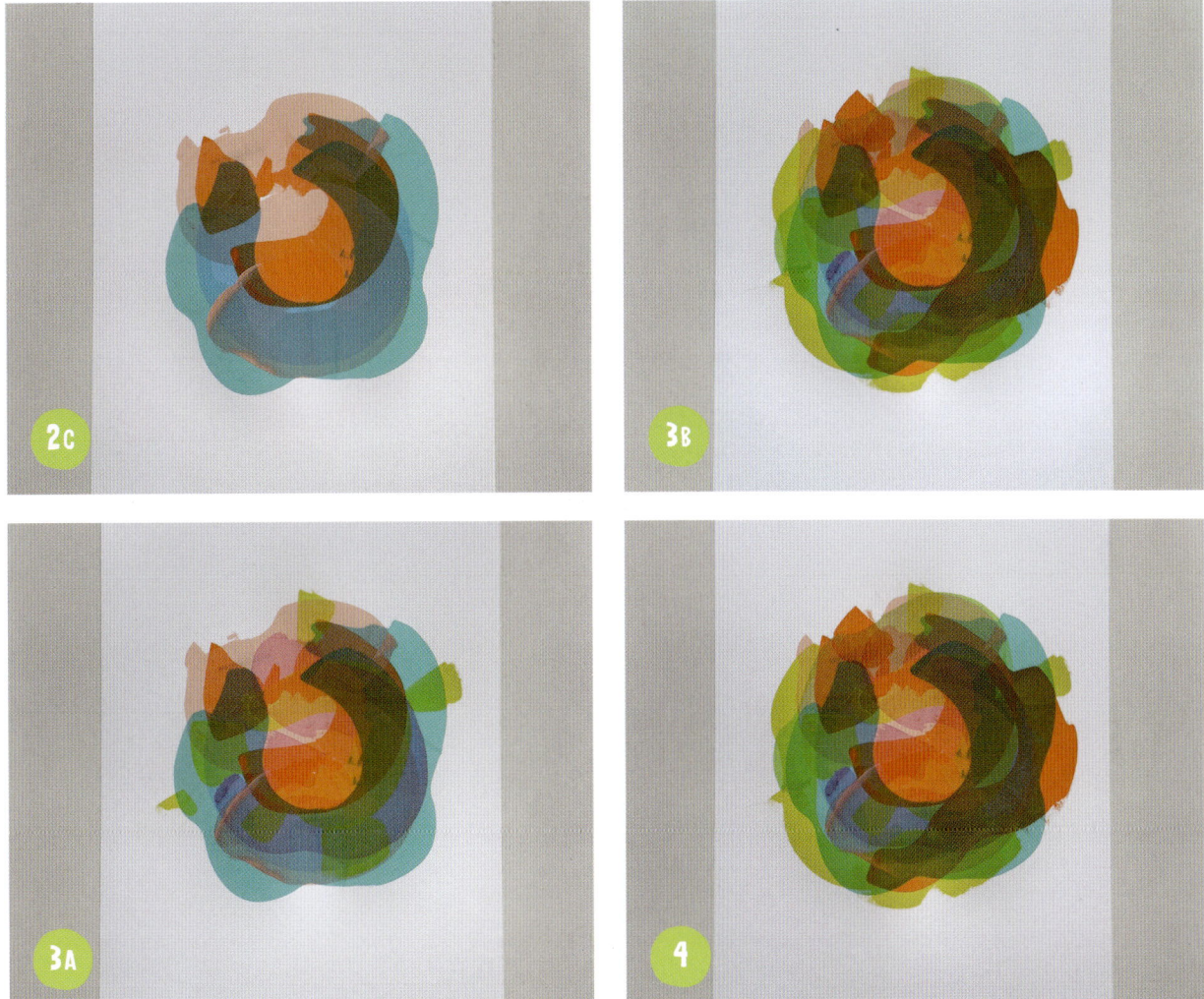

3 Take a step back from time to time to see if your picture is in the middle of the paper or not. If it isn't, you can add more layers of paint to correct the alignment. Lighter colors are more forgiving. I recommend ending with a yellow or light green.

4 Once you're happy with your layers, remove the tape and admire your beautiful marble.

11

A NEW PLANET

Here's another project for practicing concentric
stripes. Together we're going to paint a new planet.
It's based on the previous project, only this time,
we'll add some outlining.

PAPER

✘ Fine-grain 200 lb
(300 g/m²) watercolor
paper, 11" × 14"
(27 × 35 cm)

COLORS

✘ Pearl Violet
✘ Turquoise Green
✘ Quinacridone Rose
✘ Yellow Green
✘ Titanium Buff Light
✘ Azo Orange
✘ Azo Yellow Deep
✘ Turquoise Blue
✘ Venetian Rose

TOOLS

✘ Squeegee
✘ 0.7 marker (black)
✘ 1.0 marker (gold)
✘ Masking tape
✘ Damp cloth

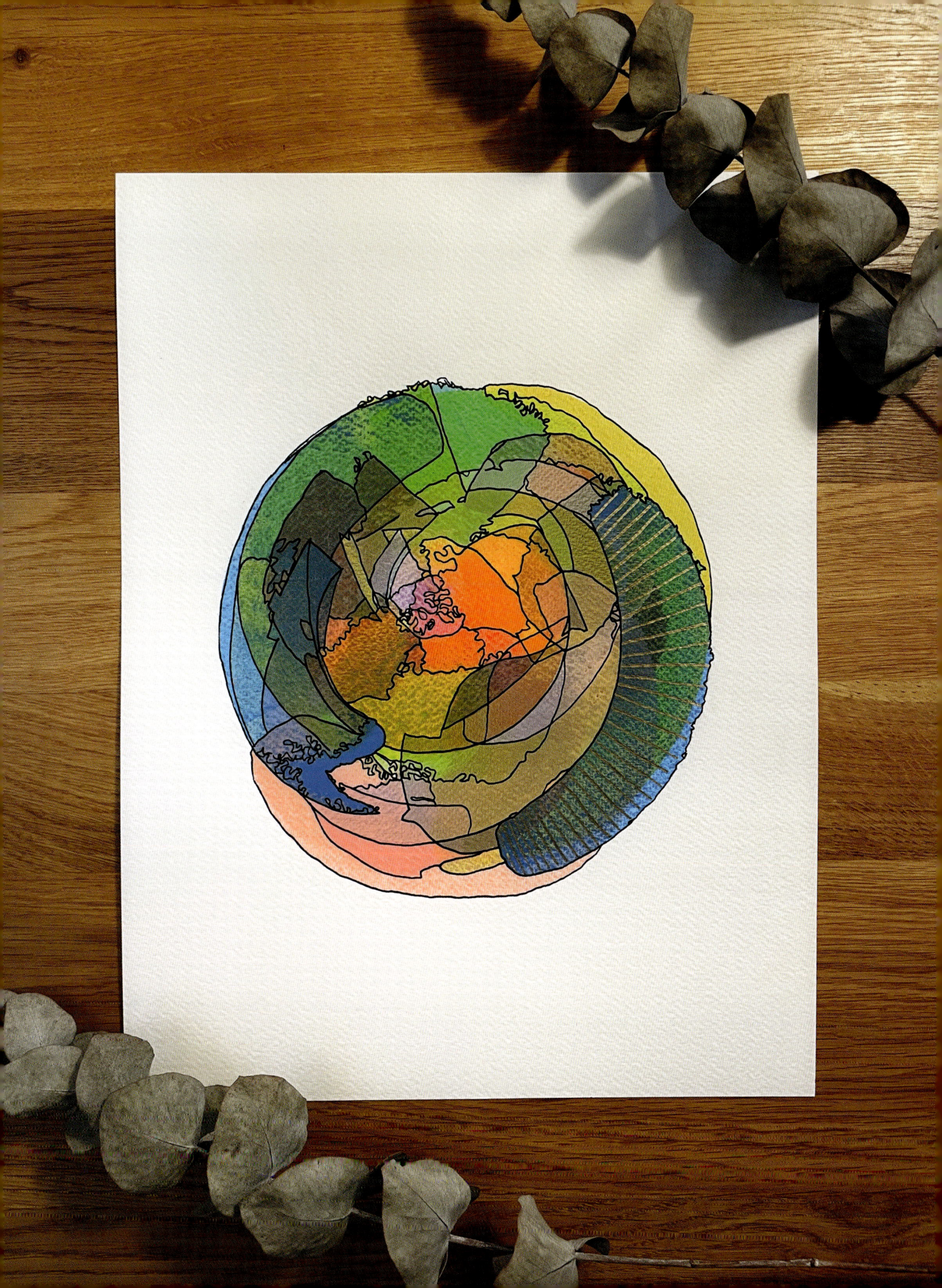

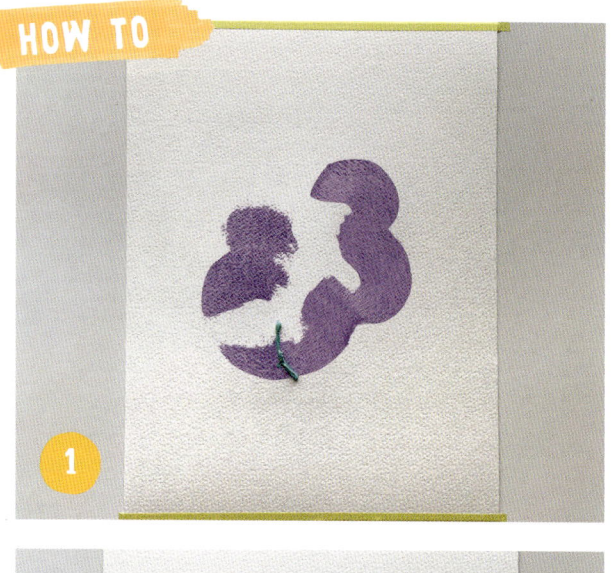

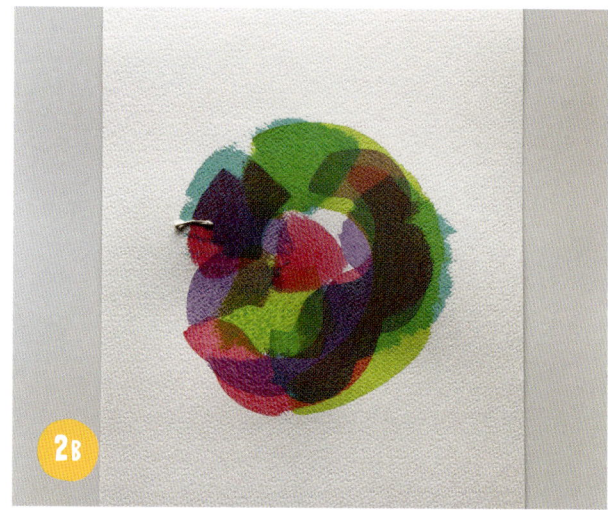

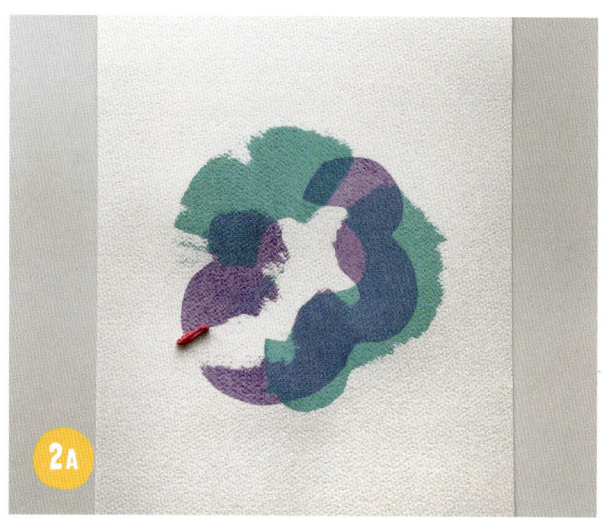

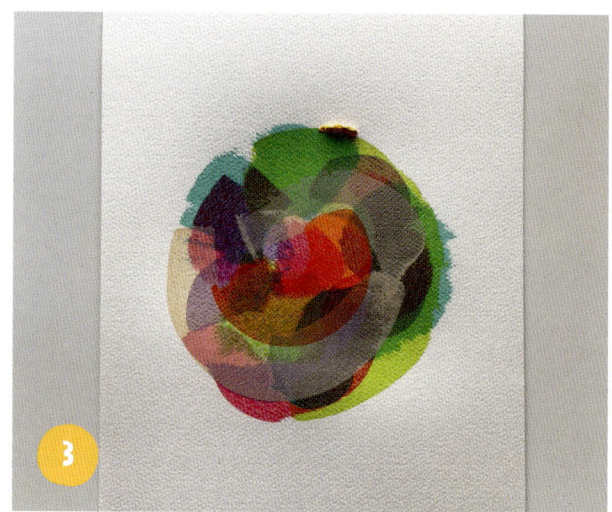

1 As in the previous project, you don't need to tape down every side of the paper. Just use enough tape to make sure the paper doesn't slip as you apply your paint. Measure the center of your paper or estimate the measurements, then start applying paint around the middle. This time, you can be more liberal with your squeegee and create a few shapes.

2 Keep applying the paint to your paper in layers and gradually make your circle bigger. If it's too dark, you can lighten it up, so trust the process and keep painting.

3 My last layer of paint makes everything look too dark, so I thought this would be a good point to add a few layers of Titanium Buff Light. It worked perfectly.

4 My circle was almost in the right position, so I added a few more layers in light pink and yellow paint to adjust its alignment slightly. I also added two additional blue stripes because the turquoise pattern was a little too prominent for my tastes.

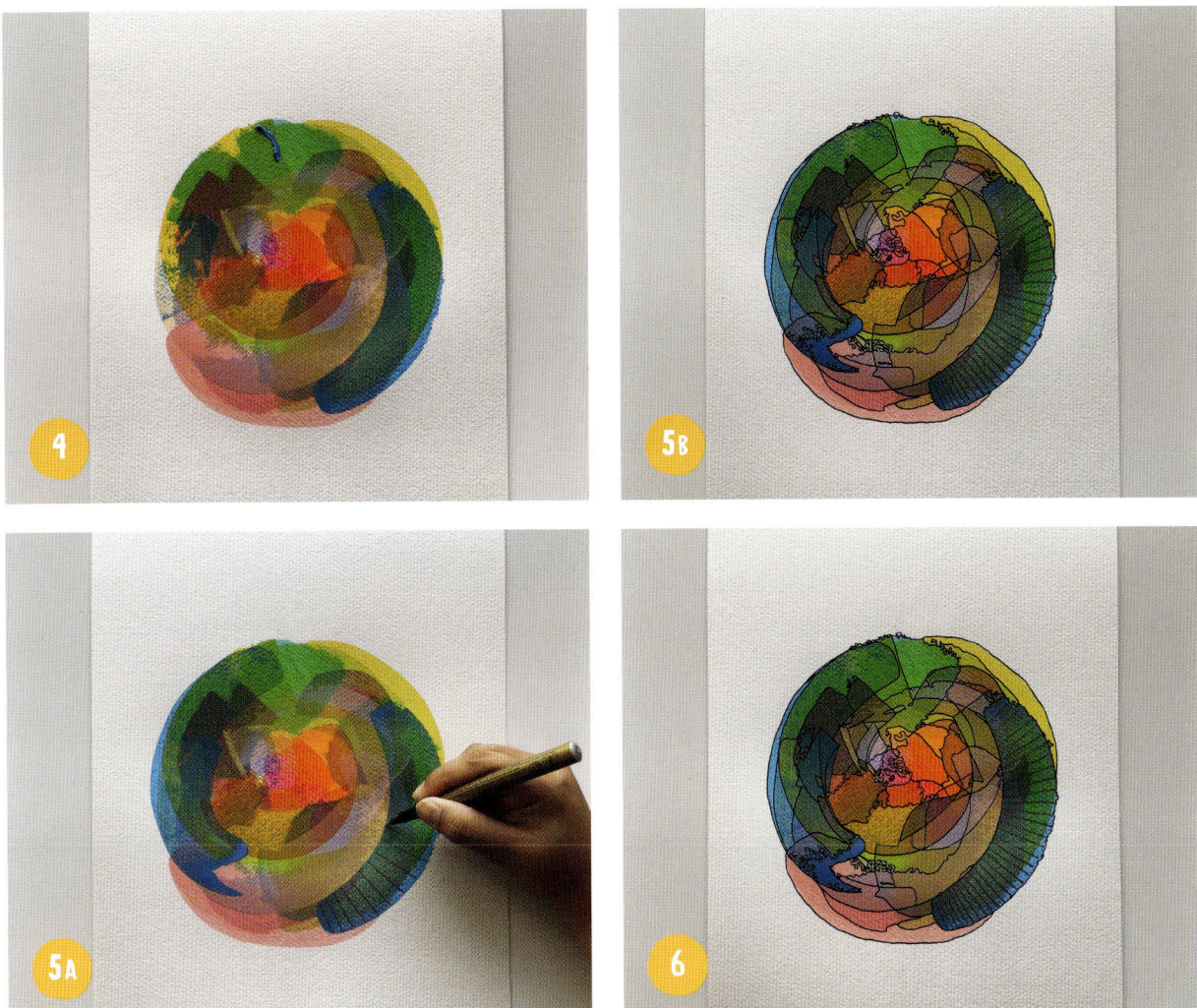

5 After completing the painting stage, I took my gold marker and drew some lines across the blue stripes. It looks great when the light shines on it. I then took my black marker and outlined every shape I could find, highlighting all the colors created by the overlapping layers.

6 Once you're happy with your design, remove the tape and enjoy your new creation.

12

AN EXPLOSION OF COLOR

In this project, we're going to create another sphere. This time, though, it'll look more dynamic, with more room for experiments and "happy accidents." We'll also use a combination of outlined and non-outlined areas. We'll even create some shadow from the same paint since the paint is unevenly distributed. The outcome is a fascinating medley of color.

PAPER

✖ Fine-grain 200 lb (300 g/m²) watercolor paper, 11" × 14" (27 × 35 cm)

COLORS

✖ Venetian Rose
✖ Azo Orange
✖ Permanent Madder Lake
✖ Yellow Green
✖ Turquoise Green
✖ Cobalt Blue
✖ Titanium Buff Light
✖ Azo Yellow Deep
✖ Quinacridone Rose

TOOLS

✖ Squeegee
✖ 0.7 marker (black)
✖ Masking tape
✖ Damp cloth

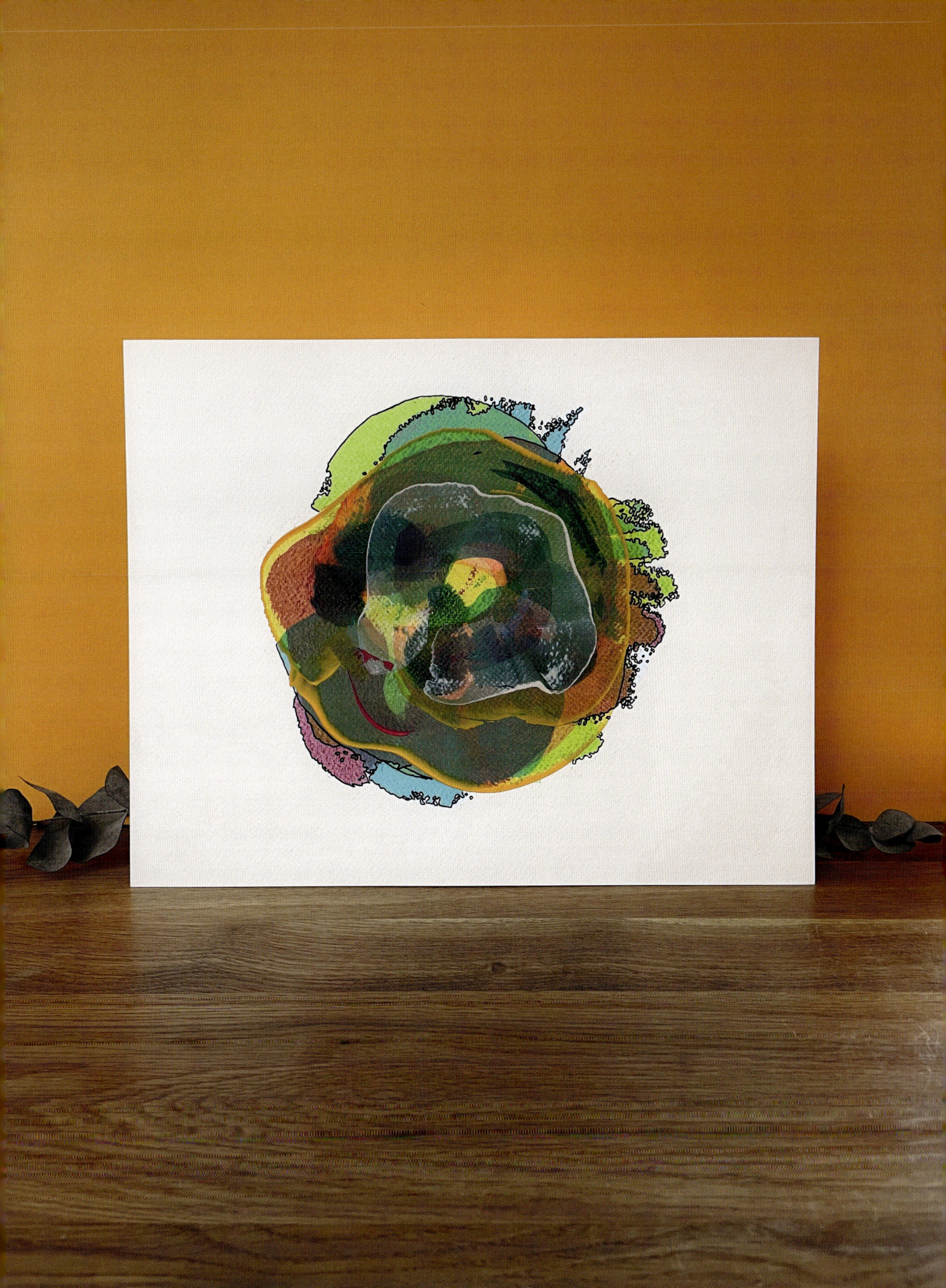

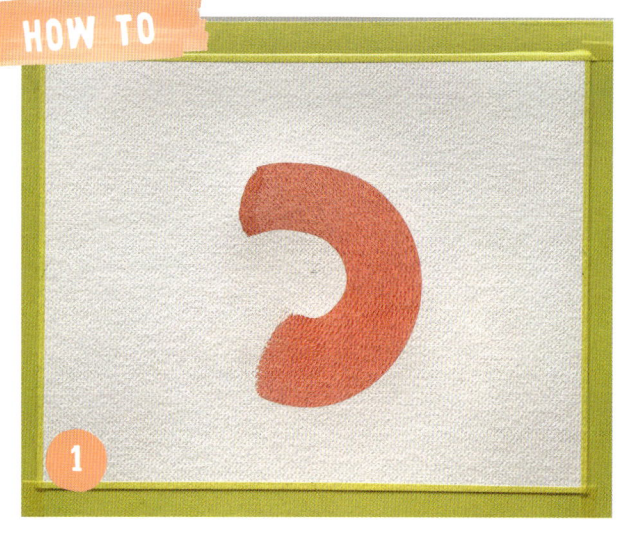

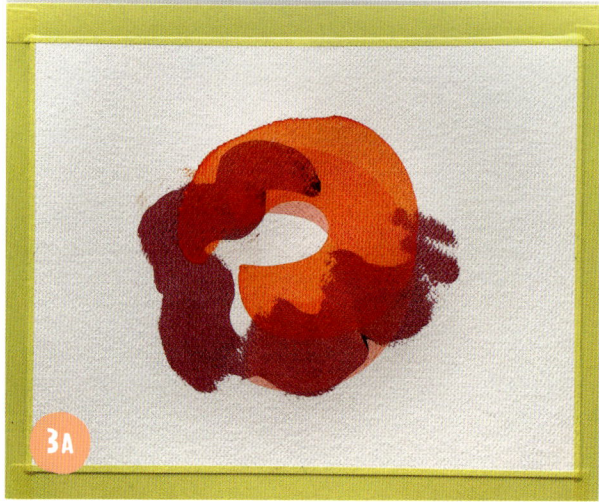

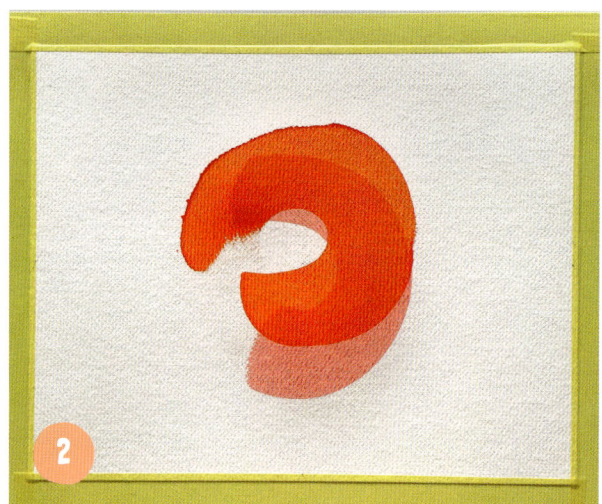

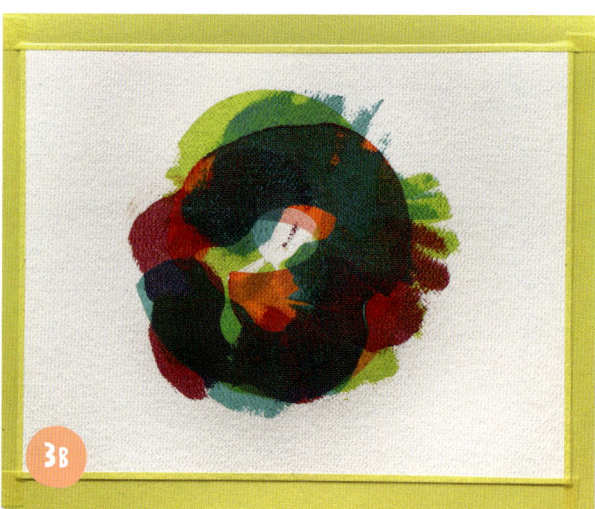

1 First, mark the center of your watercolor paper. Next we're going to create concentric shapes around this center. You don't need to tape down every side of the paper; however in this project, I wanted to experiment with the shapes some more. Therefore I made sure that the paper was taped down securely so it didn't slip as I worked.

2 I like to start with some regular shapes around the center of the paper. This gives me a better idea of how easily I can move the paint. If this is the first picture in a sitting, it might take you a while to relax.

3 As I become more confident, I make more changes to the shapes. The "mistakes"—or "happy accidents," as I prefer to call them—often occur when you tilt your squeegee to a very narrow angle, as parallel to the paper as possible.

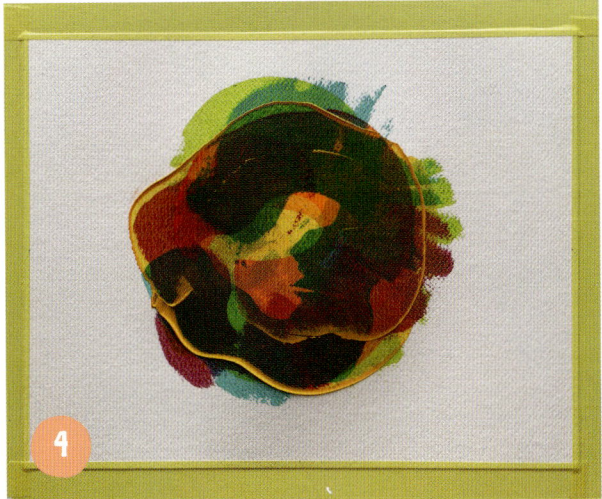

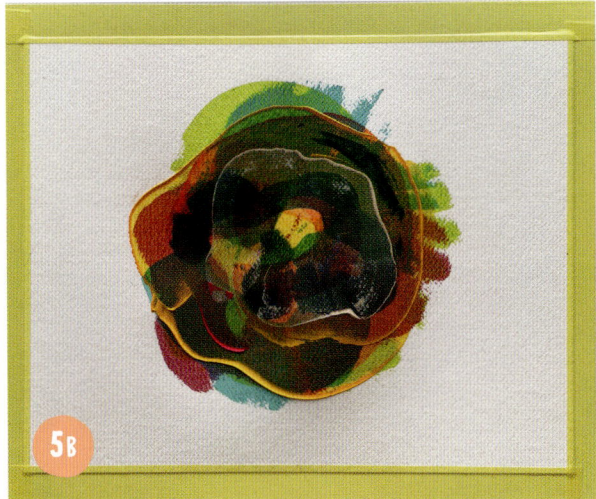

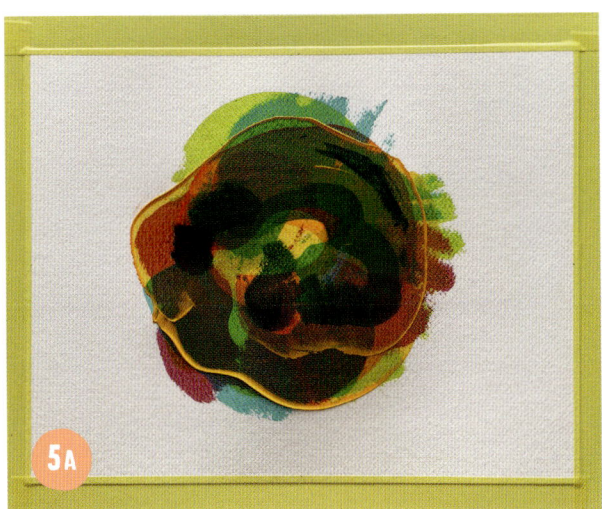

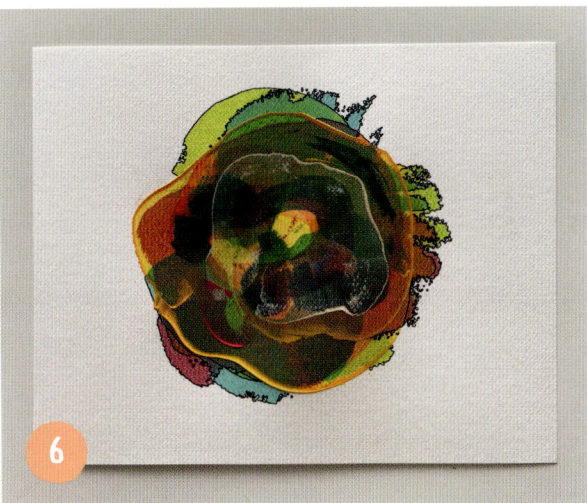

4 Something funny happened at this point. The yellow paint oozed over the edges of my squeegee, gathering at the sides of the stripe I'd just added. In this case, you can either clean your squeegee and remove the surplus paint or wait until it's dry before adding more layers.

5 I decided to leave the yellow as it was, where it was, until it had dried. I then retouched it with a darker color, as I felt it needed a bit more weight to anchor it in the picture. I then used Titanium Buff Light to add a little more contrast.

6 Once I was happy with the result, I took a black marker and added some detail around the edge of the picture. I didn't draw around all the shapes this time because I thought that would take away from the pretty yellow "accident." Here it is: yet another gorgeous picture.

13

CREATIVE LOVE

In this project, we're going to work on one of the most popular styles ever posted on my social media accounts. Here you'll learn how to write words with the squeegee technique. A quick disclaimer: For this project and the next, you'll need tubes of paint with thin nozzles so you have full control.

PAPER

- **✘** Fine-grain 200 lb (300 g/m²) watercolor paper, 7" × 5" (16.5 × 12.5 cm)

COLORS

- **✘** Quinacridone Rose
- **✘** Azo Yellow Deep
- **✘** Venetian Rose
- **✘** Pearl Violet
- **✘** Yellow Green
- **✘** Azo Orange
- **✘** Turquoise Blue
- **✘** Permanent Red Purple

TOOLS

- **✘** Squeegee
- **✘** 0.7 marker (black)
- **✘** Masking tape
- **✘** Damp cloth

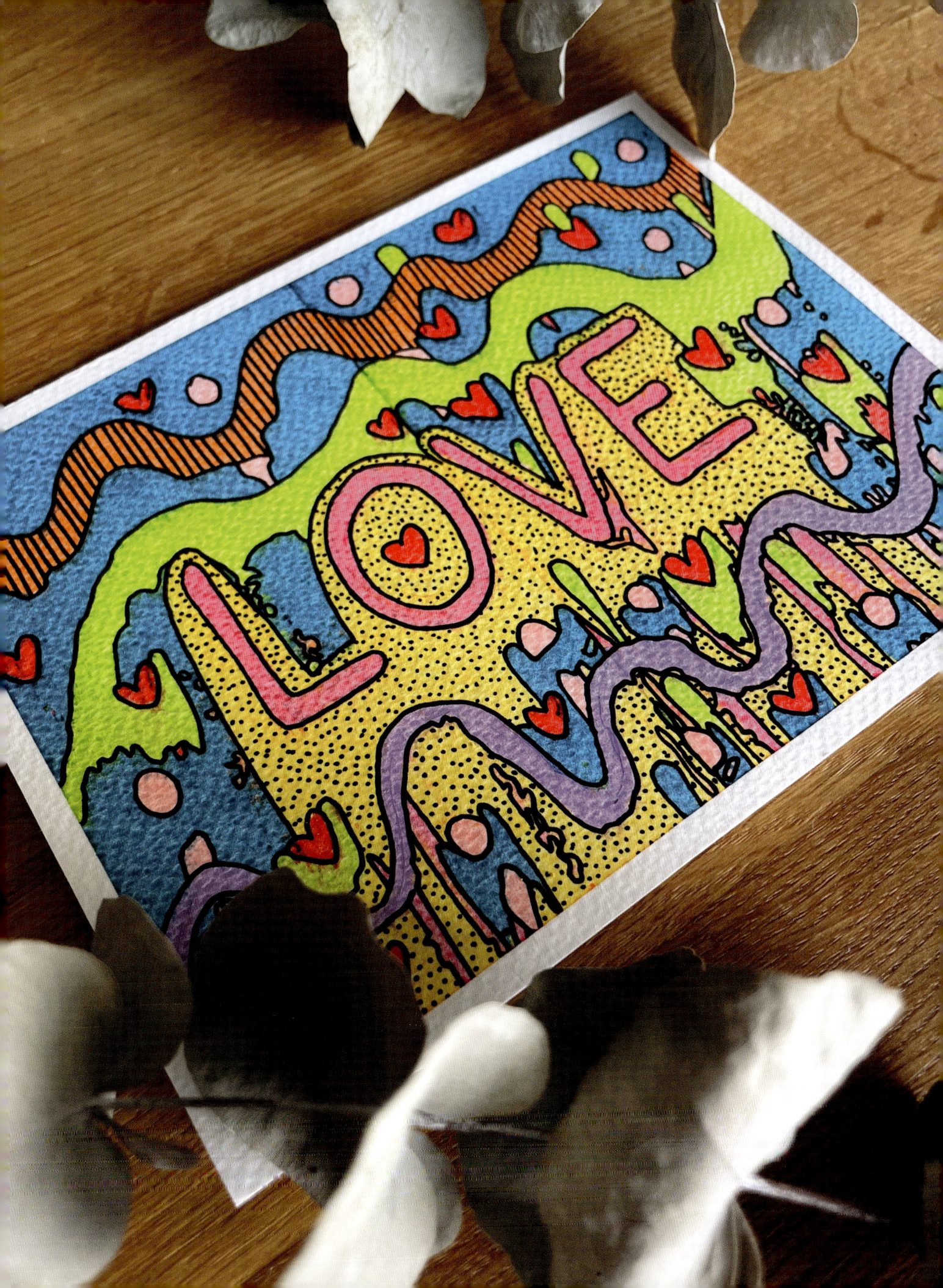

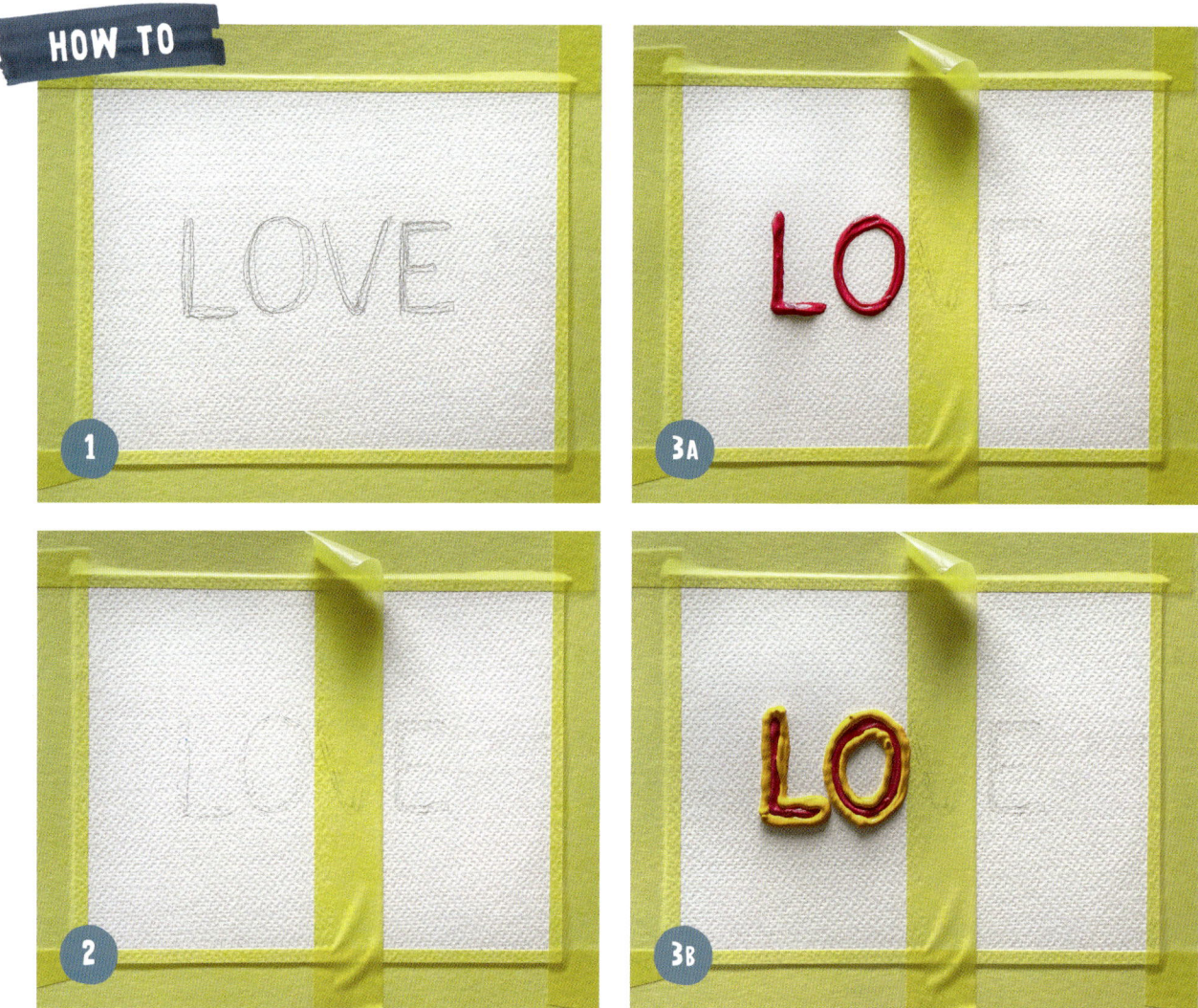

1 Tape down all four sides of your paper. Draw the word "love" on your paper in pencil. Try to draw it as lightly as possible so it doesn't shine through the paint later on. After taking this photo, I erased some of the pencil, leaving just enough for me to know where to paint.

2 If your squeegee doesn't cover the width of the paper, you can divide the picture in two with some tape. I recommend placing it between the letters rather than across the middle of them. That way, it'll be easier to bring the two halves back together.

3 Apply the paint in the shape of the letters onto the first half of the paper (3a). Then outline them in a contrasting color to make sure they keep their shape (3b).

4 Add any details you like, such as curvy lines, hearts, or polka dots. Additionally, you can apply a horizontal line in paint at the top to create a background (4a). Then scrape off the paint all in one go, using moderate to firm pressure from the top down (4b).

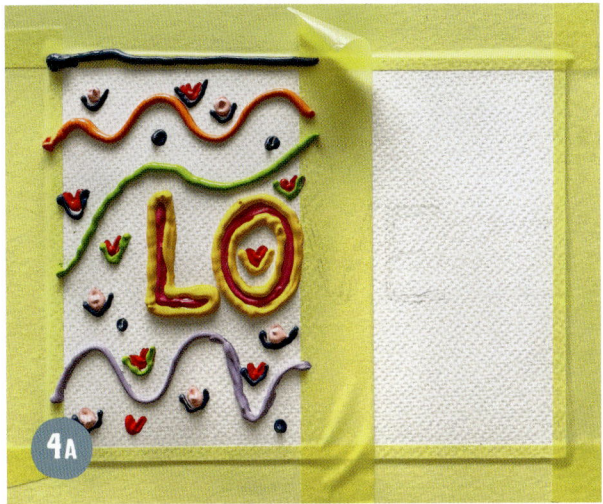

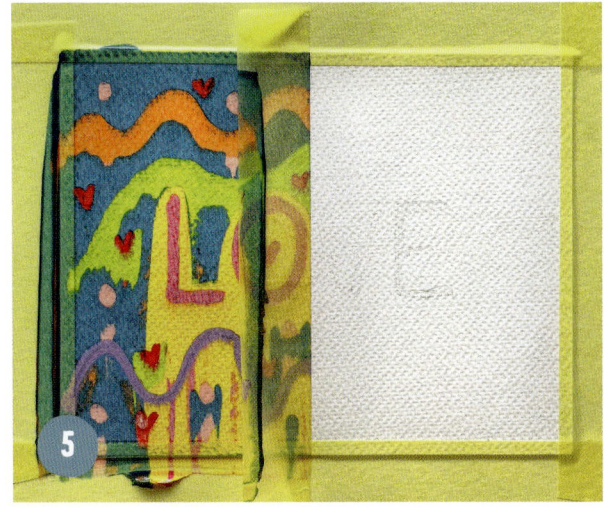

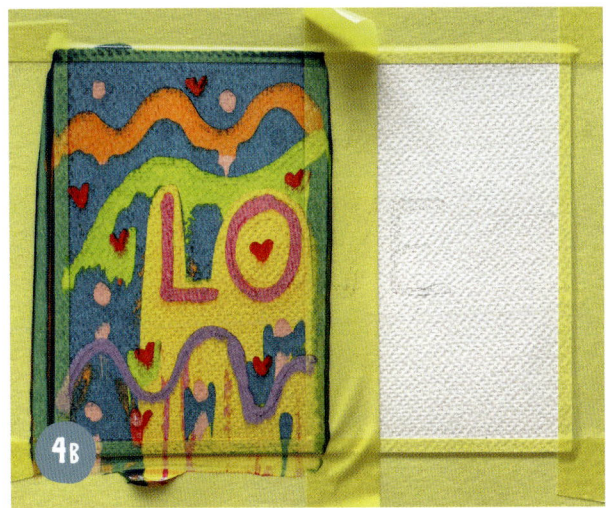

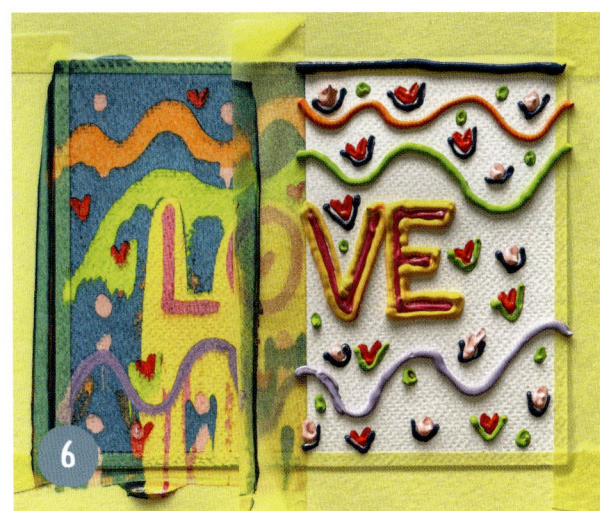

5 Move on to the second half. Make sure that you move the tape to the left and don't leave any gaps in the middle. If you do, you'll end up with a white line down the center of your picture.

6 Follow the same steps as before: Fill the letters with paint and outline them in a contrasting color. Then add any extra details. You can try to create continuity from one side to the other by using the same colors and the same style of dots and lines.

CONTINUED →

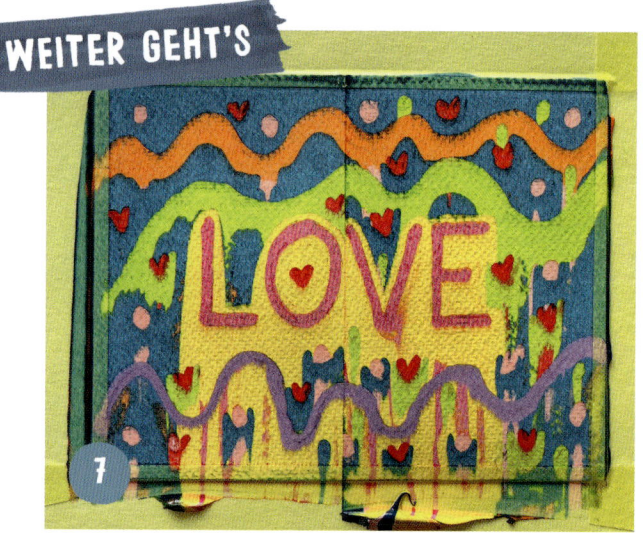

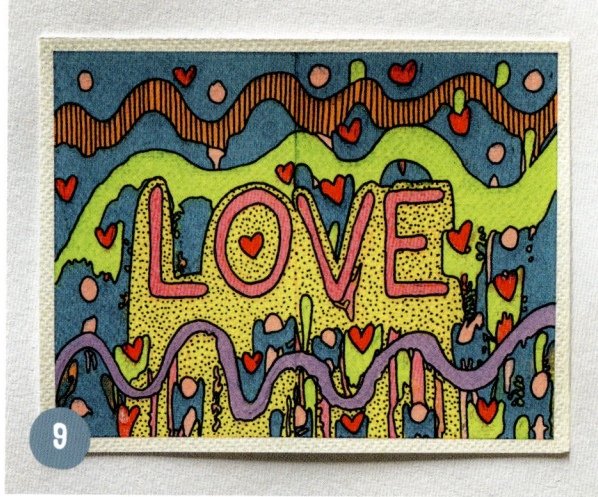

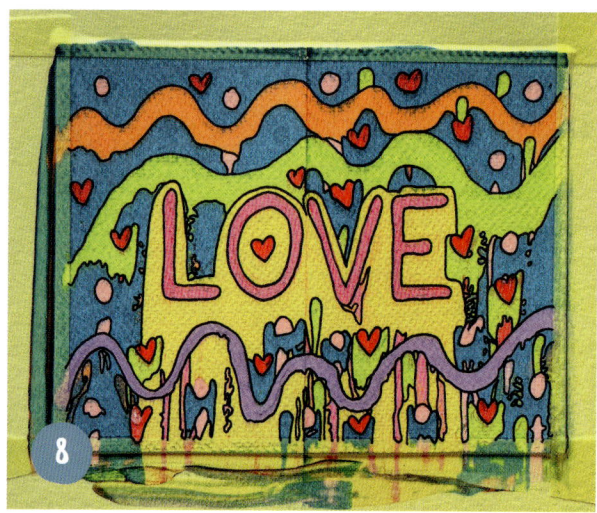

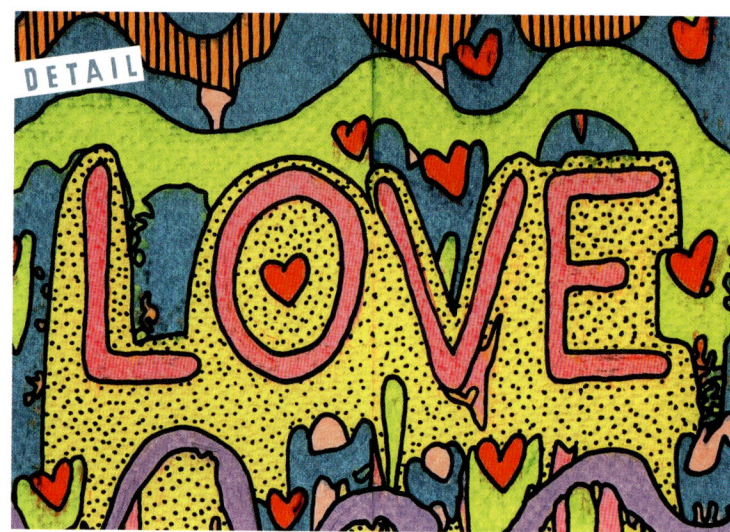

7 Once you're happy with everything, you can scrape off the paint.

8 After painting both halves, I go over the picture in black marker, adding details and outlines to all the shapes.

9 Once you've finished painting, you can remove the rest of the tape and add another beautiful picture to your collection.

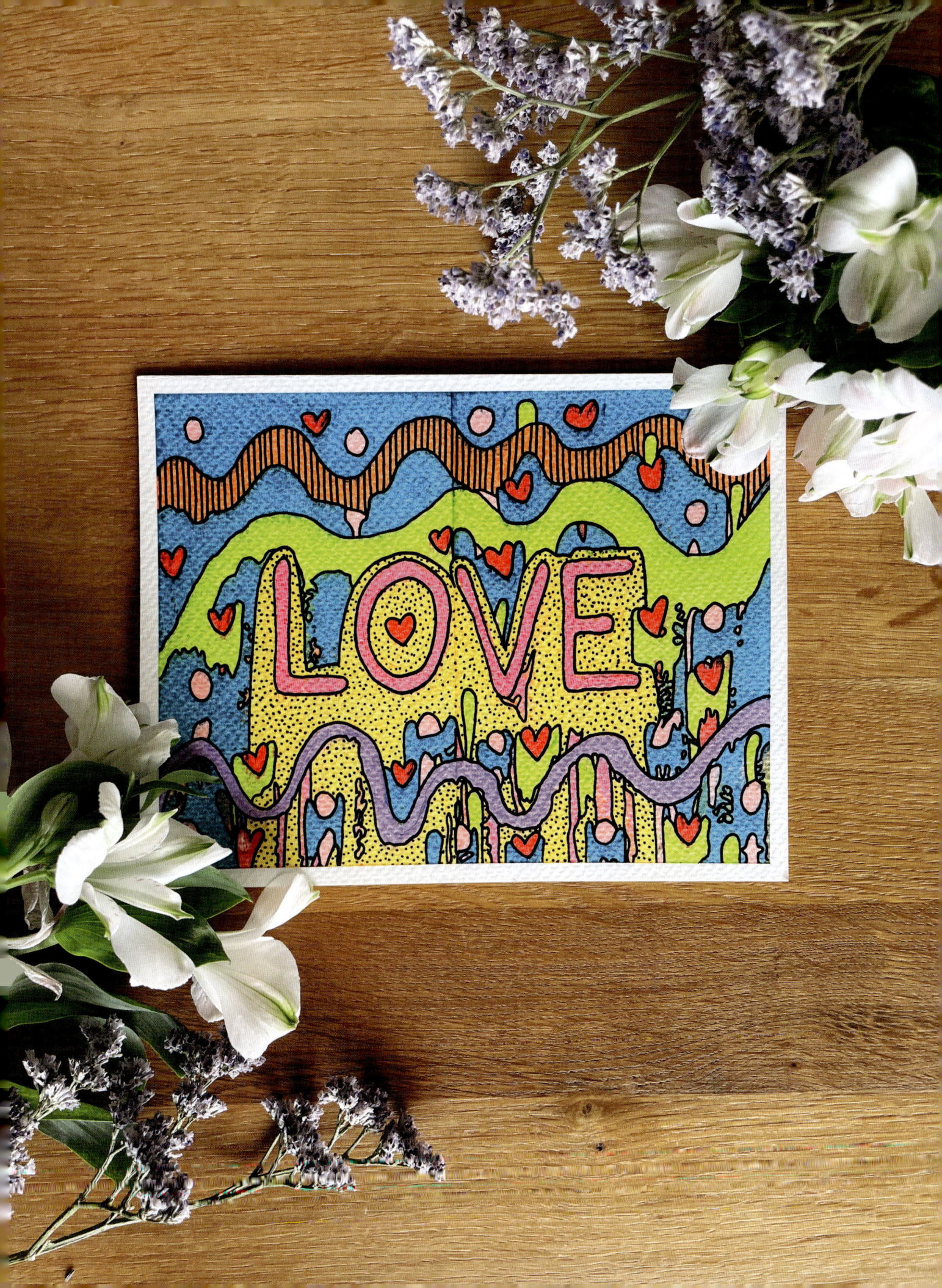

14

THE COLOR OF BLISS

In this project, we'll paint another word using the steps in the previous project so you can learn how to paint a word of your choice. I'm so happy to have had the chance to share my love of painting in this book, so for this project, I've chosen the word "bliss." How are you feeling?

PAPER

✖ Fine-grain 200 lb (300 g/m²) watercolor paper, 7" × 5" (16.5 × 12.5 cm)

COLORS

✖ Yellow Green
✖ Azo Orange
✖ Azo Yellow Deep
✖ Pearl Violet
✖ Quinacridone Rose
✖ Venetian Rose
✖ Turquoise Green
✖ Turquoise Blue

TOOLS

✖ Squeegee
✖ 0.7 marker (black)
✖ Masking tape
✖ Damp cloth

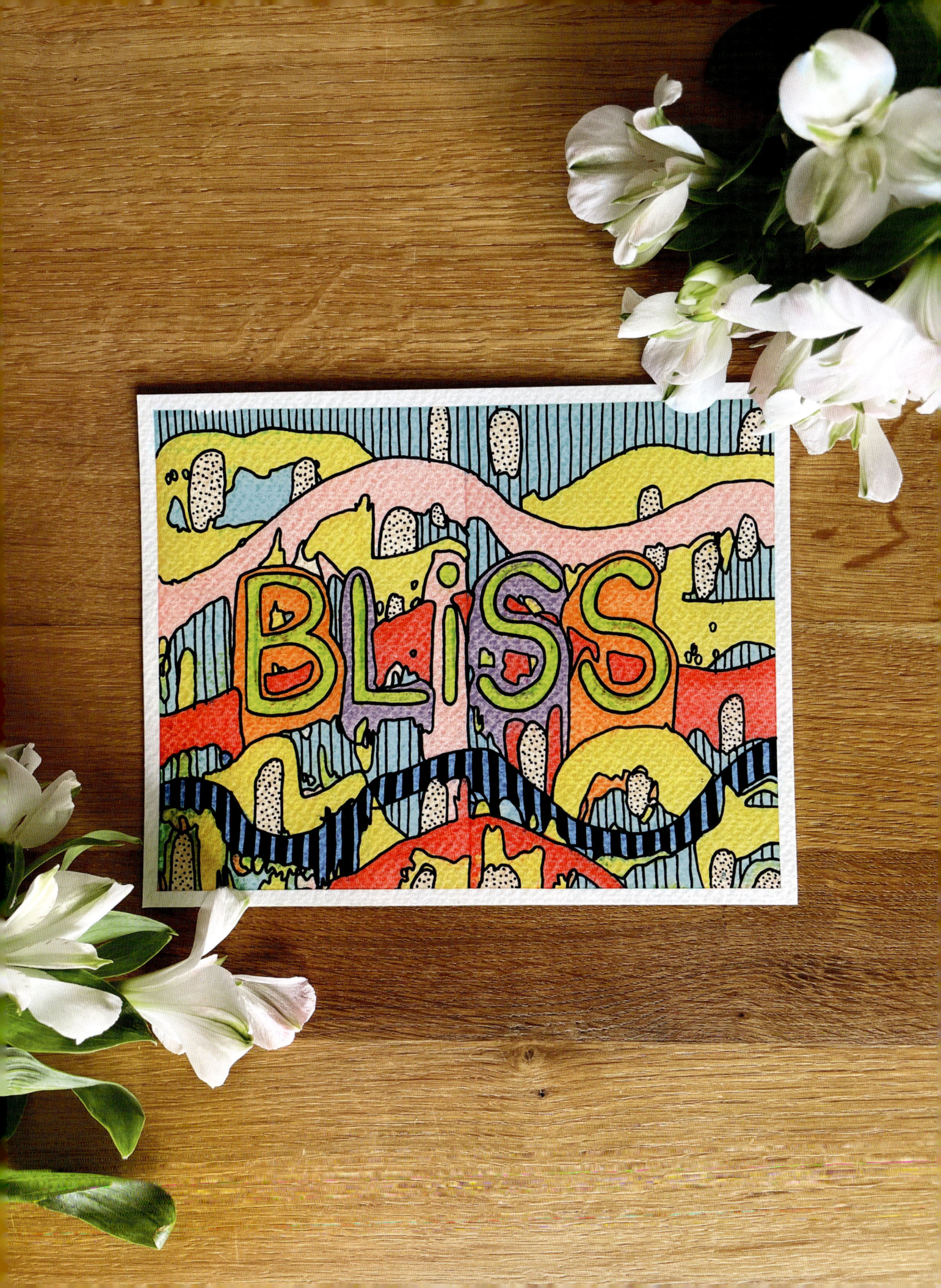

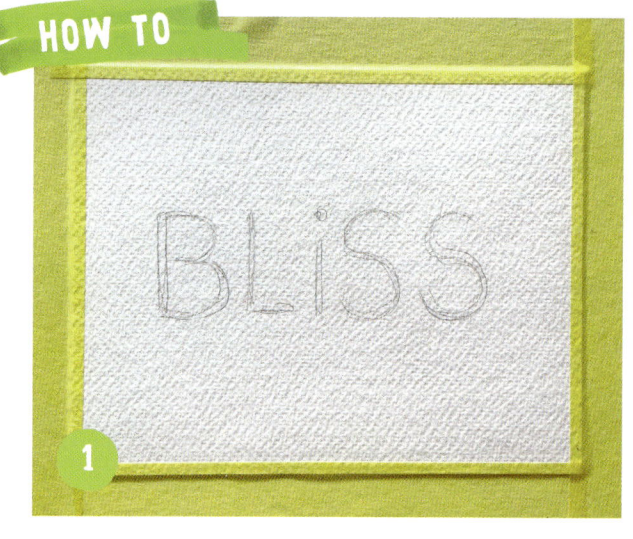

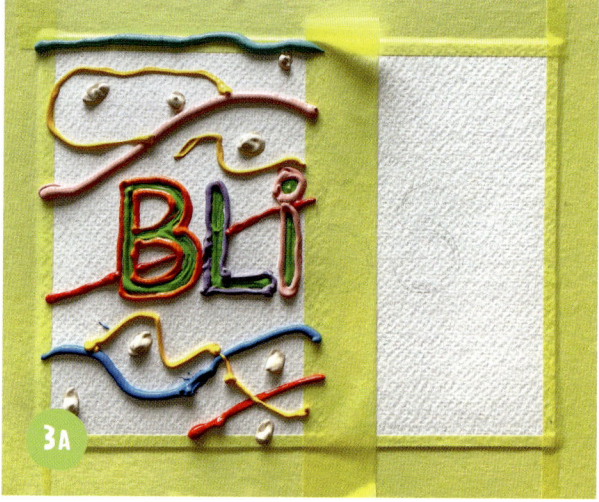

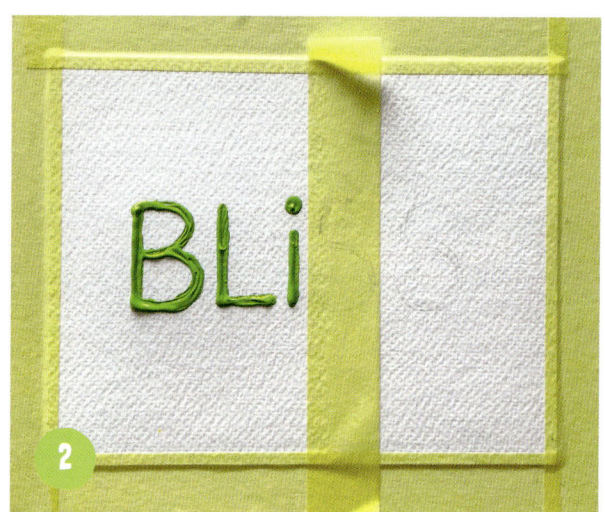

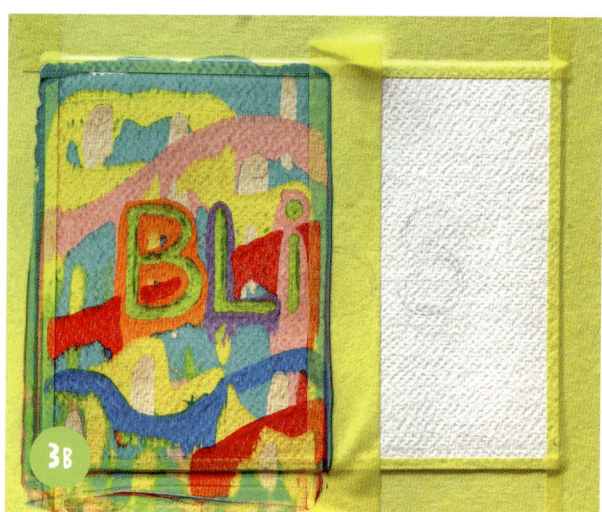

1 Start by writing the word "bliss" on your paper in pencil. Make it as light as possible so it's not visible when you paint over it.

2 Divide the paper in two so it's narrower than your squeegee.

3 Outline the letters with contrasting colors, add all of your desired details, add stripes of paint at the top for the background (3a), and then scrape off all of the paint with your squeegee from the top down, applying moderate to firm pressure (3b).

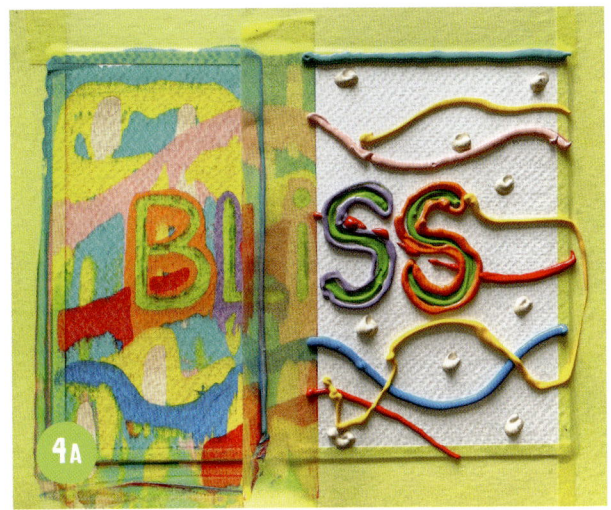

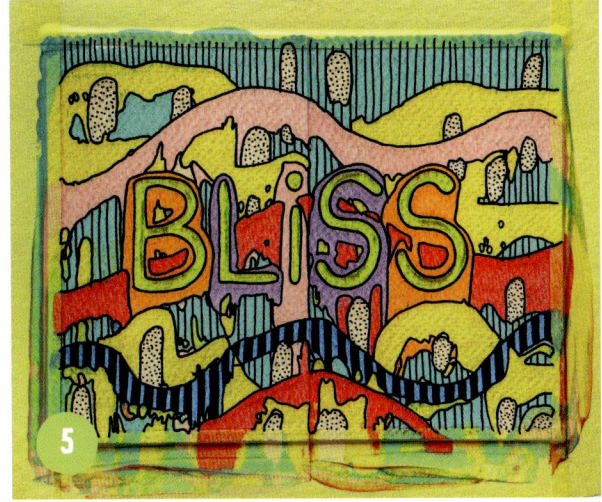

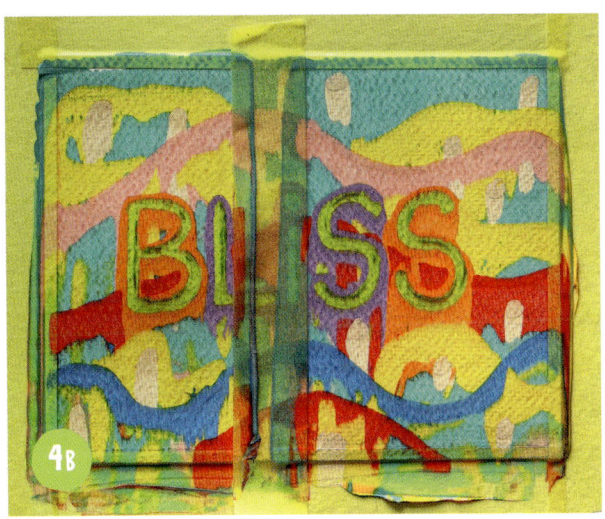

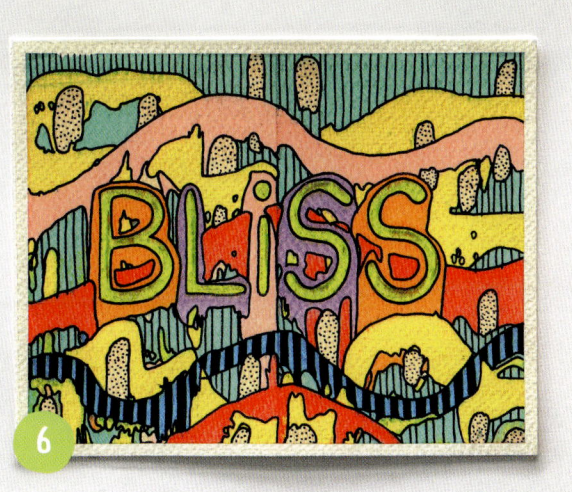

4 Move the tape to the other side, making sure there's no gap in the middle. Then paint the letters and outline them in a contrasting color. Once you've finished your composition, scrape off the paint from the top down by pulling the squeegee downwards, applying moderate to firm pressure.

5 After removing the tape from the middle of the paper, take your black marker and go around any shape you like, adding a few patterns too.

6 Once you've finished the outlines, it's time to remove the tape. Do you feel happy with the result? Or are you frustrated?

15

RIBBONS IN THE WIND

This is a simple project, topped off with a touch of gold outlining. This project is perfect for playing around with layering paint without worrying about getting the perfect wave or curve.

PAPER

- ✖ Fine-grain 200 lb (300 g/m²) watercolor paper, 11" × 14" (27 × 35 cm)

COLORS

- ✖ Sky Blue
- ✖ Pearl Violet
- ✖ Yellow Green
- ✖ Azo Orange
- ✖ Primary Magenta
- ✖ Light Rose
- ✖ Azo Yellow Lemon
- ✖ Titanium Buff Light
- ✖ Permanent Red Purple
- ✖ Turquoise Blue
- ✖ Turquoise Green

TOOLS

- ✖ Squeegee
- ✖ 1.0 marker (gold)
- ✖ Masking tape
- ✖ Damp cloth

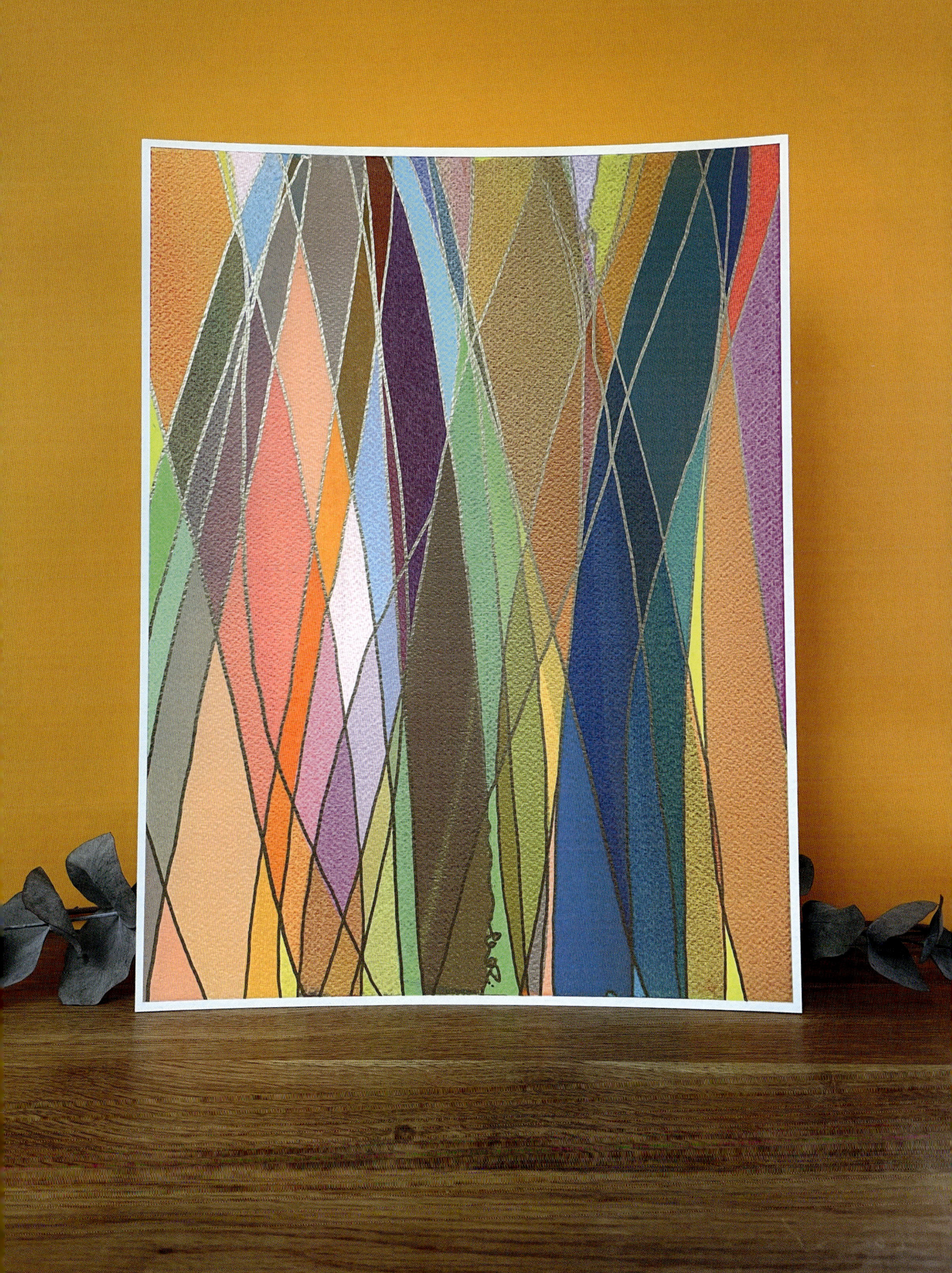

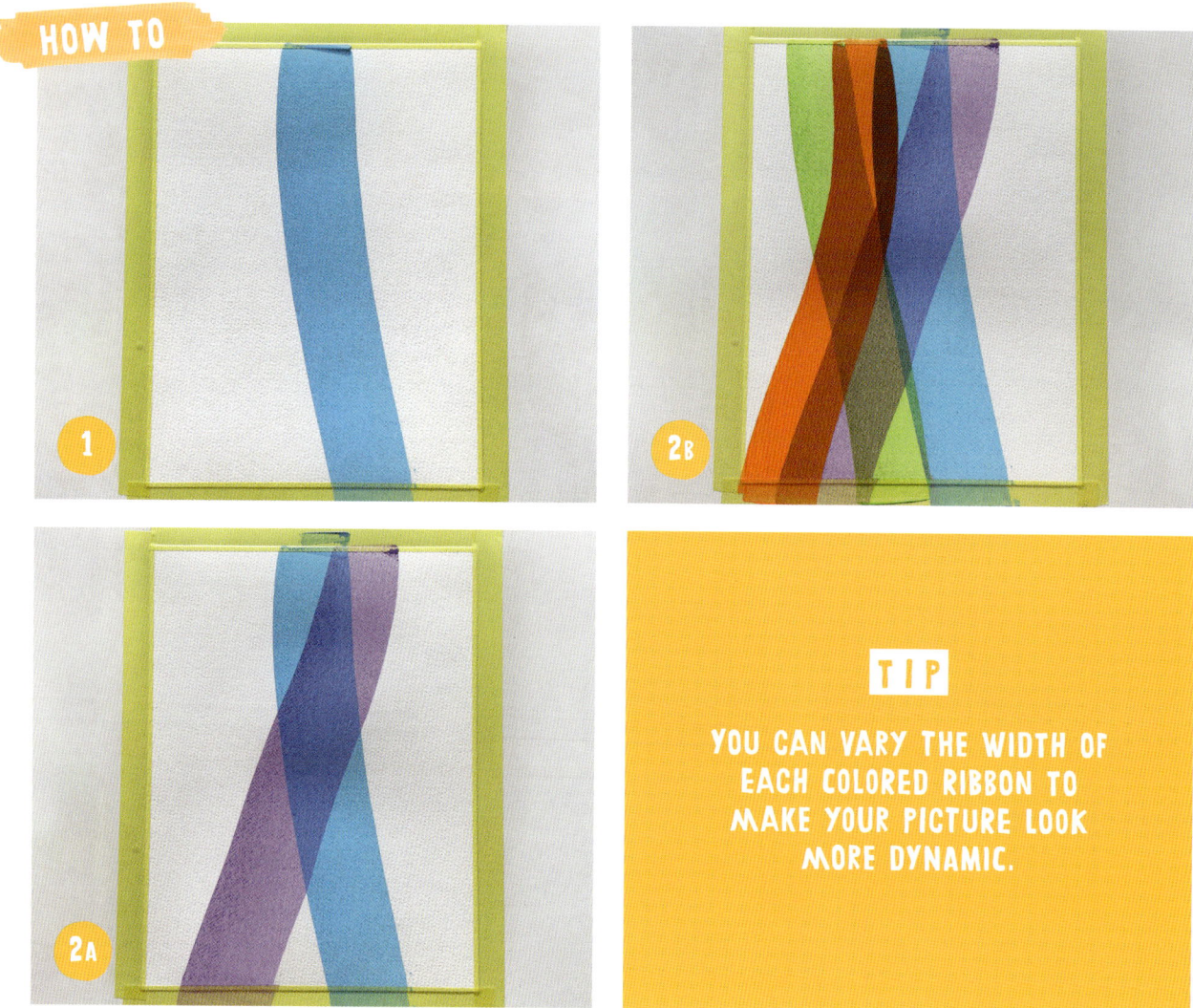

YOU CAN VARY THE WIDTH OF EACH COLORED RIBBON TO MAKE YOUR PICTURE LOOK MORE DYNAMIC.

1 If you've painted each project in order, you'll be able to relax and enjoy this one, just because it's so simple. The steps are the same for the whole picture: Tape down all four sides of your paper. Apply the paint along the top edge of the paper and, with a gentle motion, scrape it to one side like a ribbon being kissed by a gentle breeze.

2 Repeat until your paper is full of ribbons. You can apply the paint to the bottom edge of the paper too and scrape it up to the top. This can be helpful for covering up gaps, without the pressure of having to cover everything 100 percent when scraping from the top down.

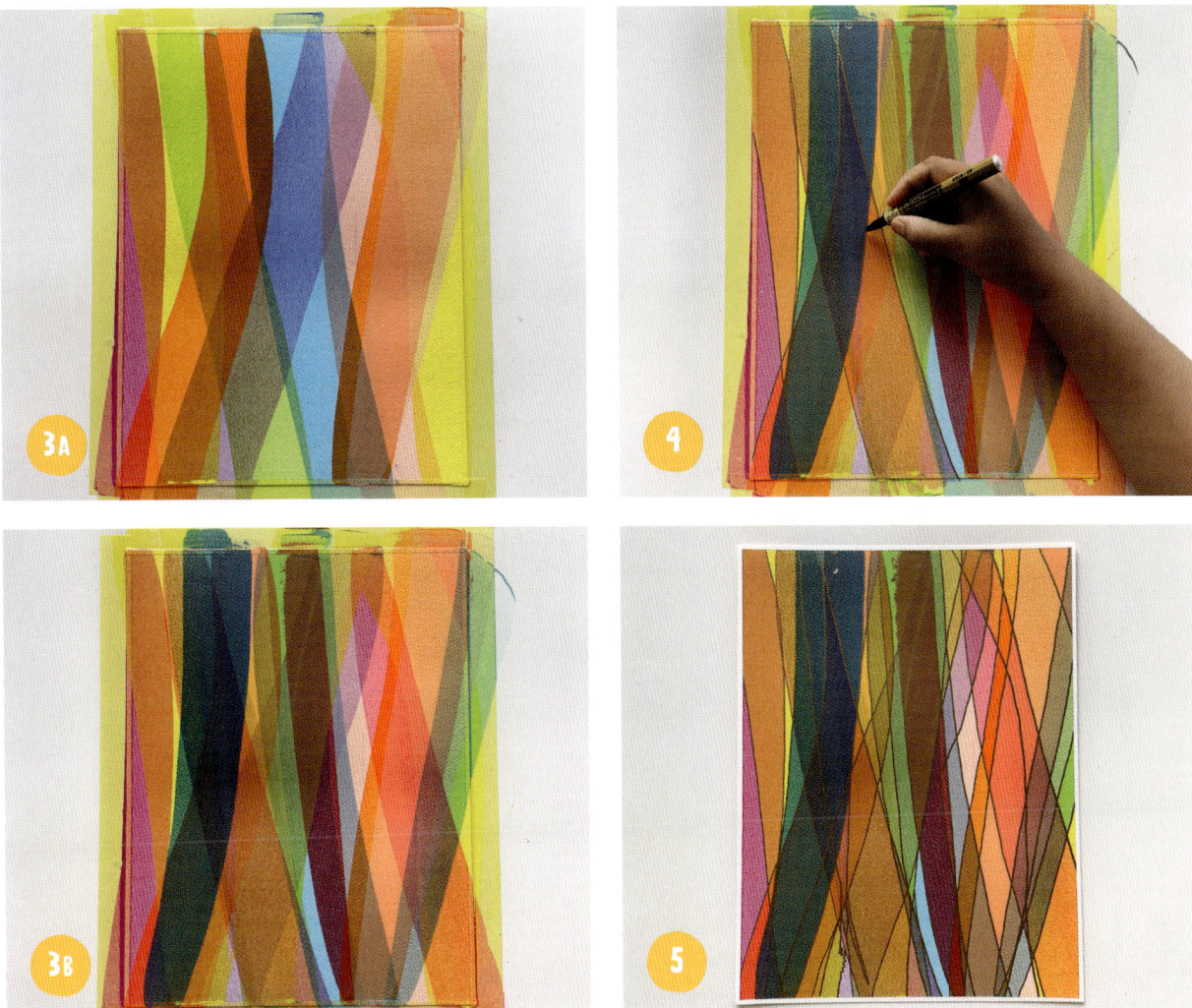

3 Apply your layers until you feel like you have enough "ribbons." Add a dark and a light color to increase the depth.

4 Then take your gold marker and draw around all the edges you can find.

5 This painting looks especially vibrant when the sun shines on it. You'll be amazed!

16

FIREWORK

Now we're going to paint a colorful firework together. In this project, the squeegee motion is very subtle and easy to control. The various layers of paint, applied in the correct order and in a variety of widths, give your picture an attractive depth and movement.

PAPER

- ✘ Fine-grain 200 lb (300 g/m²) watercolor paper, 11" × 14" (27 × 35 cm)

COLORS

- ✘ Turquoise Green
- ✘ Azo Orange
- ✘ Pearl Violet
- ✘ Quinacridone Rose
- ✘ Brilliant Green
- ✘ Azo Yellow Deep
- ✘ Permanent Red Purple
- ✘ Turquoise Blue
- ✘ Titanium Buff Light
- ✘ Cobalt Blue

TOOLS

- ✘ Squeegee
- ✘ 0.7 marker (gold)
- ✘ Masking tape
- ✘ Damp cloth

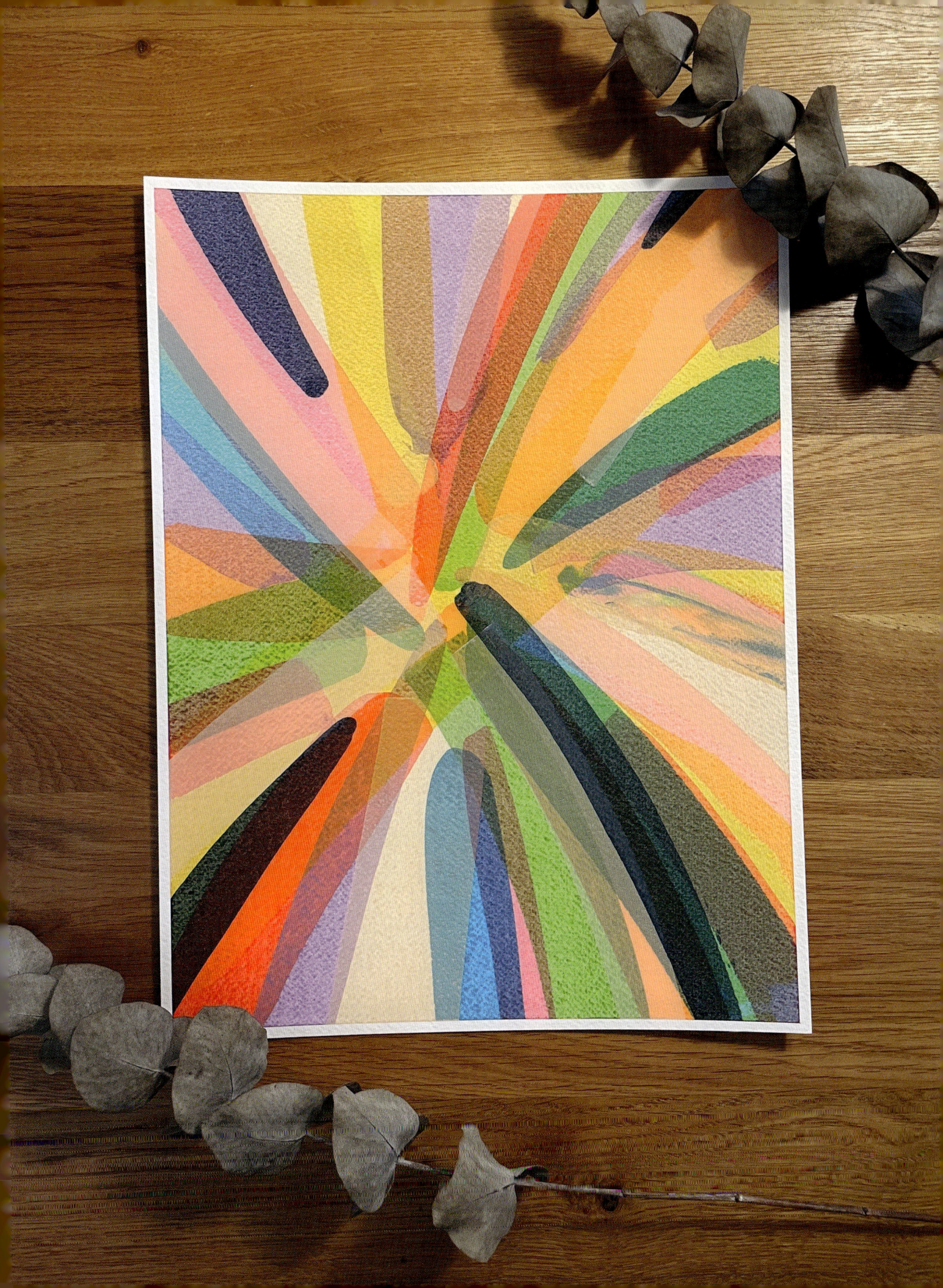

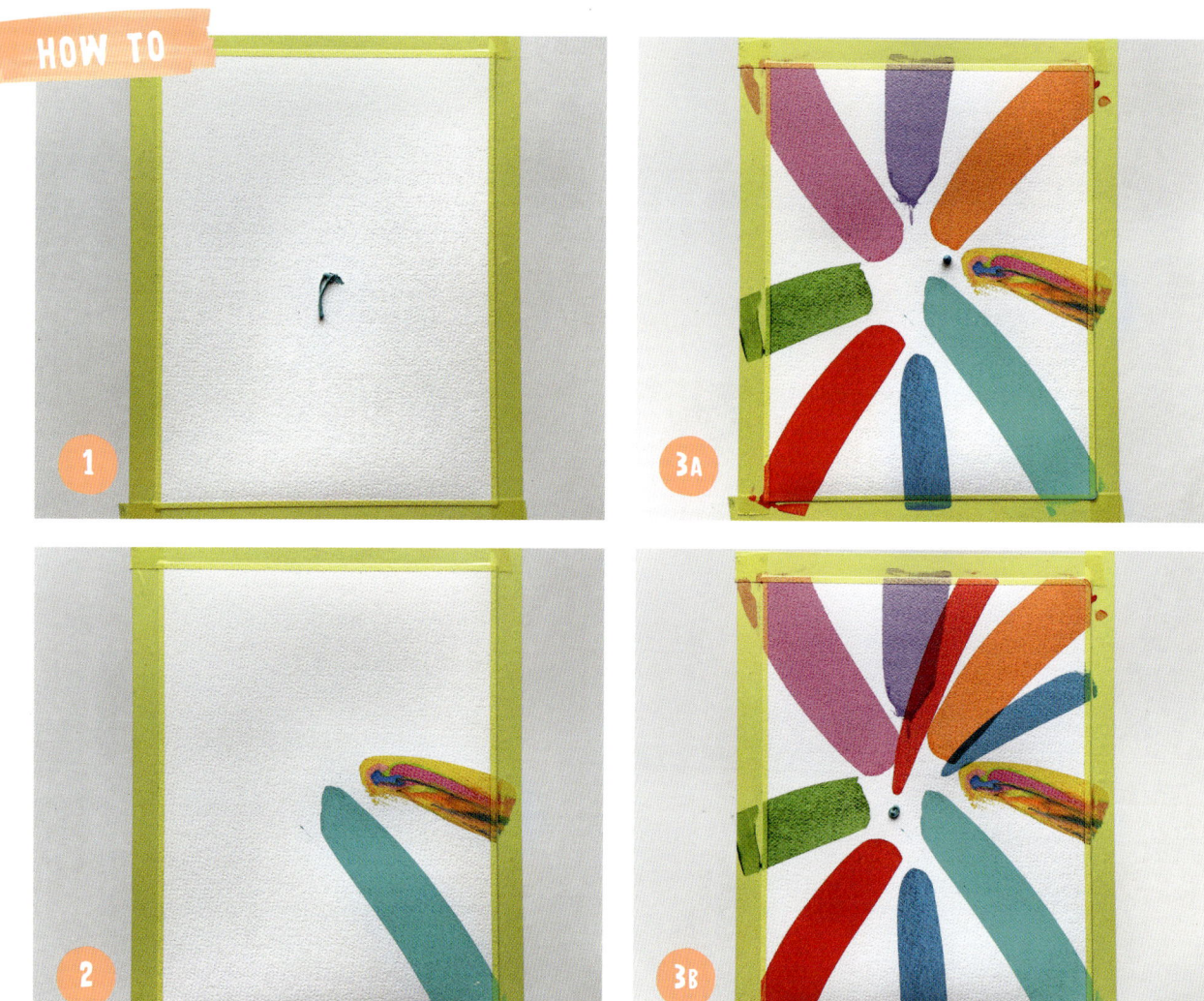

1 In this project, every layer of paint starts from the same place. You then scrape the paint outward from this central point. You can choose the actual center of the paper if you want, or you can start somewhere else. The most important thing is that all the stripes start from the same place. Begin by taping down all four sides of your paper and applying some paint to the paper and scraping it outward.

2 In the second step, I experimented with creating a marbled stripe from some leftover paint. However, it looked a bit dull among all the other layers, so I recommend choosing a pure color instead.

3 Now distribute the stripes across the page to highlight the center or starting point of your picture. Then fill in the gaps with other colors. I recommend using less paint to make these stripes thinner than the previous ones.

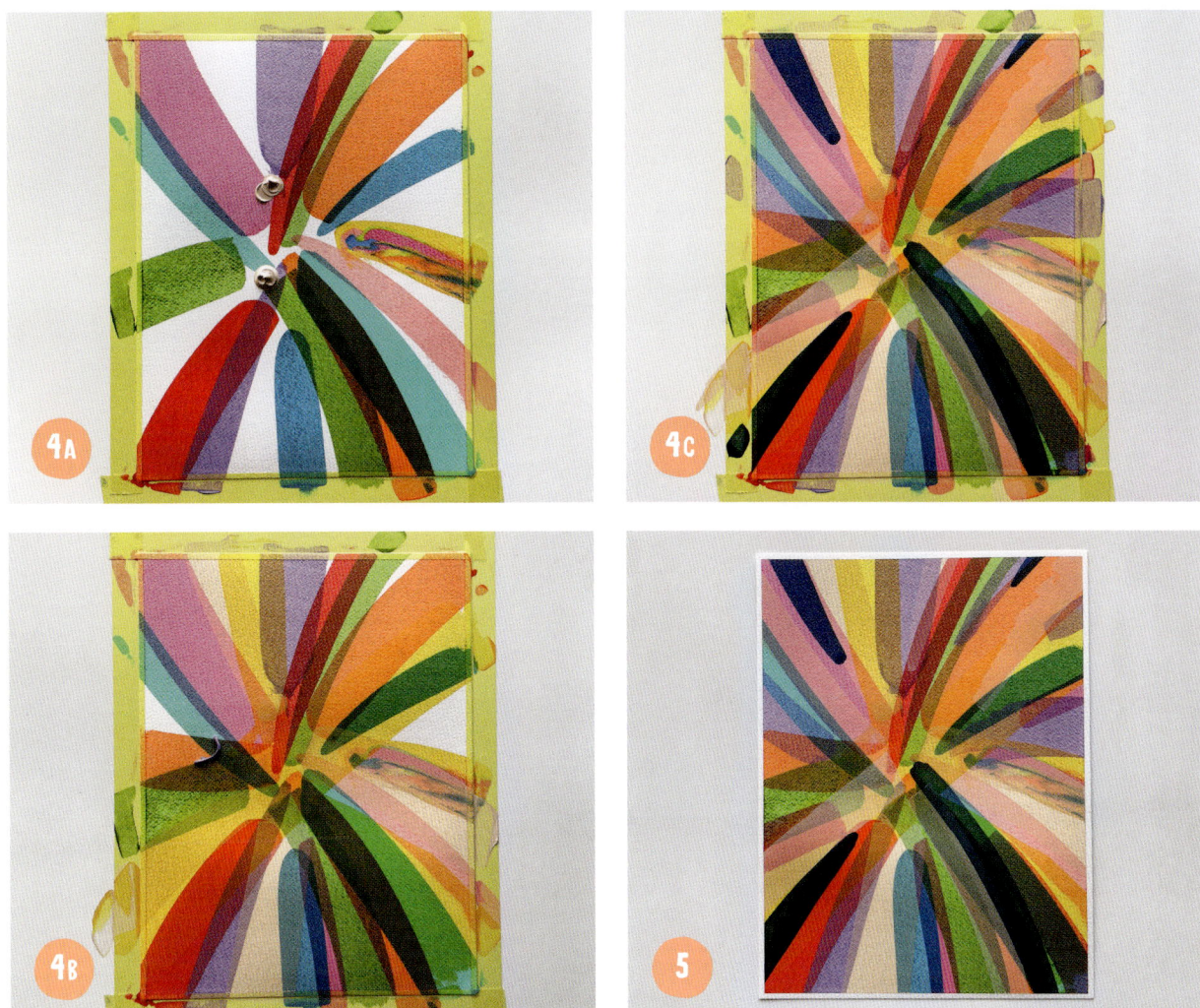

4 Keep filling your paper, varying the width of your stripes. If a certain area needs more contrast and emphasis, try adding a layer of yellow (4a). If an area is too dark, I try a layer of Titanium Buff Light (4b). If the picture needs more weight, I try darker colors like in the third image (4c).

5 Once every element is in place, your colorful firework is done!

17

RAYS OF COLOR

In this project and the next, we'll create a new picture that takes advantage of the versatility of masking tape. We'll use it to isolate the areas where we're going to apply the paint, creating an interesting combination of shapes.

PAPER

- ✖ Fine-grain 200 lb (300 g/m²) watercolor paper, 11" × 14" (27 × 35 cm)

COLORS

- ✖ Quinacridone Rose
- ✖ Pearl Violet
- ✖ Turquoise Blue
- ✖ Yellow Green
- ✖ Azo Orange
- ✖ Titanium Buff Light
- ✖ Cobalt Blue
- ✖ Oxide Black
- ✖ Brilliant Green
- ✖ Light Rose
- ✖ Sky Blue
- ✖ Permanent Green Deep
- ✖ Permanent Red Purple

TOOLS

- ✖ Squeegee
- ✖ Masking tape
- ✖ Damp cloth

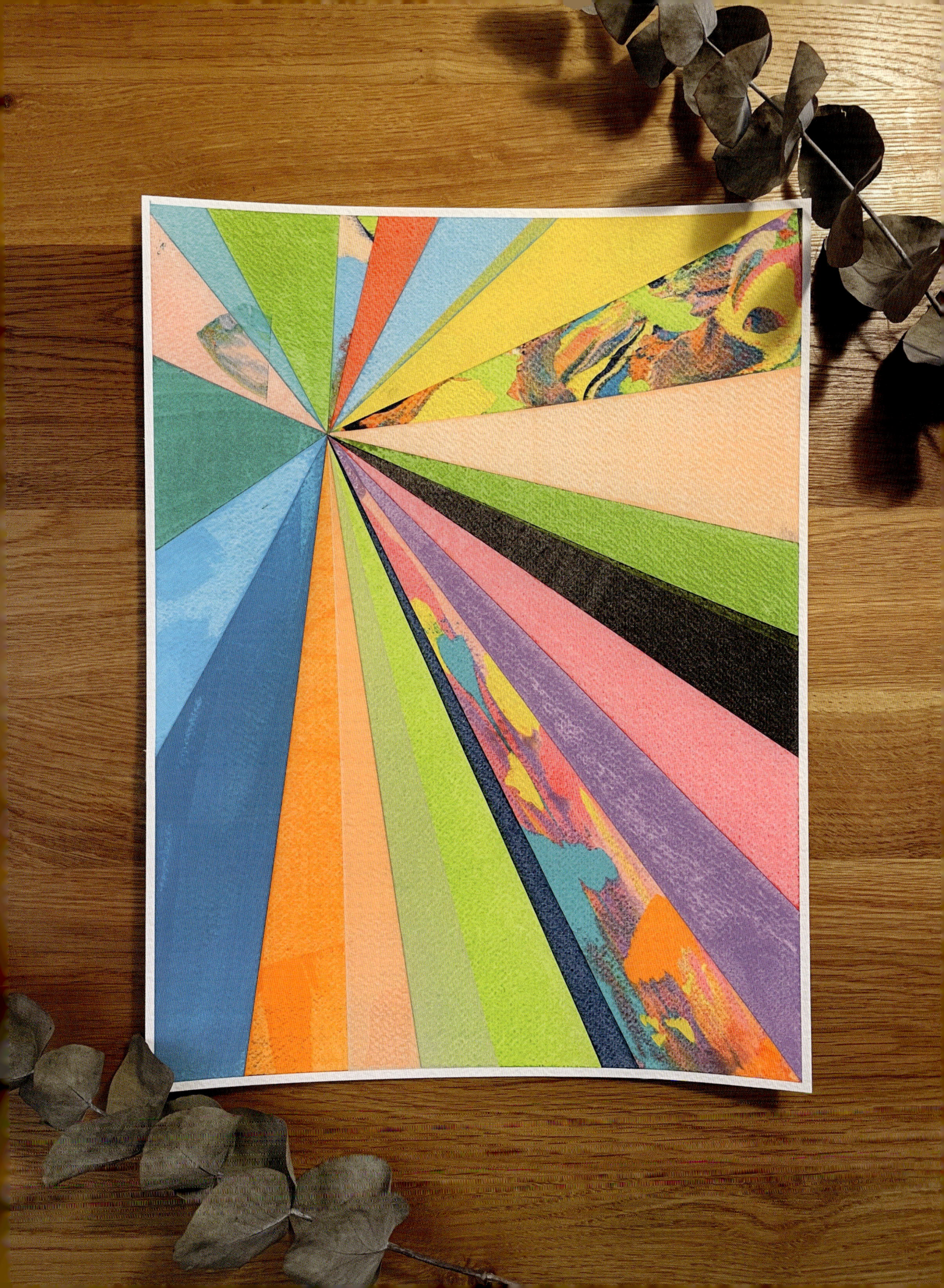

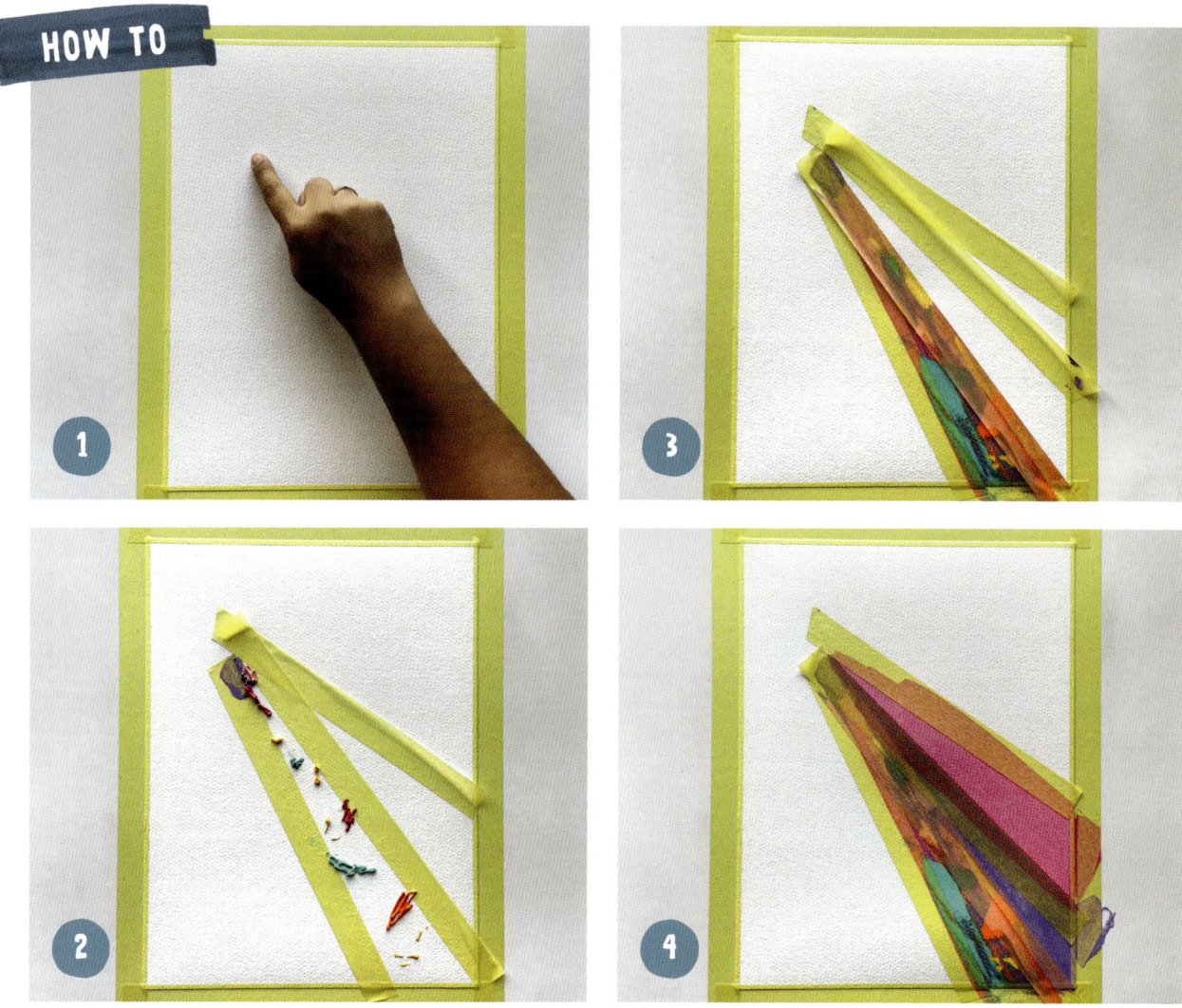

1 Decide on the location for the source of your rays and make a small mark on your paper.

2 Tape down all four sides of your paper. Mask the first section with tape to create a triangle. You can then start laying down the various colors inside this triangle. Make sure that the widest part of the triangle is narrower than your squeegee. If, like me, you've started spreading the paint only to discover that your triangle is too big, remove the paint with a palette knife, place some tape down the middle, and paint over the top.

3 Scrape the paint through your triangle, then change the position of the tape and paint the next step.

4 Repeat the above steps, filling the paper with your colorful little rays.

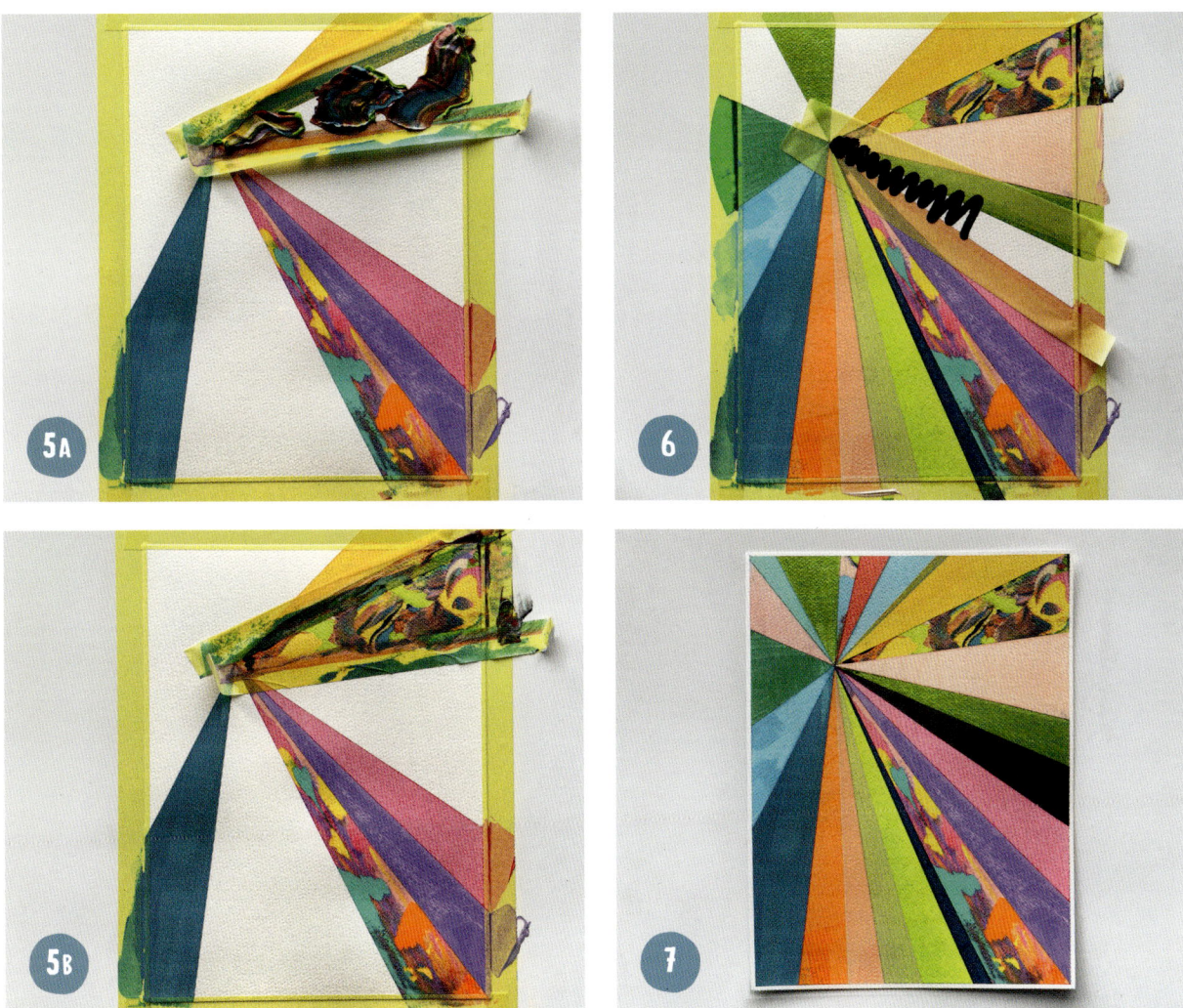

5 You can use leftover paint to create an interesting pattern too.

6 Black adds a little more drama and contrast to the surface.

7 Now you have some lively colors to brighten up every corner of your home!

18

CHAOS DIAMOND

It's magical how a new shape can emerge just from using masking tape to interrupt the flow of color. For this project, we'll paint a diamond-shaped picture to demonstrate what you can achieve by experimenting with a squeegee and some masking tape.

PAPER

- ✖ Fine-grain 200 lb (300 g/m²) watercolor paper, 11" × 14" (27 × 35 cm)

COLORS

- ✖ Quinacridone Rose
- ✖ Pearl Violet
- ✖ Turquoise Blue
- ✖ Yellow Green
- ✖ Azo Orange
- ✖ Titanium Buff Light
- ✖ Cobalt Blue
- ✖ Oxide Black
- ✖ Brilliant Green
- ✖ Light Rose
- ✖ Sky Blue
- ✖ Permanent Green Deep
- ✖ Permanent Red Purple

TOOLS

- ✖ Squeegee
- ✖ Masking tape
- ✖ Damp cloth

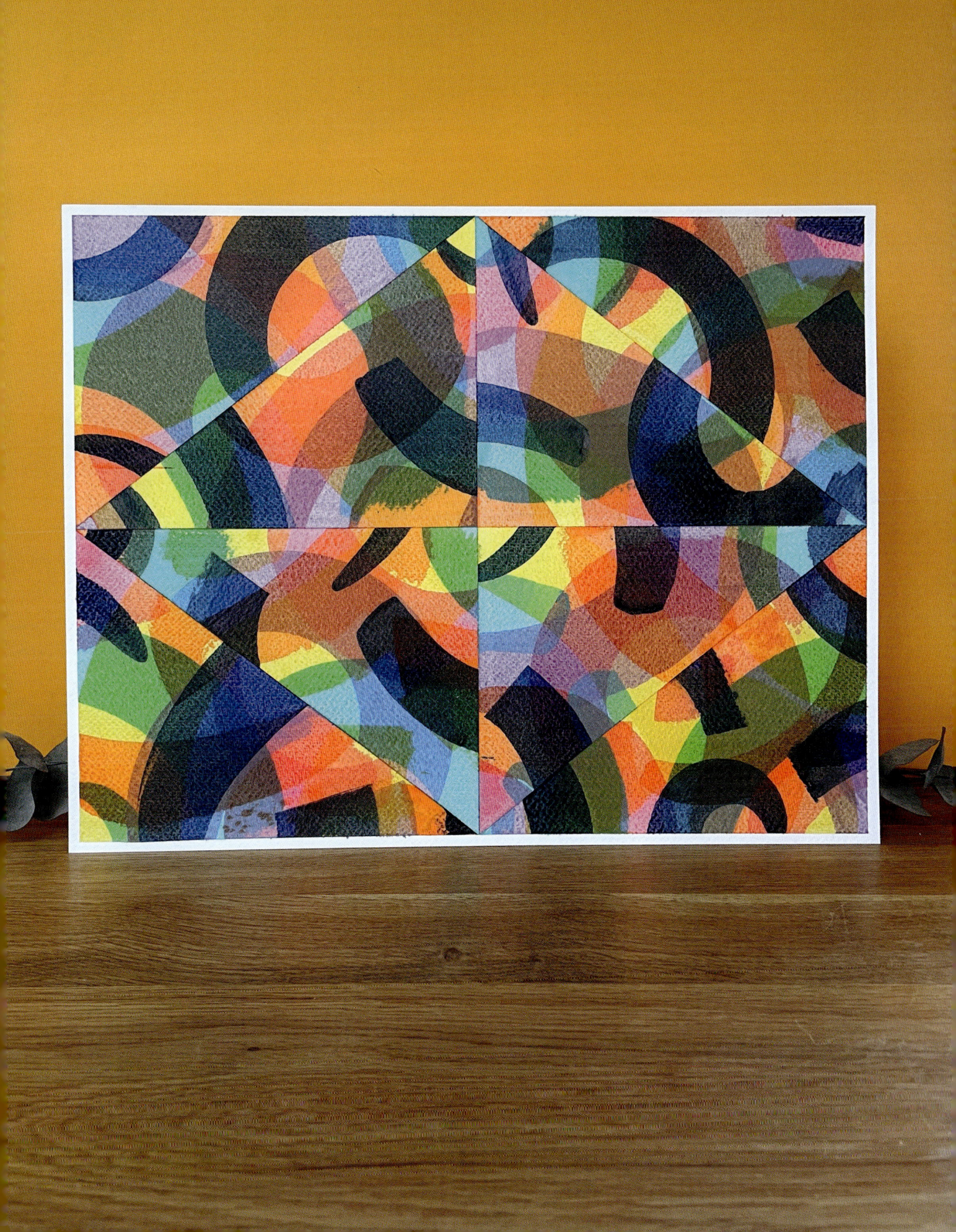

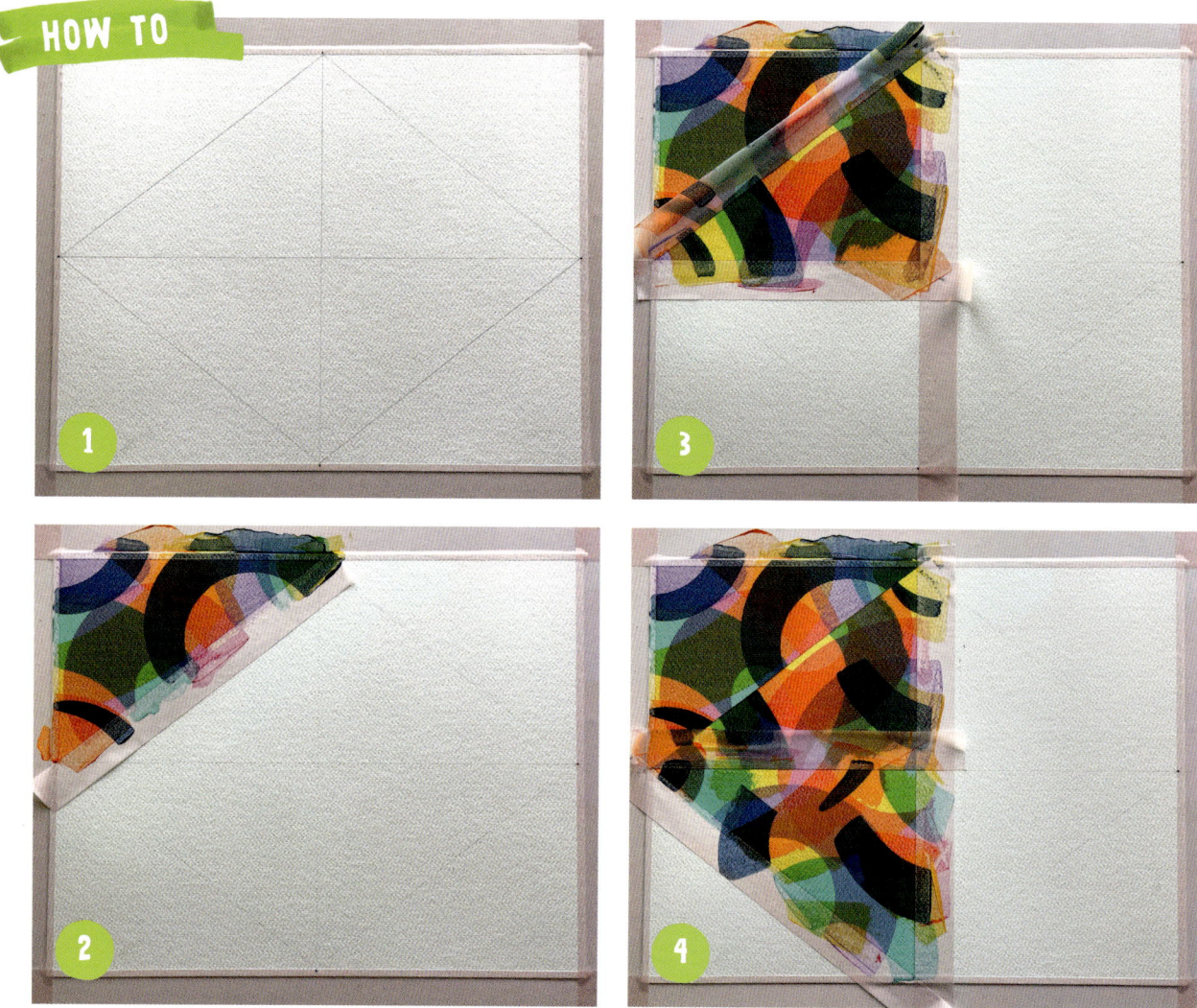

1 Tape down your paper. Use a pencil and ruler to mark the center of all four sides of your paper. Then connect these points to create a diamond in the middle of your paper. Draw one horizontal and one vertical line through the center to create a total of eight right-angled triangles. Draw the lines using gentle pressure so the lines don't shine through the paint once you're done.

2 Take a piece of tape and isolate the first triangle. Then fill with shapes and colors to your liking.

3 Once the first section is complete, you can move on to the next one. I recommend marking the center of the vertical line on the paper with tape first and then taking another piece of tape and isolating the next triangle. Use the same colors as you used for the first triangle, only this time, try to break up the shapes so they don't continue seamlessly to the other side.

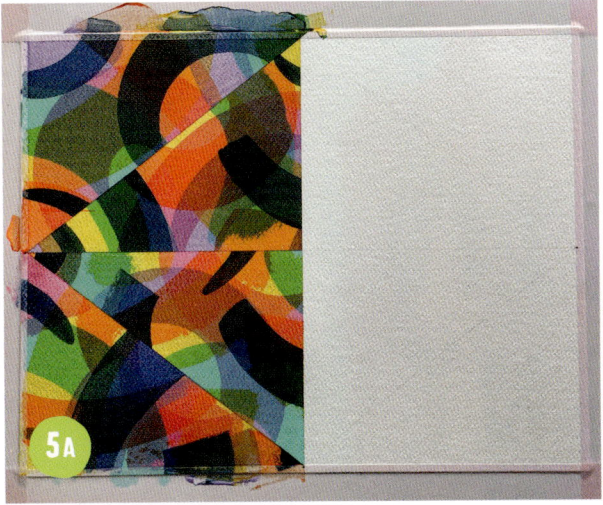

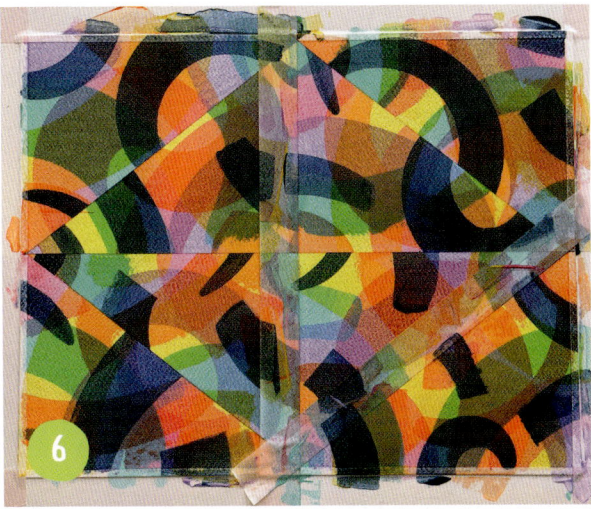

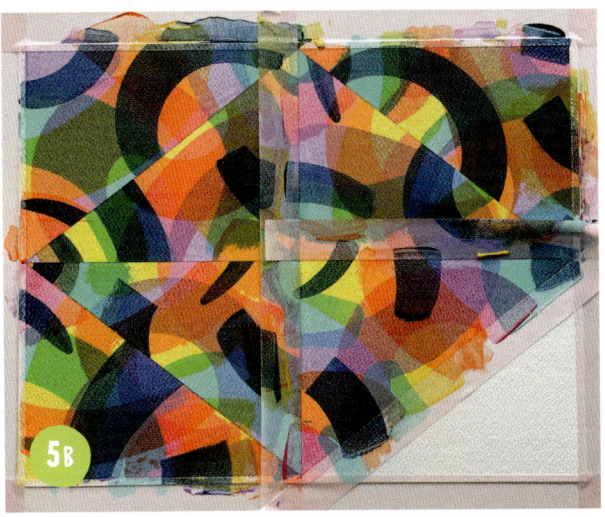

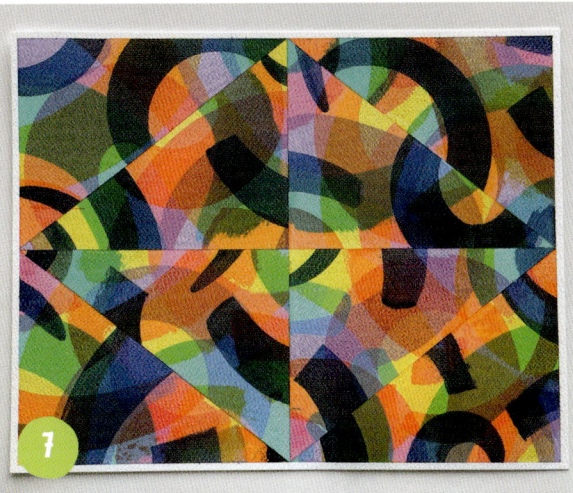

4 Now you can move the tape to the next section, isolate the next triangle, and apply your paint. Remember not to carry over the shapes from the adjacent triangle to the triangle you're currently working on. We want to make an invisible line along the edge of the triangle, a visual effect created by the transition between colors.

5 Apply the same principle to all eight sections until the entire page is full.

6 Finish the last triangle and remove the tape.

7 Now you have a sparkling diamond. If you want to have another go, you can use paint to create a shape that runs seamlessly across all sections too. I'm sure this picture will look just as interesting.

19

A COLLECTION OF MINI PAINTINGS

Now we're going to paint four mini paintings using a variety of color combinations, textures, layers, and techniques. In a single sitting of three to four hours, you can paint dozens of them. The longer you paint, the more interesting they become. They look great together: You can mount them, put them in a frame, and hang them up around your home.

PAPER

- ✖ 4 pieces of 245 lb (360 g/m²) acrylic paper, 4" × 4" (10 × 10 cm) each

COLORS

- ✖ Yellow Green
- ✖ Azo Yellow Deep
- ✖ Turquoise Green
- ✖ Turquoise Blue
- ✖ Azo Orange
- ✖ Cobalt Blue
- ✖ Permanent Red Purple
- ✖ Pearl Violet
- ✖ Quinacridone Rose
- ✖ Brilliant Green
- ✖ Titanium Buff Light
- ✖ Venetian Rose

TOOLS

- ✖ Squeegee
- ✖ Palette knife
- ✖ Masking tape
- ✖ Damp cloth

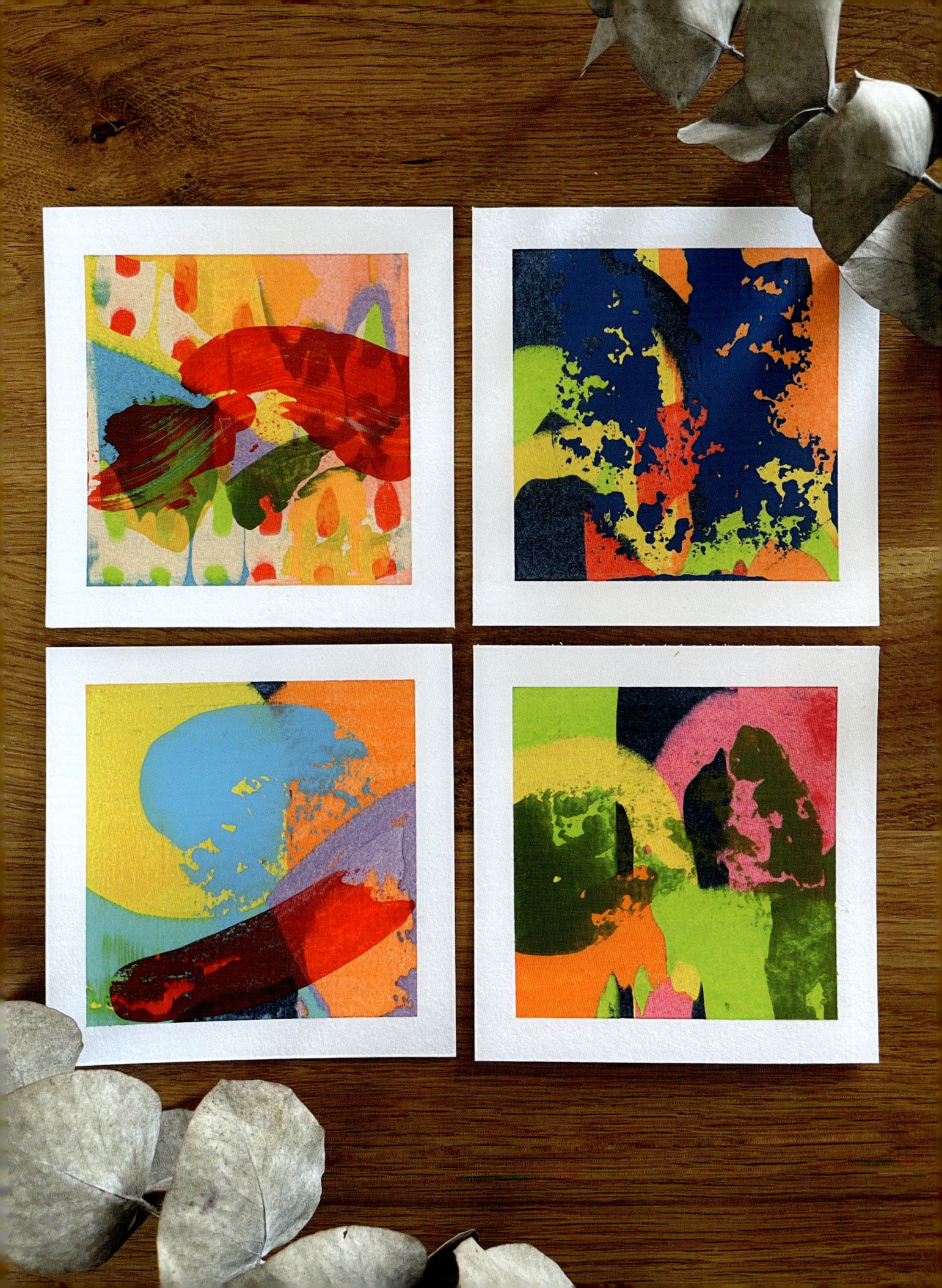

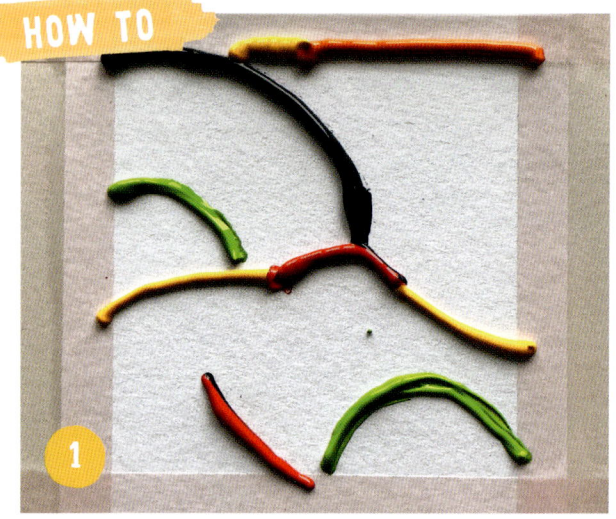

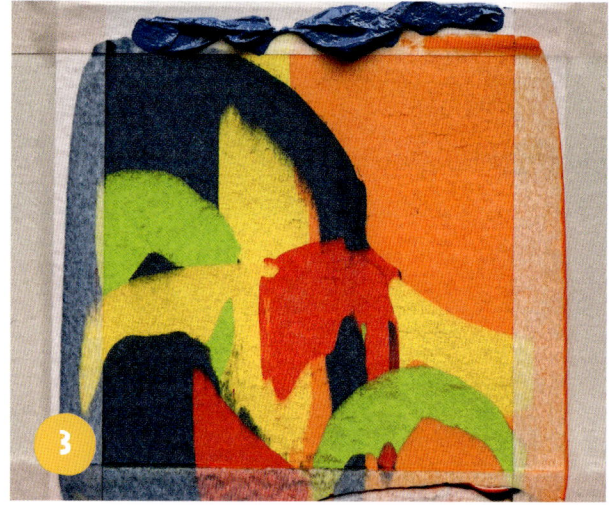

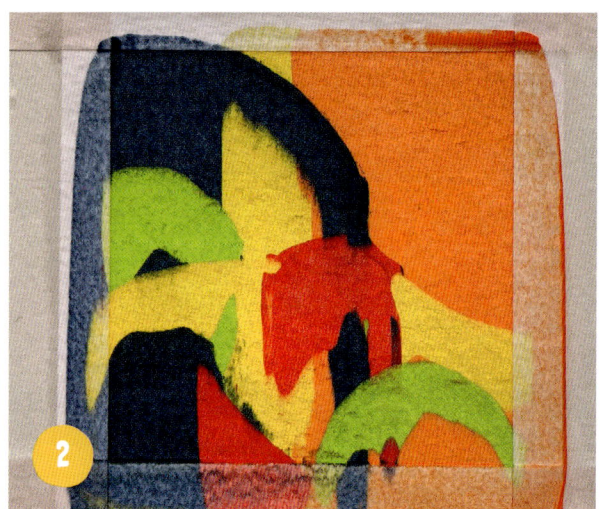

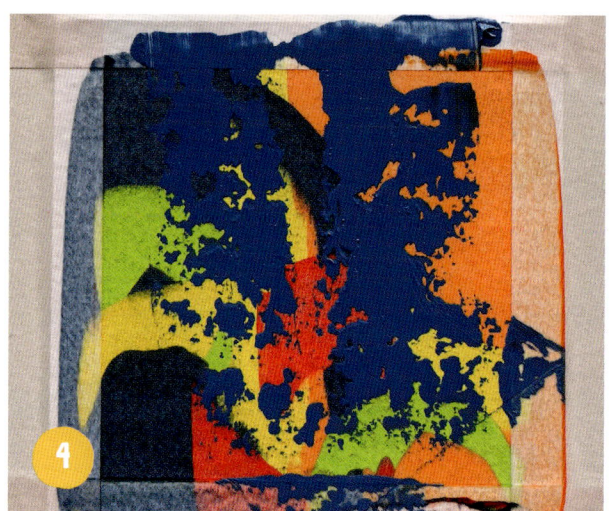

MINI 1

1 Start by taping down your paper and laying down all your desired colors and shapes.

2 Once you've applied your paint, use your squeegee to scrape it off from the top down, using moderate to firm pressure.

3 Then place more paint at the edges of your picture or somewhere else on the page. Try to choose a contrasting color. This can be more effective if you use acrylic paints like I do. The texture can look more interesting.

4 Take your squeegee and, holding it at a very acute angle, almost parallel to the page, spread the extra paint across the paper, applying very light pressure. You can apply more paint and repeat the process if you're unhappy with how your picture looks.

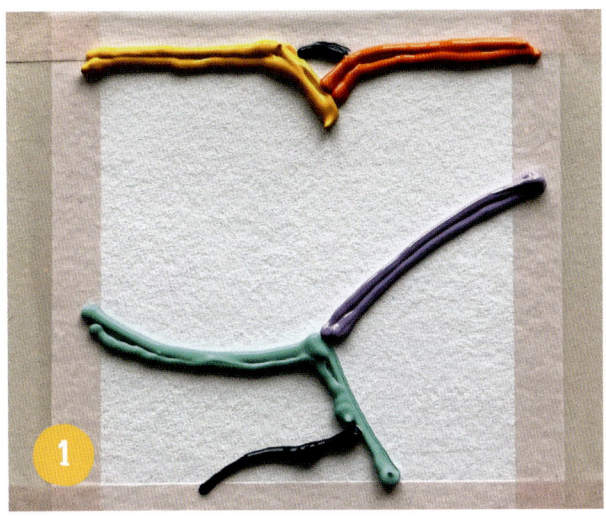

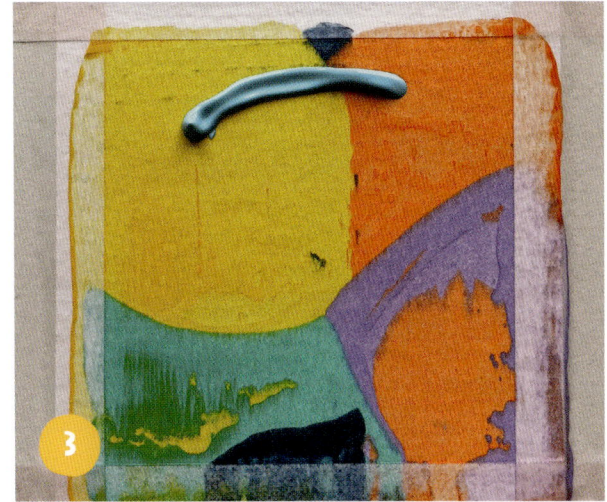

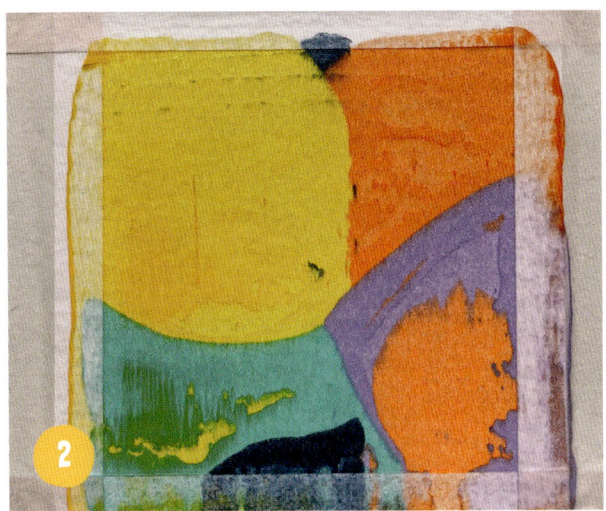

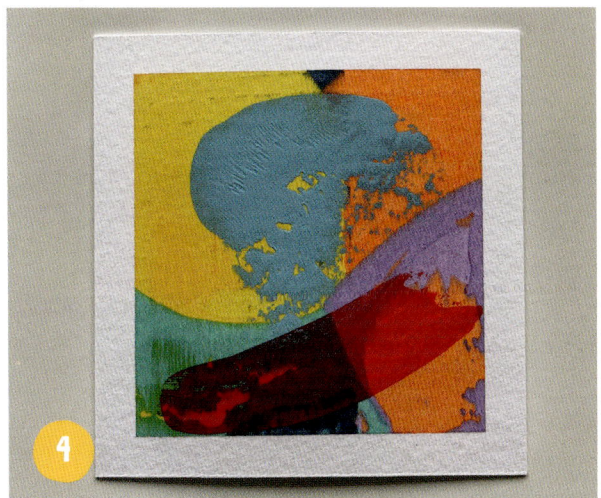

1 Place the paint on the paper. Experiment with different shapes to get a better feel for how the paint behaves as it's scraped off.

2 Now scrape off the paint from the top down and compare the lines in this composition with the one you did before. This will give you a sense of how the paint behaves.

3 Now you can try out a new color to give your picture some added "oomph." Apply the paint where you think it makes most sense.

4 Scrape the paint, using light pressure, in the desired direction. I've repeated the same step twice, once in blue and once in red.

CONTINUED →

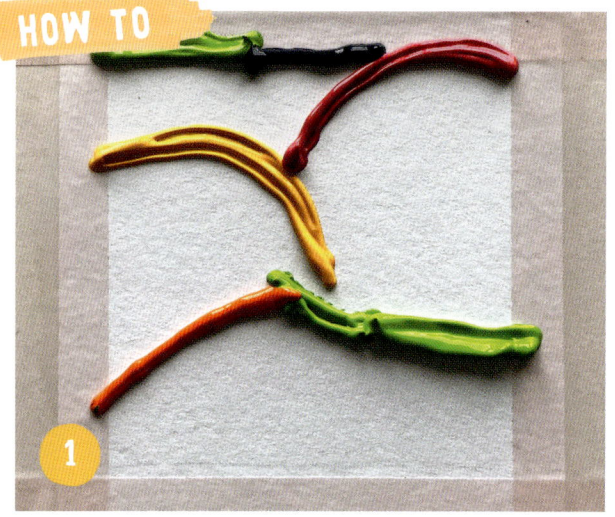

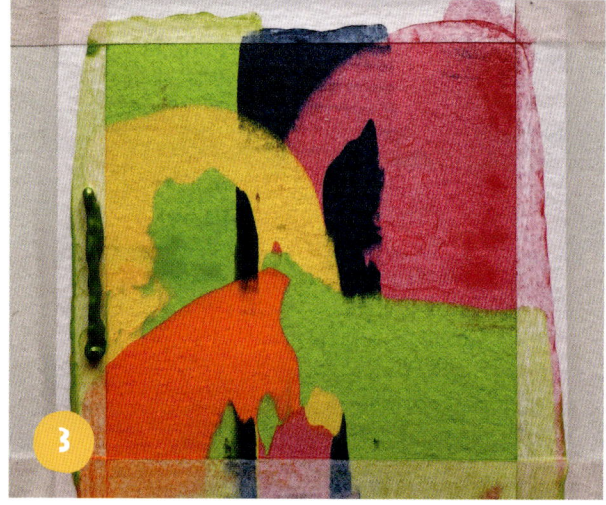

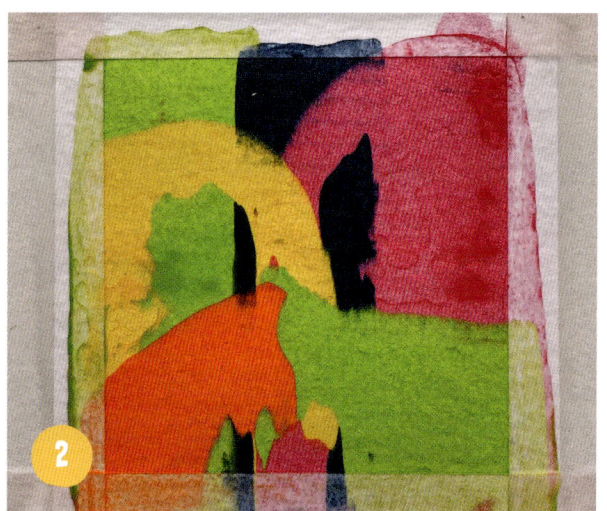

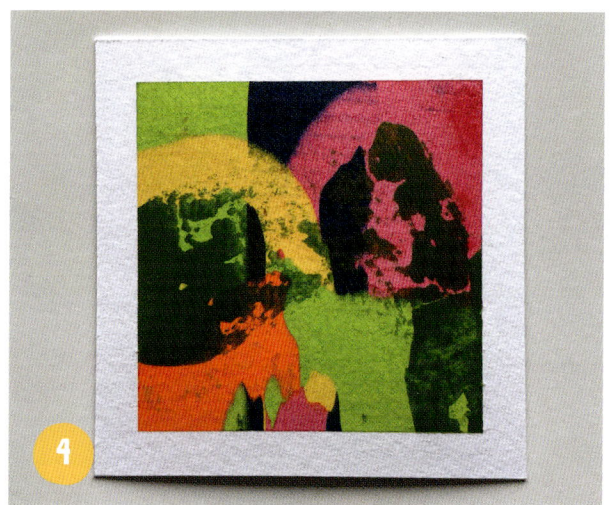

MINI 3

1 Begin as you did with the previous mini paintings, experimenting with colors and shapes.

2 After scraping the paint from the top down, you can see that an interesting effect has been created with the blue. It looks as if it's in the background. This wasn't intentional, but I like the result.

3 This time, I chose a metallic paint to add along one of the edges. If you have some, you can try it out too.

4 Here I created lots of blotches by moving the squeegee from left to right. The metallic paint looks particularly striking when the light shines on it.

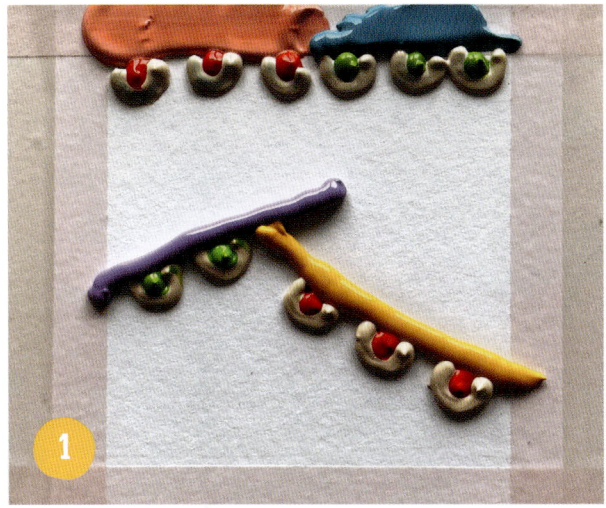

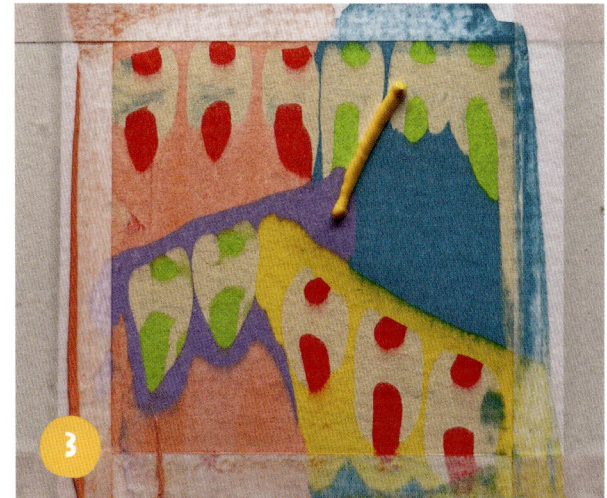

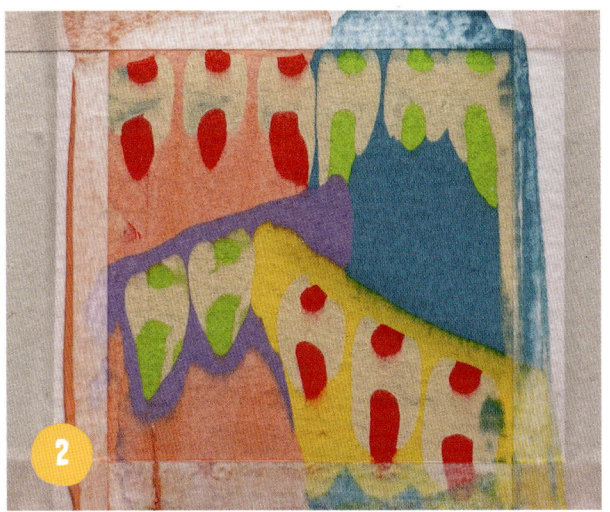

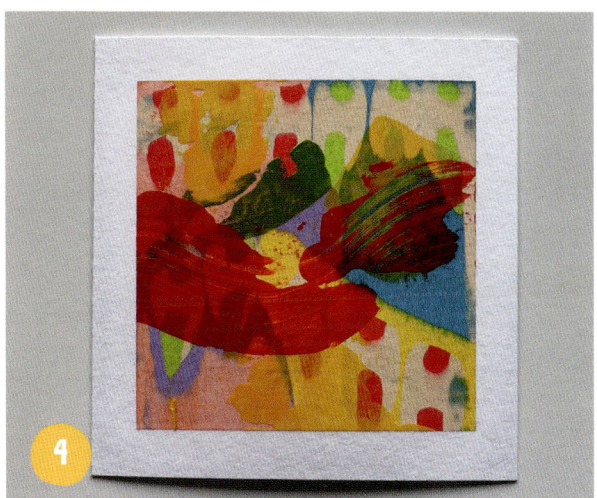

MINI 4

1 This time, I chose to incorporate lots of different shapes: I now know that the result will look really eye-catching!

2 When scraping off the paint, things didn't go quite as I'd expected, and I got a few strange results. This could be down to how much paint I put on the paper.

3 Add contrasting colors or highlights wherever you want on the paper.

4 Try to scrape off the extra layer of paint with an organic, dynamic motion. You've now made four mini paintings: If you're feeling inspired, why not make a few more? I'm sure you'll encounter lots of wonderful surprises.

20

BLACK HOLE

This project needs a bit more time, but the result is stunning and can be very dramatic. We're going to combine a colorful background with a black shape in the foreground. For added wow factor, you can even replace the black circle with a flat mirror.

PAPER

- 245 lb (360 g/m²) acrylic paper, 17" × 13" (42 × 32 cm)

COLORS

- Yellow Green
- Azo Yellow Deep
- Turquoise Green
- Turquoise Blue
- Azo Orange
- Permanent Red Purple
- Pearl Violet
- Titanium Buff Light
- Quinacridone Rose
- Permanent Madder Lake
- Sky Blue
- Brilliant Green
- Venetian Rose
- Olive Green Light
- Oxide Black

TOOLS

- Squeegee
- Palette knife
- Compass
- Ruler
- Paintbrush
- 0.9 marker (black)
- Masking tape
- Damp cloth

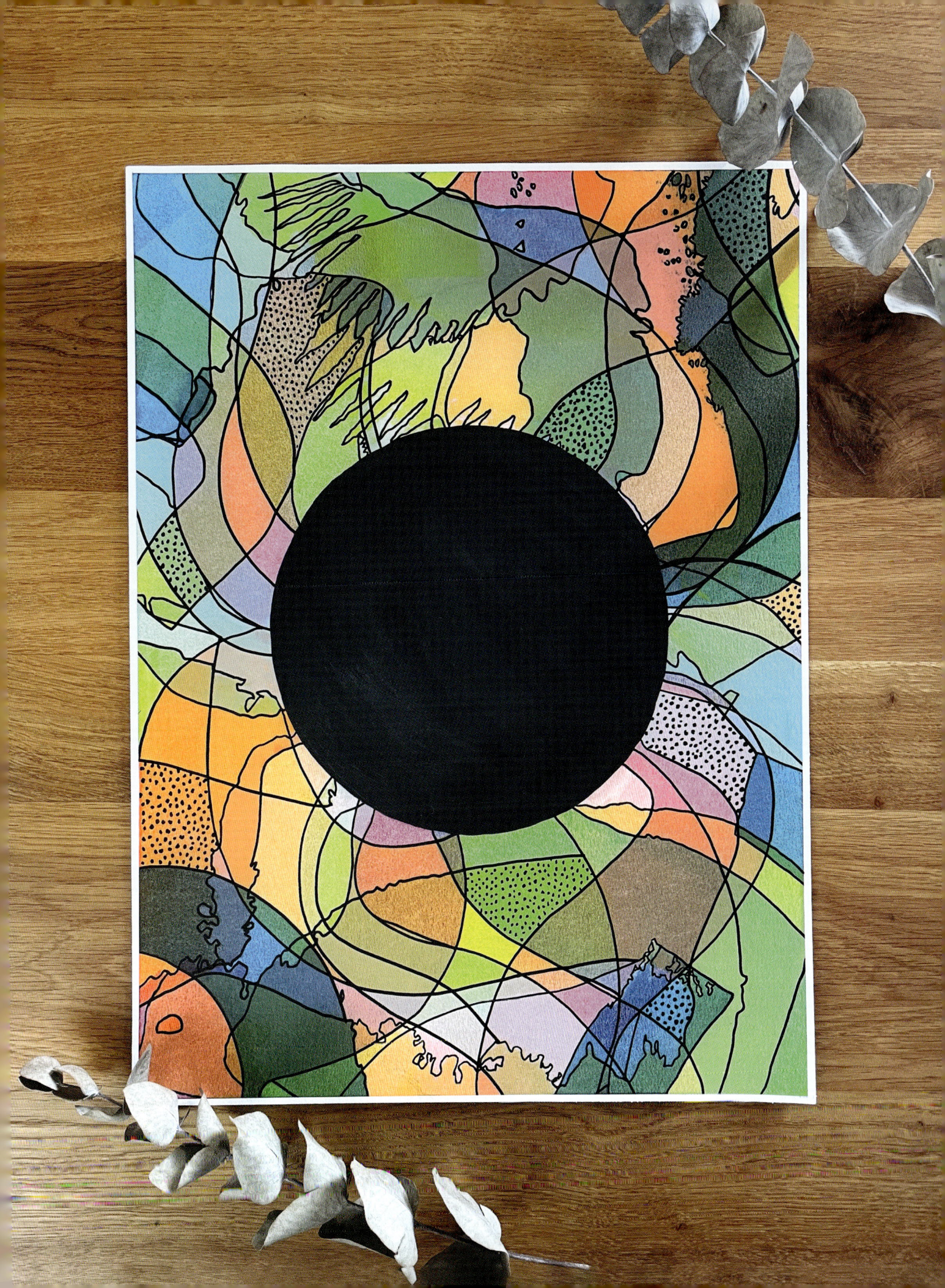

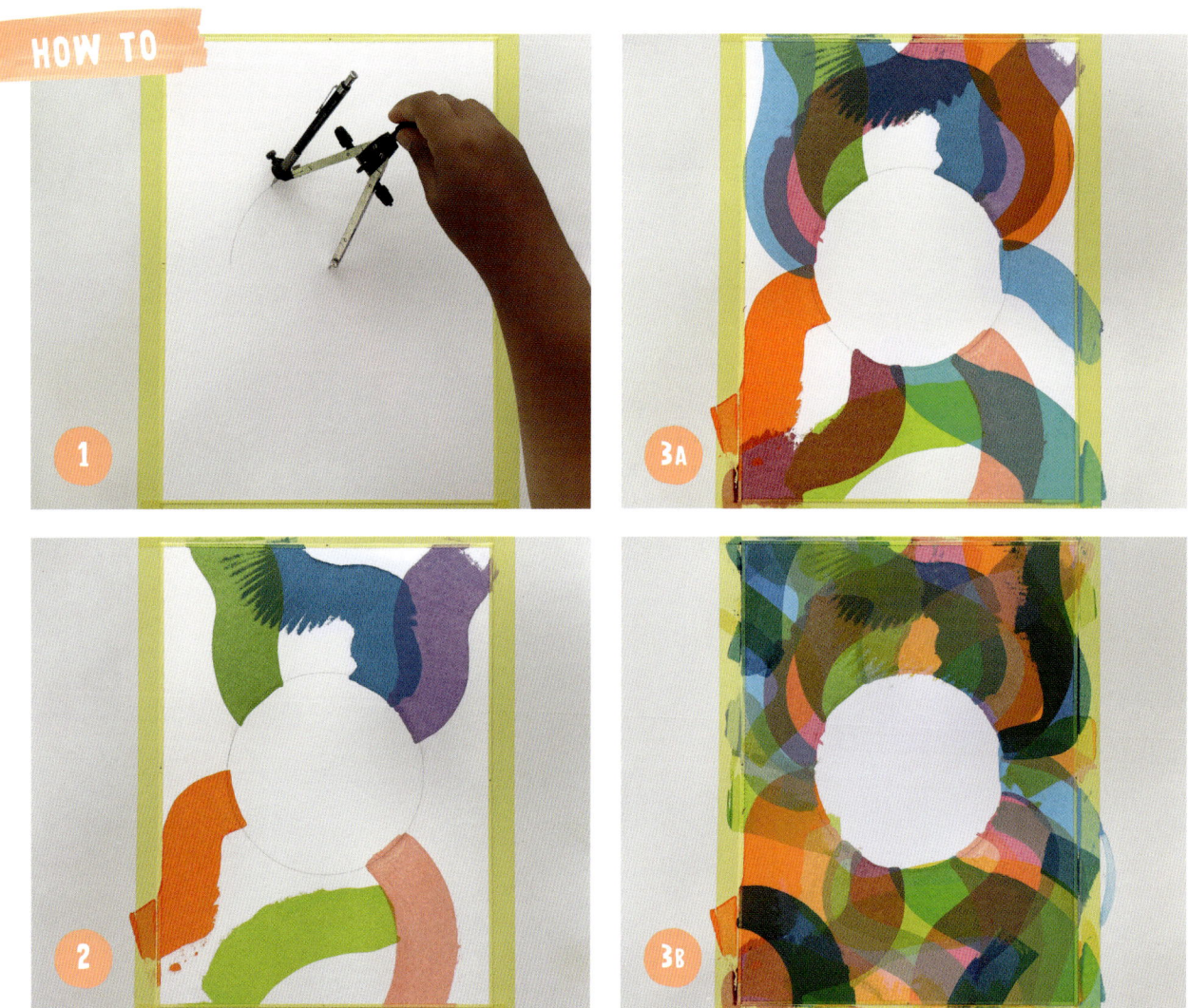

1 Tape down your paper. Start by measuring the paper to find the center of the page. After you've marked the center, draw a circle around this point. Decide for yourself how big you want your circle to be.

2 Now start applying your layers of paint: You can even start from the circle and move outward. It's okay if you go inside the circle a little, as we're going to cover it up with black paint later.

3 Add as many layers as needed to cover all the paper, excluding the circle in the middle.

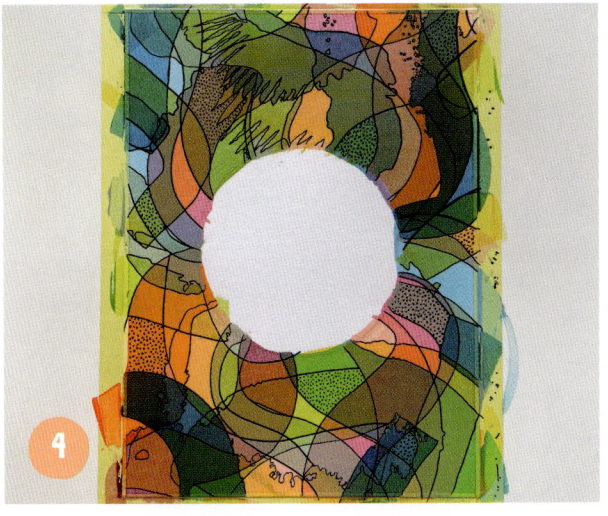

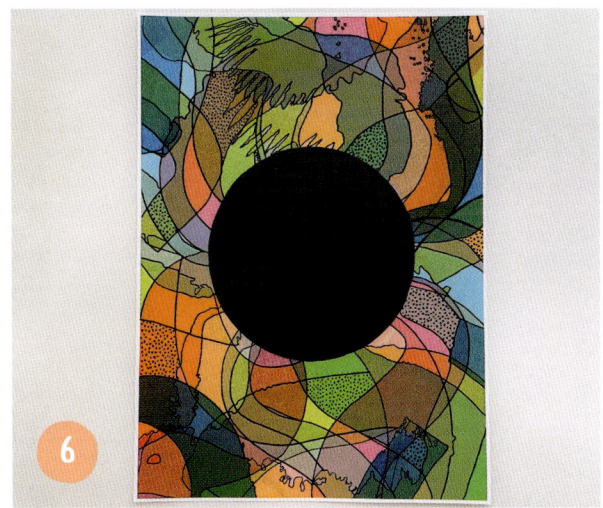

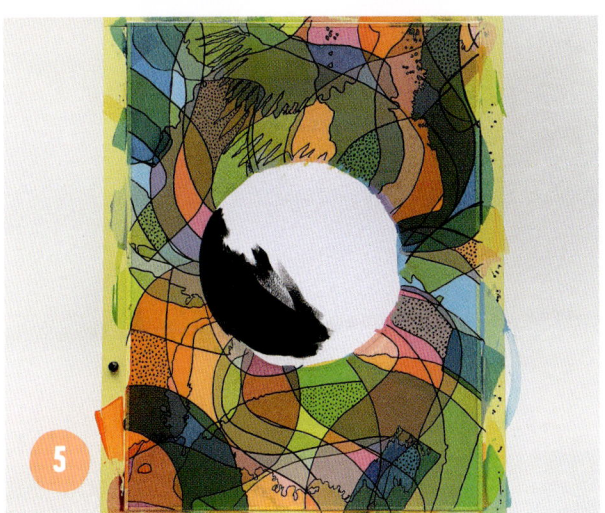

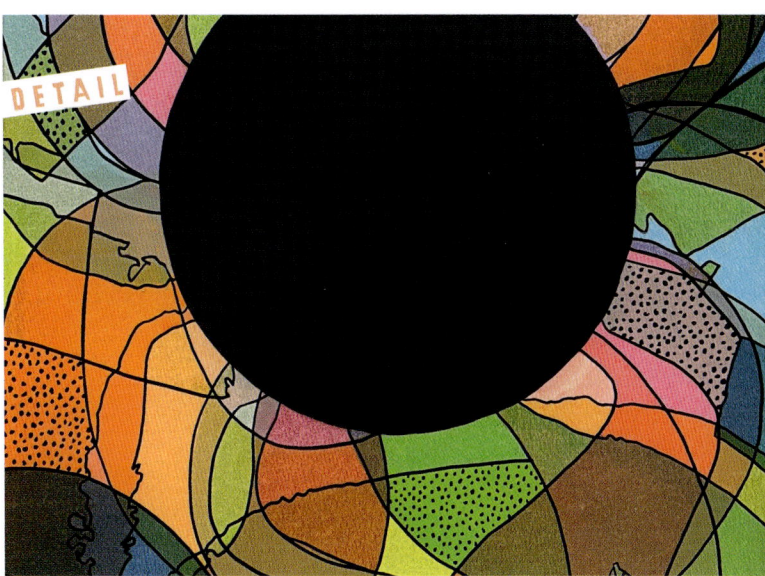

DETAIL

4 Once you've finished all the different layers, take your marker and go around all the shapes you'd like to draw an outline around. It's important that you complete this step before painting the circle, as the marker will be visible against the black paint if you go over it.

5 Once the outlines are done, you can start filling the circle with black paint. Take your time here so the outlines are as neat as possible. The more precise you are, the better the result will be.

6 And now, your new picture is complete. If you want to go a step further, you can cover the circle with gold leaf, or even a round mirror, and then frame it.

21

MELTING ROLLER COASTER

This exercise is about tying together different elements in a painting. In this simplified version, we're going to paint four sections on the same piece of paper. We'll link together the different sections with one color that runs through each section, giving the impression of a line holding the whole together.

PAPER

- 245 lb (360 g/m²) acrylic paper, 8" × 8" (20 × 20 cm)

COLORS

- Yellow Green
- Azo Yellow Deep
- Turquoise Green
- Azo Orange
- Pearl Violet
- Quinacridone Rose

TOOLS

- Squeegee
- 0.9 marker (black)
- Masking tape
- Damp cloth

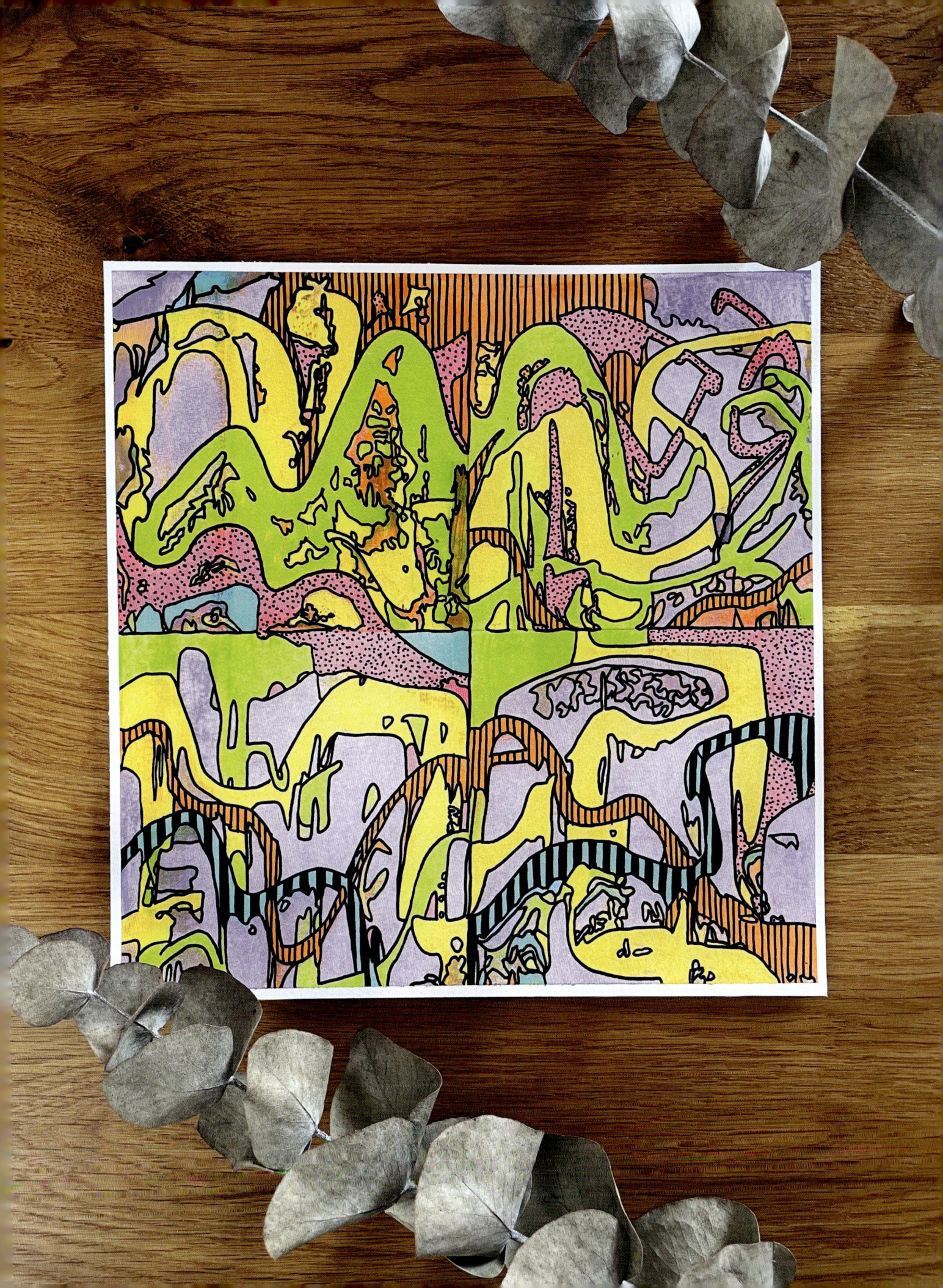

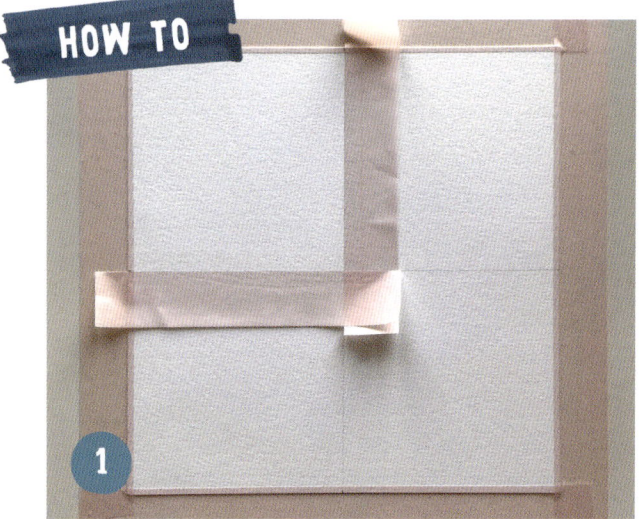

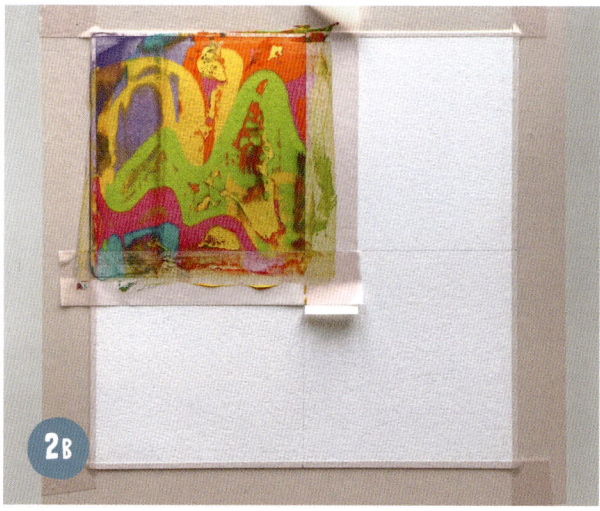

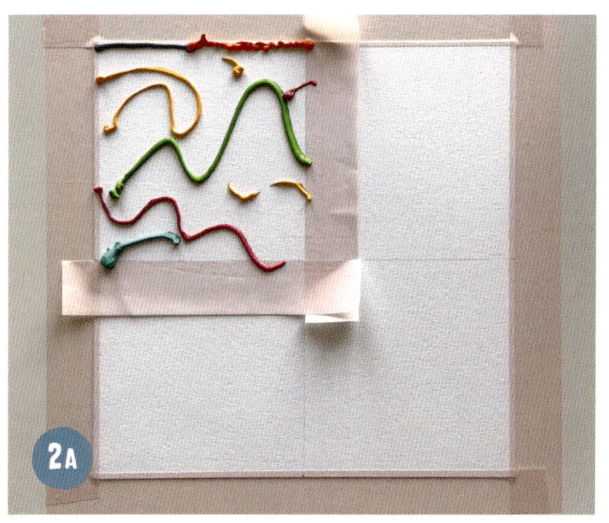

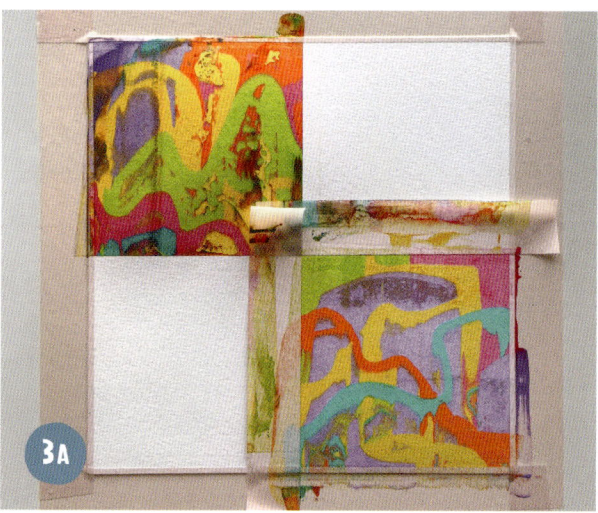

1 Tape down your paper and divide the paper into four sections. Make sure that each section is narrower than the width of your squeegee. Then isolate a section with tape.

2 Apply paint to the paper however you like. I recommend drawing a few lines to make it look like a roller coaster. Once you've added the paint, scrape it off all in one go from the top down, applying moderate to firm pressure.

3 Move the tape to isolate subsequent sections and repeat the process three more times (3a). Try to use one or two colors to link each section and let the "roller coaster rails" run through them. In 3b and 3c, you can see how green and orange paint have been used to create this effect.

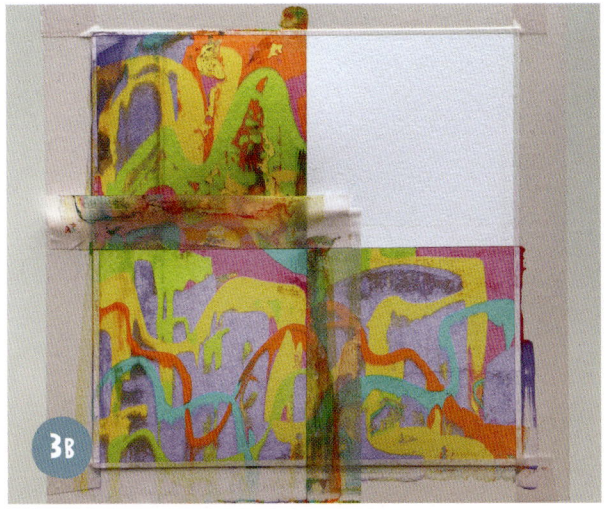

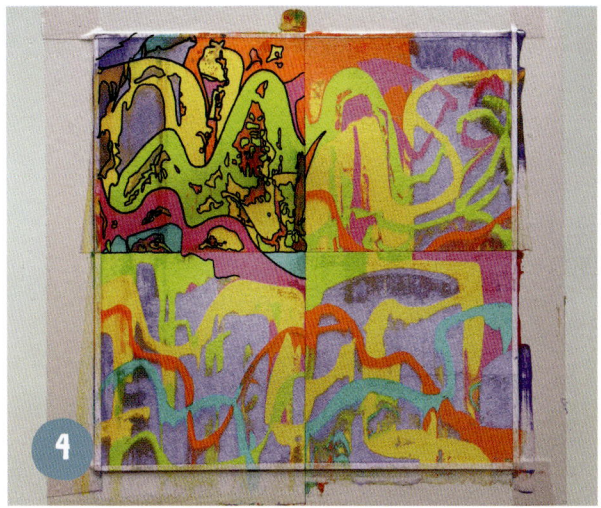

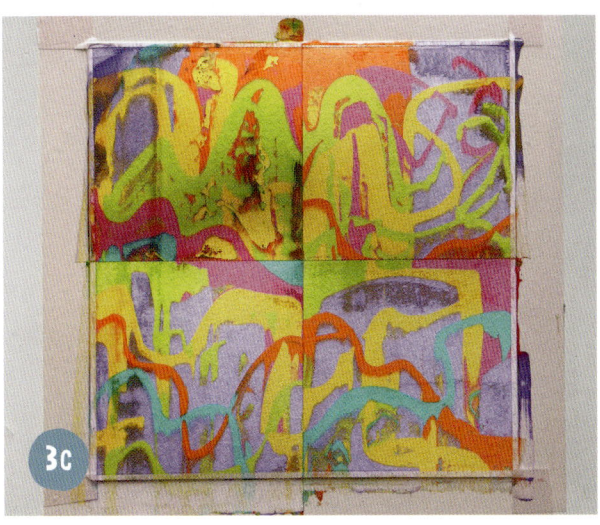

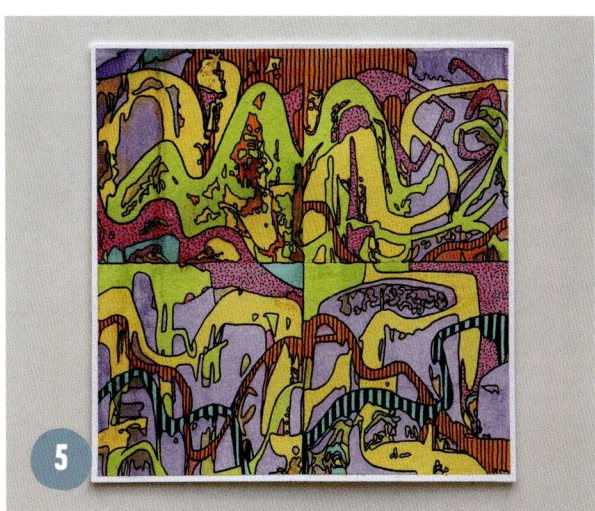

4 Go around the various shapes with your marker and add some patterns, especially where the same color crosses several sections. This will hide any traces left by the tape when dividing the paper.

5 That's it! Congratulations on your first trippy squeegee painting!

22

COLORFUL GREETINGS

To round off our sequence of projects, we're going to create an exciting, colorful painting and turn it into a greeting card. How about writing a thoughtful message inside and gifting it with your first squeegee painting? That would really make somebody's day!

PAPER

- ✖ Fine-grain 200 lb (300 g/m²) watercolor paper, 9" × 6" (23 × 14 cm)

COLORS

- ✖ Sky Blue
- ✖ Permanent Orange
- ✖ Reflex Green
- ✖ Azo Yellow Lemon
- ✖ Turquoise Green
- ✖ Primary Magenta
- ✖ Light Rose
- ✖ Ultramarine Violet

TOOLS

- ✖ Squeegee
- ✖ Masking tape
- ✖ Paper cutter
- ✖ Paper-creasing tool
- ✖ Damp cloth

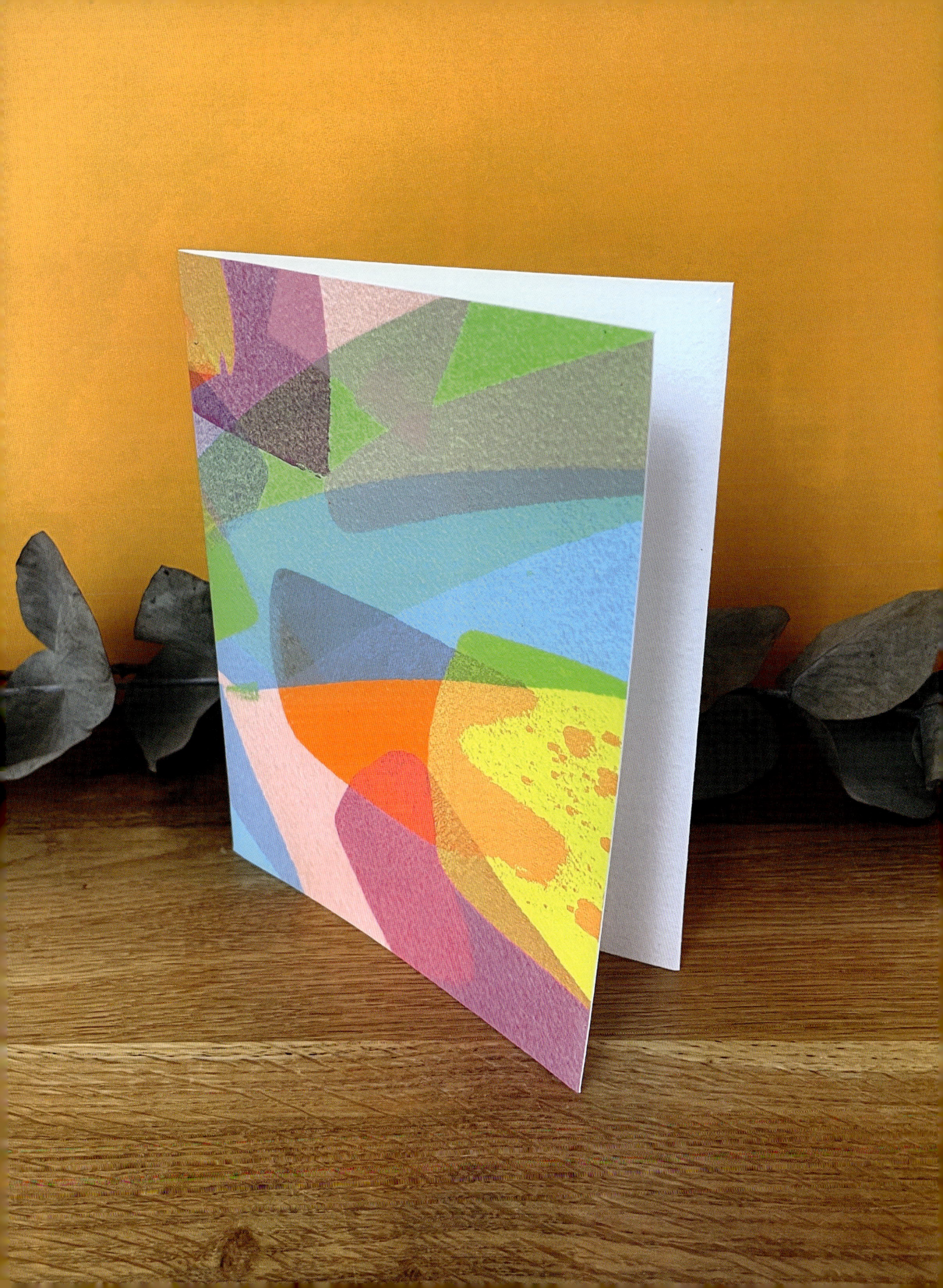

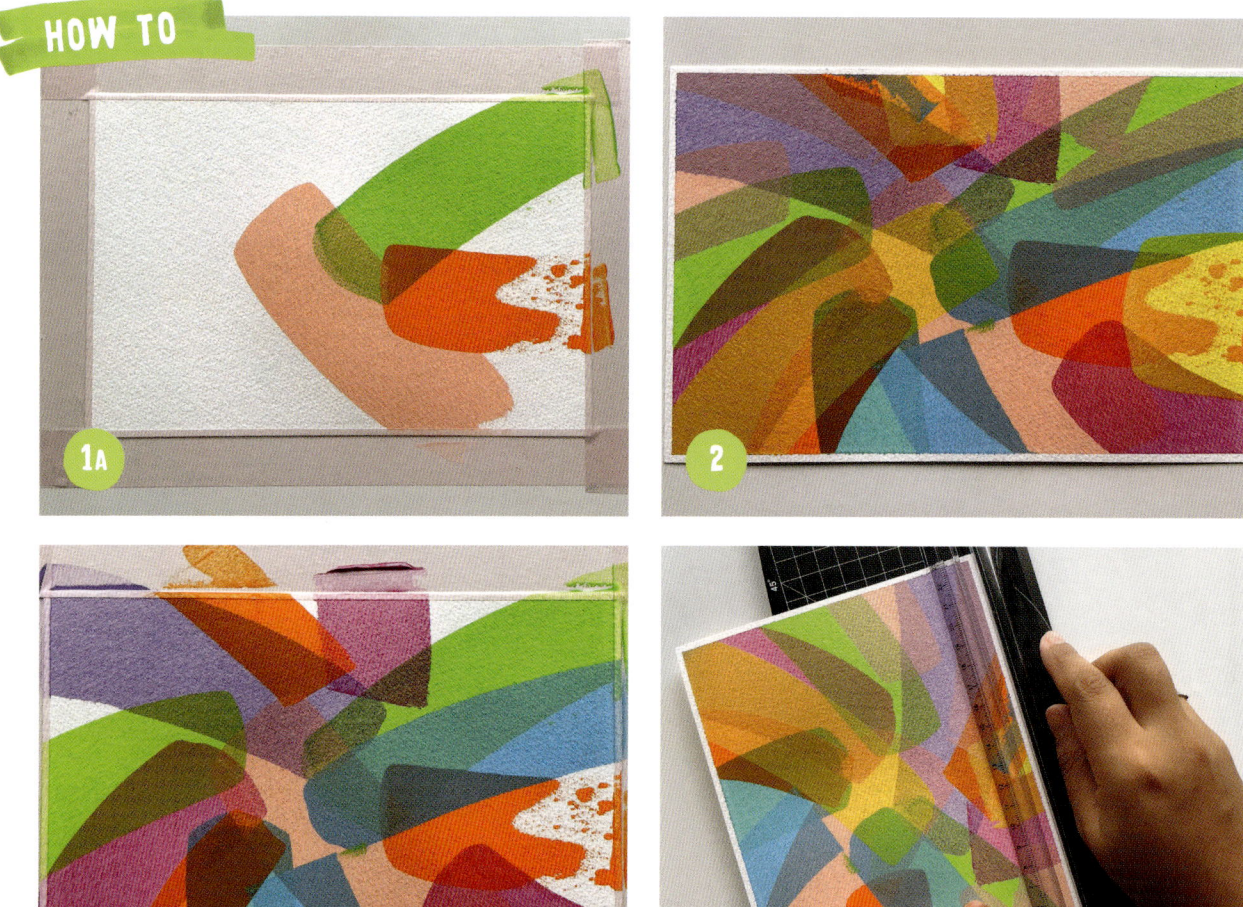

1 No new techniques are introduced in this project: You're welcome to go back to your favorite project in this book and repeat it if you like. For this project, though, I'm going to use a similar technique to the one from the "Firework" painting. Only this time, all the stripes will be the same width.

2 Once you're happy with your paint layers, you can remove the tape.

3 Now remove the white edges using a paper cutter or a metal ruler with a cutter. It's important to hold it straight to get an accurate cut. Otherwise, the sides will be uneven when you fold it.

4 Measure your paper to find where the center is and form a crease by scoring along the centerline with the paper-creasing tool. Then fold your paper.

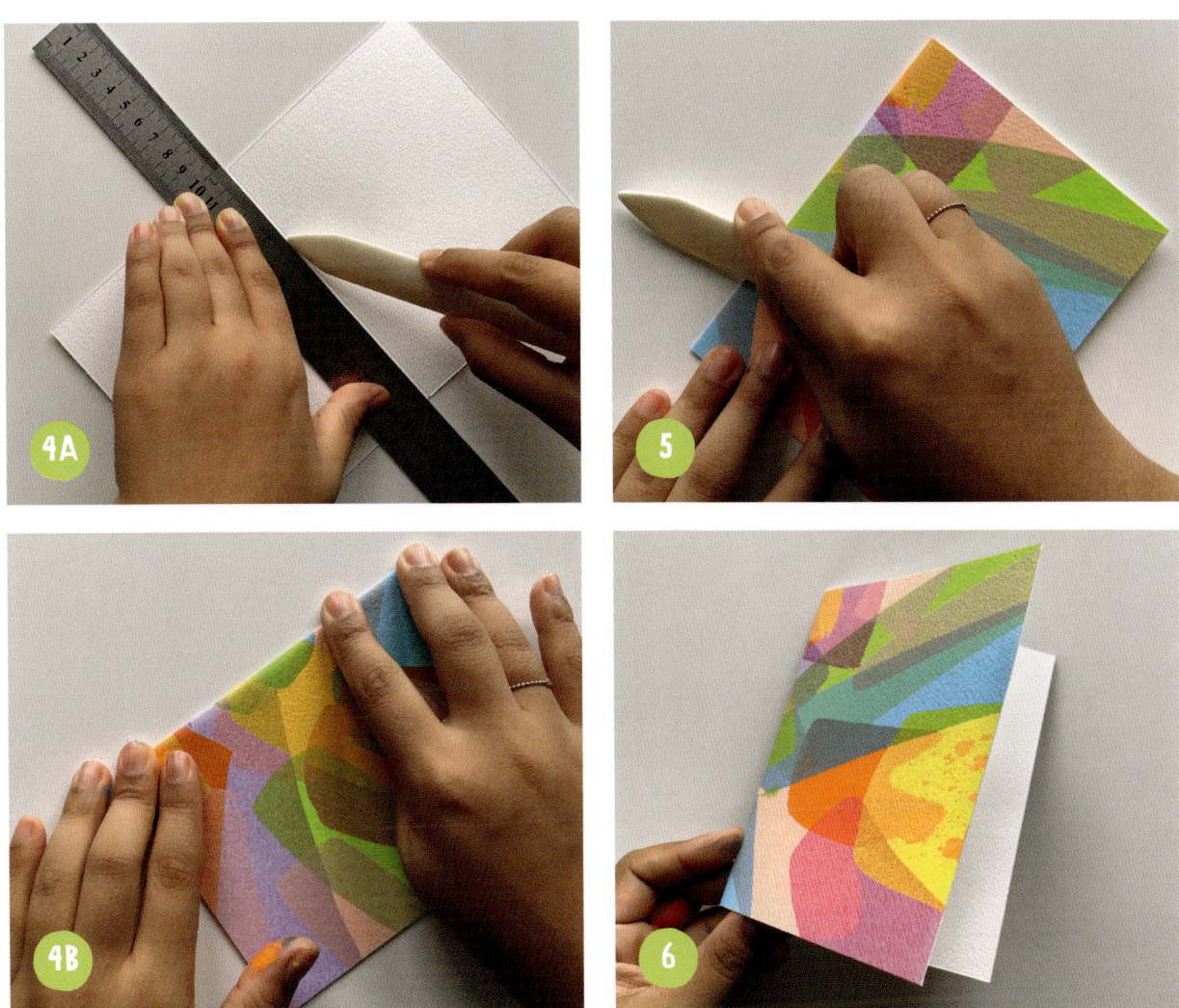

5 Make sure the edge is creased properly so the card doesn't open by itself.

6 Now you have a colorful, artistic, personalized greeting card to give to a friend.

ACKNOWLEDGMENTS

Not a day goes by that I don't think about my beloved granny Ildete and uncle Cassemiro. I dedicate this book to them.

I'd also like to thank Saskia Hauck and EMF Verlag for making all this possible and for their immense support throughout the process.

A big thanks also to Royal Talens who sponsored a considerable amount of the material for this book, giving me complete creative freedom. It feels great to have a brand that you already know and love sponsor your work.

Thanks to my family and friends for their support in the months leading up to finishing this book. It was a great incentive to know I had so many people cheering me on.

Last but not least, I would like to thank all my followers and supporters on Instagram and TikTok, as well as all the collectors who have purchased my art over the years. Without you, none of this would have been possible.

Love,
Clara

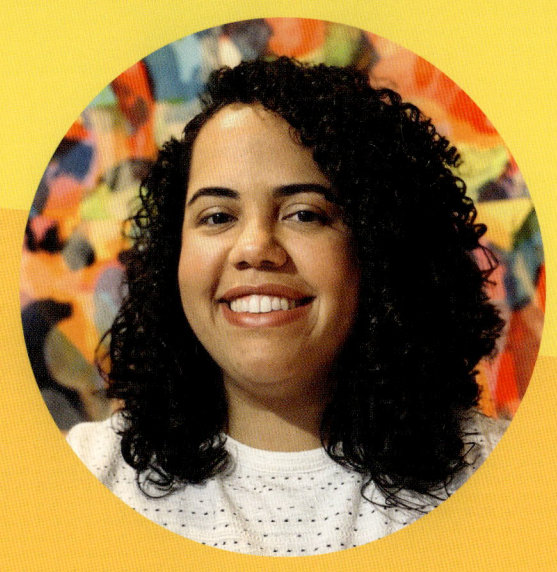

ABOUT THE AUTHOR

Clara Cristina de Souza Rêgo (@aclaracris) was born in Brazil in the 1990s and has had a love of creativity ever since she was a child. She did lots of DIY projects with her granny and one of her aunts. She studied industrial and graphic design at the University of Brasilia and now works as a user experience designer in Germany, where she has been living since completing her master's in integrated design in 2016.

Clara's sunny, carefree attitude sprouts from her Brazilian roots and positive outlook on life, traits that also come through in many of her pictures.

From childhood to her teenage years and adulthood, she's consistently turned to art, a passion that she ultimately consolidated into a regular practice at the start of the coronavirus pandemic. She had more free time available since she didn't need to go into the office every day.

Clara grabbed the opportunity. Like a scientist in a lab, she did a lot of research and a lot of experiments. Clara paints as often and as much as she can, always with the aim of having fun and sharing a colorful moment with others in her social media videos. Her motto is "*Pinte o que te diverte e faz feliz*" (Paint what you like and what makes you happy.).

Instagram: www.instagram.com/aclaracris
TikTok: www.tiktok.com/@aclaracris
Website: www.aclaracris.com

Quarto.com • WalterFoster.com

© 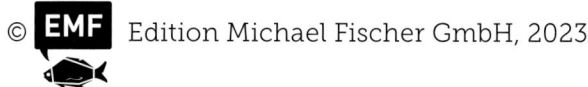 Edition Michael Fischer GmbH, 2023

www.emf-verlag.de

This translation of ABSTRAKT – SUPER EASY first published in Germany by Edition Michael Fischer GmbH in 2023 is published by arrangement with Silke Bruenink Agency, Munich, Germany.

Published in 2024 by Walter Foster Publishing, an imprint of The Quarto Group, 100 Cummings Center, Suite 265-D, Beverly, MA 01915, USA.
T (978) 282-9590 F (978) 283-2742

Walter Foster Publishing titles are also available at discount for retail, wholesale, promotional, and bulk purchase. For details, contact the Special Sales Manager by email at specialsales@quarto.com or by mail at The Quarto Group, Attn: Special Sales Manager, 100 Cummings Center, Suite 265-D, Beverly, MA 01915, USA.

28 27 26 25 24   1 2 3 4 5

ISBN: 978-0-7603-8813-6

Digital edition published in 2024
eISBN: 978-0-7603-8814-3

Text, Artwork, and Photography: Clara C. de Souza Rego,
except Thomas Schenker on pages 7 and 126
Design: Silvia Keller
Translation: Jessica West

Printed in China